Jamaican Hands Across the Atlantic

Jamaican Hands Across the Atlantic

Elaine Bauer
and
Paul Thompson

Ian Randle Publishers
Kingston • Miami

First published in Jamaica, 2006 by
Ian Randle Publishers
11 Cunningham Avenue
Box 686
Kingston 6
www.ianrandlepublishers.com

© Elaine Bauer and Paul Thompson

National Library of Jamaica Cataloguing in Publication Data

Bauer, Elaine
    Jamaican hands across the Atlantic / Elaine Bauer and Paul Thompson

        p.;   cm

    Includes index

    ISBN 976-637-246-2 (pbk)

    1. Family – Jamaica   2. Transnationalism   3. Emigration and
        immigration
    I. Thompson, Paul   II. Title

    305.85097292   dc 21

Cover photographs by Elaine Bauer, Neil Kenlock and Armet Francis.
Used with the permission of the photographers.

Book and cover design by Ian Randle Publishers
Printed in the United States of America

To
Tony, Nicholas and Anthony
From Elaine

To
Sophia
From Paul

Contents

Preface

Firstly and most fundamentally, we wish to thank all those members of our Jamaican transnational families, who have given us their time, help and hospitality, and have allowed us to record their life stories. All but two of them are quoted in this book under pseudonyms, in order to maintain confidentiality.

We owe particular debts for advice and support to Harry Goulbourne, Mary Chamberlain, Jean Besson, Delroy Murray, Catherine and Stuart Hall, and Chris Phillipson; for their constructive comments on our manuscript from Daniel Bertaux and Catherine Delcroix and from our publisher's anonymous reviewers; and for help in finding interviewees, Holger Henke of the Caribbean Research Center, Medgar Evans College, City University of New York (CUNY), and Anthony Henry of the Jamaican Canadian Association. We especially want to thank Ian Randle for giving his backing to our project. And more privately, we have been crucially encouraged by the warm support of Elaine's own transnational family, her children, sisters, uncle and cousins.

We are especially grateful for the financial support which we have received for our own interviewing on the 'Transnational Jamaican Families' research project from the Young Foundation (then the Institute of Community Studies) with its award of a Research Fellowship to Elaine Bauer. We also wish to thank the British Academy, the Canadian High Commission, the Fuller Bequest and the University of Essex for their financial help with our fieldwork and transcribing. The four 1970s interviews were carried out by Harry Goulbourne for Paul Thompson's 'Oral History and Black History' project supported by the Nuffield Foundation, and are now available in the British Library National Sound Archive (C707).

Finally, we should like to thanks those journals which during the period of our fieldwork published earlier explorations of some of the themes of this book. They provided foundations for Chapters One, Three, Six and Seven, and the first and last articles include extended literature reviews. These articles are: Paul Thompson and Elaine Bauer, 'Jamaican Transnational Families: Points of Pain and Sources of Resilience', *Wadabagei: A Journal of the Caribbean and its Diaspora* 1 (Summer/Fall 2000): 1–37; 'Recapturing Distant Caribbean Childhoods and Communities: the Shaping of Memory in the Testimonies of Jamaican Migrants in Britain and America', *Oral History* 30, no. 2 (2002): 49–59; 'Evolving Jamaican Migrant Identities: Contrasts Between Britain, Canada and the United States', special issue on Caribbean families, *Community, Work and Family* 6, no. 1 (2003): 89–102; and '"She's always the person with a very global vision": The Gender Dynamics of Migration, Narrative Interpretation, and the Case of Jamaican Transnational Families', *Gender and History* 16, no. 2 (2004): 334–75.

We have researched and written this book between us. Meeting these 45 families, listening to their stories, visiting their neighbourhoods and villages in Jamaica and beyond, has for both of us been an incredibly rich experience, which we hope we can share through this book.

ONE

Jamaican Transnational Families

Donetta Macfarlane has lived for over 30 years in Toronto, where she works as a hospital food supervisor, but she lives as part of a much wider family web. Donetta grew up with her parents in Jamaica on a small farm, but she now describes herself as a 'Jamaican Canadian'. This complexity in identity resulting from migration goes back at least to her parents' generation, for her mother was born to a migrant Jamaican family in Panama, only coming to Jamaica as a small child, and to the end of her life was proud to be able to count in Spanish. In Donetta's generation her sisters and brother were to cross the Atlantic in diverse directions. She was the youngest of seven children, of whom only one has remained in Jamaica throughout. The eldest and the third sister went to England, and although they have now returned to Jamaica their children remain in London. But Donetta, her brother, her two other sisters and also her mother all migrated to Canada rather than England. Another close relative, her mother's sister's daughter Joyce Leroy, migrated first to England and then moved on to New York. Yet despite the vast distances separating them, Donetta's relatives remain in close contact, whether in Britain, North America or Jamaica.

It is this kind of family, maintaining close relationships across national boundaries, with members often holding more than one citizenship, which we call a 'transnational family', that has inspired our project and is the central focus of this book.[1] We wanted to understand how far grandparents and parents, brothers and sisters, could still operate as families despite being split up by migration, and whether the family patterns and sense of identity remained simply Jamaican after migration, or new forms are emerging. In chapter two we shall outline the historical context of these transnational families, point to the most relevant literature around the theme, and describe our own oral history project to record the life stories of family members. But to make our central theme clear from the start, we want to begin in this chapter by sketching out some of the key features of transnational Jamaican families.

Transnationalism and Family Bonds

Firstly, for these Jamaican families whom we interviewed transnationalism is not a figment of the researcher's imagination, but a reality both in the mind and in practice. Obviously the continual fracturing, both in terms of migration and of multiple partnering, means that contacts are often lost, and there are often gaps in people's knowledge. In any case it is only practicable to keep in active touch with a limited number of kin over such distances. Nevertheless people were certainly always aware of their Jamaican, British and North America relatives and usually in touch with some of them.

These families are rarely easy to delineate, particularly because it has long been so common in Jamaican families for either fathers or mothers or both to have children with more than one partner. Such multiple partnering is so widespread that very many families become complex structures. Thus the starting point of one of our first families was four half-sisters by the same mother, each with different fathers who had other children. The fathers of two of them had altogether some 30 children from at least ten different mothers. It is impossible to compress this kind of family into the narrow spaces of a conventional Anglo-American family tree. And often it may require a long discussion to unravel precisely how two people are related. Selvin Green recalls how as a child in Jamaica he went to school with 'many, many cousins by my mother's side.... Some of them I can't even remember their names, there's so many of them'. Quite often because of distance or breaches the whole kin network cannot be known. Thus Yolande Woods grew up in Britain believing that she belonged to an unusually small Jamaican family, and only as an adult discovered she had a 'mega-family' of relatives in rural Jamaica. This means that there is always the possibility of unfinished business in setting out these kin patterns: someone unexpected who may suddenly be discovered, or come 'knocking at her door'. These are kin systems which more than most are continually on the move. The sheer difficulties of comprehending such kin links may be one possible reason why Jamaicans tend to simplify. Typically, they do not distinguish half from full siblings, or indeed use these terms, and they call aunts cousins or vice versa with little concern. But when one looks more closely, it becomes apparent that this imprecision is in fact a distinctive structural feature of the Jamaican kinship system.

It is particularly striking that in the Jamaican countryside this broad concept of family has been paralleled in practice by a traditional usage of 'family land' on which any member of the family has a right to come and live — thus creating both a bond and also sometimes a source of conflict. Family land is freehold land owned in common by the family, most of which was acquired by former slaves in the post-emancipation period.[2] It is usually transmitted by custom rather than formal law, and all recognized descendants through both sexes of its original owners have accepted rights to use it and to build a house on it. The land should be transmitted undivided, so that the co-heirs have joint rights to the whole rather than actual pieces of it. It is also traditionally regarded as inalienable. This reluctance to sell is strengthened by the fact that in many cases family members are buried there, so that their graves give an element of sacredness to the family land. Often children were also linked to the family land through the planting of 'navel trees,' as Dick Woodward remembered:

> It's an Ashanti practice in West Africa, that the umbilical cord, when you're born, is cut off, and a piece of it is kept in the room until you're old enough to understand, and then it's buried in the ground and the tree is planted on it. That is your link with this spot, ... your link to the place, as your family, your responsibility.

In practice, however, priority is given to those family members who are most in need, and those who occupy and cultivate particular bits of the family land, especially over more than one generation, may come to be seen as owners of it. On the other hand, those who have migrated or otherwise done better are expected to suspend their claims. Nevertheless these absent members are recognized as having a latent right to return to use the land, for example on retirement. 'Thus it is the *entitlement* to freehold land which is the crucial aspect of family land, rather than the *activation* of such rights.'[3] In short, in terms of land, 'family' is seen as encompassing all those descended from the same ancestors, with no formal or gender distinctions accepted between them in terms of rights, but prioritization based on individual need and circumstance.

This concept closely matches the working of the overall kin system in other ways. For example, in terms of the mutual aid which is such a strong feature of these families, such as helping with migration or caring for children or for the old, two features are striking. The first is that help sometimes comes from or is given to quite distant kin in the complex wider family structure, including kin by marriage. But this inclusiveness is countered by the second feature, selectivity. Thus while most migrants feel an obligation to send regular money and gifts home, they are likely to focus on those they feel are most in need. For example, one New York Jamaican explained how he sends remittances not to his mother, but to a younger sister: 'Of all the family members, she is the one who is struggling most to make ends meet.' We view this combination of complexity with pragmatic selectivity not as a sign of weakness in the kin system, but as a positive characteristic, which enables its resilience in supporting family members. The flexibility of Jamaican kin relationships is empowered by their pragmatism and informality.

The same flexibility characterizes the naming of kin. Eva McNeep, now a cook in Toronto, explains how as a child in Jamaica, 'I used to live with my "aunt" — which is my mum's first cousin — so we would say that's my great-aunt's daughter, but I call her my auntie, because she and my mum were like two sisters.' In the same spirit Eva gives family names to some particularly close friends. 'We had close family friends around, that weren't real family. Up to this very day, this girl that we grew up with, she will always say we are her "sisters" and "brother". I send for her here on visits.' This pragmatism in naming also commonly applies to substitute parents and to half siblings: the term chosen reflects the individual case.

Thus gradually one begins to see that within this familialism there is also an equally crucial individuality. Kin networks in any family have to be seen from the starting points of individuals, but re-partnering means that the resulting kin maps are likely to differ much more sharply, even between siblings. In the face of this, on the one hand people accept the possibility of help from many directions, so that Dahlia Noble, later a nurse in Britain, remembers feeling no sense of loss when as a child in Jamaica she moved on the death of her grandmother to a great-aunt: she felt secure because she was 'still within the family circle'. At the same time, however, particularly for adults, there is a sense that kin relationships need to become real through significant social contact and potential or actual exchanges of help. Hence fathers who have abandoned their offspring are largely disregarded, and may not find it possible to win back a parental relationship later in life. Blossom Grant's father, who lived in America and had no contact with her as a child, came to Jamaica to find her when she was 27: 'He tried to give me material things, but that's not all.... He wasn't there for me when I was small ... I didn't have any love for him as a father.'

Remembering Points of Pain

It is worth exploring a little more deeply how emotional loss is handled, both because it is a central issue for migrants, but also because it highlights the workings of the Jamaican kin system. For it seems that this similar pragmatism in attitudes to kin helps to explain why the crucial points of pain in their lives of which our migrants spoke were often not the separation from fathers or mothers, with the continuing sense of parental loss, which have been stressed by comparable studies of white children who grew up with a missing parent.[4] In these Jamaican families three different primary sources of pain are highlighted.

There is, firstly, certainly a kind of grief intrinsic in migration itself, even when made in a spirit of hope for betterment. Some migrants for years continued to feel a general sense of loss, which they expressed in terms of feeling socially isolated. Migrant women were particularly likely to feel the absence of family and close local community at times of childbirth, but sometimes men spoke of similar feelings of loss. Thus Linton

Black, now an American pensioner, nostalgically describes a Jamaican childhood where he was part of a large extended family living close together: 'We all took part in looking after each other. Well, they see to it that I didn't get in trouble, and if I do get in trouble, they were there to help me out.' Now he is in the United States he has just one cousin nearby to whom he could turn for help.

These feelings of loss were much more acute when they concerned separations between parents and children. When she was 17 Verity Houghton's mother left for Canada, preparing the way for the rest of the family, but to Verity 'It felt like someone — someone had died.' Isabelle Woods' mother left London for New York when she was under 5, but she still remembers her distress: 'I was bitter towards that. I didn't see the need for her to leave.' Roy Cripps did not see or hear his mother for five years after she migrated ahead to England: 'My mother — I miss my mother dearly, dearly, I really did.'

On the parental side, Stella Wadham remembered her four-year separation from her three-year-old daughter after migrating to New York. 'It was tough. But I think I consoled myself by saying, "I can give my child this".... It was very tough.' 'So I left the kids there with my mum,' said Pearl Selkirk of her leaving for London. 'Because it was my mum, and I know my mum, she will look after them, that side didn't bother me too much. But I did miss them. I did miss them.... It was heartrending.' Sarah Chisholm similarly reflects on how she felt leaving her son in Jamaica as a small child when she went ahead to Canada:

> It was a mixed feeling that I was going through, a feeling of guilt, leaving him back home, sadness, missing him. But on the other hand, I felt quite relieved that I was able to be here to work, and I could afford to buy the things that I would see in the store, and I would say, "Oh yes I would love this for him," and send it.... If I was in Jamaica, I could never afford to buy it for him.

The other most notable points of pain sprang from the widespread practice, both in migrant families and in Jamaican families generally, of children being brought up by substitute parents, typically grandmothers or other older kin. It is clear that in most instances these older caregivers proved more than adequate substitutes for mothers. Selvin Green stands for many others when he says, 'I was pretty close to [my mother], although I was closer to my grandmother.' Connie Dixon calls her grandmother 'a saint'. But because of their greater age grandmothers were more likely to die than mothers, and for Connie the day her grandmother died was 'the first time I've ever felt my heart ache, and it was literally, my heart was aching'.

For a very unfortunate few, to this grief from loss could be added the misfortune of being placed with a much less sympathetic relative. For Connie Dixon it was an aunt who would beat her and sent her own child to school while forcing Connie to work in the fields. Blossom Grant similarly was sent to an uncle whose wife favoured her own two children, beating Blossom, discriminating against her in terms of food and clothing, and sending her to work in the fields while the other two were at school. Such aunts are described with the acute dislike usually reserved in European family stories for wicked stepmothers.

There is, on the other hand, rarely any emphasis on pain through absent or missing fathers. In general, when a father is absent but 'owns up' to being a parent, exchanges photographs and sends occasional money and gifts to his children, his behaviour is regarded as acceptable. The contact and gifts are seen not only as helpful but as important symbols of caring. Thus Selvin Green described how he sustained contact in this way with children he had left behind through migrating to England: 'So it's continuous communication with barrels and letters and money.... You just keep communicating. You can't lose track of them.'

By contrast, fathers who failed to maintain contact seem to have eventually lost any potential emotional significance. Charlene Summers was not much moved when in her thirties she heard that her father, whom she had never known, had been searching the local Jamaican countryside looking for her. She did not trace him at the address in Kingston which he left. 'My father is not a problem for me ... I don't force it. Because if it is God will, some day I will know him.... If I see my father now, I'll prefer ask him to help my two kids more than even me?' Yolande Woods, who grew up with her grandmother in London, stands for many when she reflects, 'It would have been a lot more disruptive for us.... It probably would have been a lot more headache if he'd been around, by virtue that I grew up in a very stable environment ... I felt protected ... I missed the role. I don't miss him.' So while there are many missing fathers in these life stories, there is *not one* whose absence was described as a major source of grief, pain or longing.

Interpreting Jamaican Transnational Families

The special characteristics of the Jamaican family system meant that in writing about Jamaican migrant families we were very soon confronted by two linked problems. The first is that of terminology. While we had no hesitation in avoiding the hostile labels given to Jamaican families by European commentators in the past, we still faced the difficulty that there is a set of formal descriptive words — such as 'half siblings' — which are used by Europeans but are not normally recognized in Jamaica, although as we found they are taken up by some migrants. We have nevertheless sometimes used these terms when there was no precise Jamaican alternative. On the other hand we have generally avoided terms which have strong resonances of European family structures. These include in particular 'single mother' (a mother bringing up her children without their father) and 'stepfamily' (a family unit including one remarried parent). Here we feel that the European term is not only by implication pejorative, but equally importantly, fails to see these household units within the context of the wider extended family. In the same spirit we avoid the strongly pejorative terms 'bastard' and 'illegitimate', which some Jamaicans did use in the past, but we do sometimes use the more neutral 'outside', to describe children born from one of a couple to another partner.

A second and linked problem is the prejudice which has for so long been expressed by many commentators on Jamaican family life. For more than two centuries, most commentators have been much more critical than flattering. Initially the critics were most concerned about the prevalence of sexual relationships between black slaves and white colonists, and the creation of a 'mongrel' mixed population. Later the focus shifted onto the low level of marriage and the high proportions of single mothers and multiple partnering, commentators describing such Jamaican families as 'incomplete', 'denuded' or 'disintegrate.'[5] From such perspectives, migration only made things worse. Indeed, scattered across the seas between the Caribbean, Britain and the North American continent, very often divided by parental separations as well as vast distances, Jamaican transnational families may seem to fit all too well into the white social worker's image of the classically dysfunctional and literally 'broken' family. Moreover not only white but also Jamaican social workers were strongly influenced by such critical attitudes. Thus in one of her earliest works, written in 1974 from a social policy perspective long before she became one of Jamaica's leading novelists, Erna Brodber linked child adoption or the 'passing on' of children between relatives with child abandonment, seeing them all 'as a logical phase in the development of a cultural pattern'. She cites the case of a 13-year-old girl abandoned by a transnational family as a particularly serious instance of this negative pattern:

> Lived with father and mother. Mother went to England. Sent to grandmother in Trelawny. Because of late nights sent to father in Kingston. Father goes to U.S. Child is left with a cousin. Has become a member of the "Dirty Dozens" gang which sleeps with questionable men, etc. Father not heard from; mother sends maintenance.[6]

Such a case of abandonment was in fact very rare in Jamaican families, and not at all typical.

Our purpose by contrast is to focus primarily on what is normal or typical in Jamaican family life. It is important to remember that the great majority of complex families, whether from a white European or a Caribbean background, function well enough without the intervention of social workers. And indeed these include some families which generate men or women who make outstanding contributions to the wider society. From the European past we can cite among others Isaac Newton and Leonardo da Vinci, both brought up as stepchildren. A Jamaican parallel would be Bob Marley, raised by his grandparents in the Jamaican countryside, a mixed race child of a transnational family, with kin in both the United States and Britain.[7]

Rather than impose yet another researchers' viewpoint, our most fundamental intention has been to set against the prejudice of some earlier commentators the voices of these Jamaicans, recounting their own feelings and experiences. From chapter three to chapter ten, the heart of this book, the sequence is primarily shaped by the flow of the life stories, from memories of Jamaican childhoods, through migration and work abroad to the dream of return. Through these accounts we can understand the experiences of the individual transnational family members whose lives together made the patterns of the wider family system. Equally important, these life stories offer a new kind of Jamaican social history, centred on Jamaica's migrant families, a social history which combines both the familiar and the unexpected in a new overall shape. At the same time we explore a range of questions. How far have memories of family origin or Jamaican communities or the environment been reshaped by the experience of migration? What factors pushed or pulled men or women into migration, and when whole family groups migrated, who were the activators? How did migration affect the identity of Jamaicans who went to different countries? How crucial were family backgrounds, education or religious faith to those who succeeded as migrants? What were the characteristic roles of men and women in Jamaican families, before and after migration, and what strengths and difficulties did this bring? And then in their later years, how easy was it for Jamaican migrants who wished to resettle in their homeland to realize their dreams?

Then in our final chapter we return to a second overview of Jamaican transnational families, exploring their complexities in greater depth. We end by asking whether they should be seen simply as a transitional form, with survivals from Caribbean practice which are unlikely to last beyond the first migrant generation; or alternatively as an innovative family pattern, pioneering new forms of identity and living, including interracial unions and of global living in parallel with the rapidly globalizing economy.

Contexts: Past to Present

Today, 'travelling' abroad is seen by West Indians as a normal part of growing up, and typically part of the transgenerational family story. Although migration statistics do not give us precise figures, it is said that half of all Guyanese live as migrants abroad, and the two and a half million Jamaicans in Jamaica are probably matched by over a million living overseas.[1] We have already indicated how despite the typically vast distances separating them, men and women in most migrant transnational families continue to exchange emotional and practical support. Such transnational families are often assumed to be a new feature resulting from globalization. However, it should be emphasized that there are many historical precedents for them. For example, in the early eighteenth century French Protestants who had fled religious persecution to settle in Britain could be found returning to Protestant villages in southern France to seek their wives, just as today young London Bangladeshi men look for brides in Bangladesh. Nevertheless, in the European colonial period transnational families typically belonged to the white elites, who had the financial means to travel and the cultural literacy to sustain relationships through long correspondence. The late twentieth century advent of cheap air travel and phone contact has allowed the development of active transnational family patterns among poorer migrants, and among them notably migrant families from the Caribbean.

The Caribbean in general is a very good field for exploring issues in the history of migration, for during the last four centuries its societies have been repeatedly characterized by both in- and out-migration. This is certainly true of Jamaica, which is the largest of the formerly British islands and accounts for half of the contemporary English-speaking migration currents. Small but fertile, some 150 miles long and dramatically mountainous, from the mid-seventeenth century Jamaica was mainly colonized by a mixture of white plantation owners and staff, black slaves brought from Africa to work on the plantations, and also smaller numbers of white small farmers and indentured servants, Spanish-speaking Jewish traders, and from the mid-nineteenth century also East Indian and Chinese indentured plantation labourers and traders. Although the balance has varied over time and between groups, these migrations have always involved both men and women, and have always been two-way between Europe and the Caribbean. In the eighteenth century, for example, the slave traders brought women as well as men, because the planters' aim was a self-sustaining slave labour force. But at a time when few white women came out to Jamaica, it was also the standard practice for white men to take black mistresses, to the extent that by 1830 over a quarter of slave births in many parts of the island were being recorded as 'coloured', and in over half of these instances the infant slave had a white father — the remainder presumably had a white grandfather.[2] Because most of the white plantation owners and staff who survived long enough would retire to Britain, contact with their non-white descendants in Jamaica was not usually sustained. Nevertheless sometimes a white father took an interest in his mixed race son, and arranged for him to be legally freed, and educated in Jamaica or even in Britain.

It is clear that for the black slaves further migration remained part of their imaginative world. Work songs include migration songs — about hopes of going to both Africa and England. For the older, the hope was for migration in the afterlife. 'The Negroes from some countries think they return to their own country when they die in *Jamaica*', the erudite Sir Hans Sloane, physician to the Governor, wrote in 1707; while a century later the novelist and slave plantation owner Sir Matthew Lewis noted that 'the Africans (as is well known) generally believe, that there is a life beyond this world, and that they shall enjoy it by returning to their own country' — a dream of final repatriation as ghostly returnees.[3]

For the younger and fitter, migratory dreams could be realized in life. Even before emancipation a small number of black men and women, slave or free, were also moving to and fro, particularly as servants. Thus Thomas Thistlewood, white overseer at Egypt plantation in western Jamaica, early in 1768 records in his diary how Coobah (daughter of his own black mistress Phibbah), who was a maid at nearby Paradise plantation, had returned from a spell in England looking 'very well'. She was making the rounds of her friends and lovers telling her news, and bringing with her purchases, including some cloth which Thistlewood bought from her, and a tea set damaged on the voyage which she gave to him: 'she made me a present of 6 pretty china tea cups, 3 saucers (the other 3 being broke) etc'.[4] A better-known instance is the life of the Jamaican boy Francis Barber, who at the age of 17 in 1752 became servant to Dr Johnson, author of the famous English dictionary. As an adolescent Barber went to sea, disliked it and was bought out by Johnson and returned to his service, educated at his expense. Barber stayed with Johnson and became his 'faithful servant' and 'humble friend'. He was Johnson's main heir, married an Englishwoman, and ended up running a school with her, combining this with a smallholding.[5] This recurrent migratory two-way contact from the slave era onwards was vital to the development of the transatlantic creole cultures, drawing on both black and white roots, which has become increasingly celebrated by recent scholars.[6]

It seems most likely, too, that it was during the slavery era that the Jamaican kinship system evolved as a form of protection, when formal marriage between slaves was not recognized, and family members including a child's parents could be parted by separate sales. Slave attitudes to sexuality were perhaps partly influenced by the example of the white plantation elite, for whom multiple extramarital relationships were the normal pattern. There has been considerable debate about how far the Jamaican kinship system retains African features, of which the prevalence in West Africa of 'childshifting', with children partly brought up by other kin, is the most striking example. But on the other hand, there was no survival of the elaborate kinship systems, some matrilineal but most patrilineal, which have continued in the regions from which the slaves were captured.[7] The Jamaican kinship system, as we have already suggested, is by contrast essentially informal, non-heirarchical and gender-neutral, in which bonding is based on shared experience rather than formal blood relationships.

After the abolition of slavery in 1833–38 the story of West Indian migration became less tied to Britain and less clear. Economic difficulties in the post-emancipation period sharply cut back migration from Jamaica to Britain, and the number of black Africans and West Indians in London, which had been estimated at around 20,000 in the late eighteenth century, fell to a few hundred in the dock districts of Shadwell and Canning Town. From the 1890s small communities of African and West Indian sailors also developed in other ports, including Liverpool and Cardiff. The booming South Wales coalfields employed a few West Indian miners in the 1900s. There was a brief additional influx, mainly in the ports, during World War I.[8] Between the wars too, in London there was a group of African and West Indian writers and students, political intellectuals many of whom — such as Eric Williams — became national leaders when colonial independence came after 1945. It was, however, only with World War II that a substantial and sustained new wave of migration to Britain began.

In the meantime, migrant Jamaicans, in this phase predominantly men, had sought and found work in a variety of other migration destinies. Gold mining in Venezuela brought spectacular success for a few: Devon House, still the grandest house in Kingston, was built in 1881 by George Stiebel (1820–96), who is said to have made his fortune in the gold mines, and returned as Jamaica's first black millionaire — the first of the innumerable returnees' mansions now scattered across the island's landscapes. Others migrated as plantation and farm workers to Cuba and the southern United States. The largest migration of all was to build the Panama Canal. Many came back from the migrations, but many also stayed, so that some of Central America has a coastal English-speaking fringe of settlers from Jamaica. The New York Jamaican community goes back to the 1900s, and West Indians played an important role in the inter-war Harlem cultural renaissance, and also in the later black power movement — the best-known pioneer being Marcus Garvey.[9]

World War II was to prove a crucial turning point, both in the patterns of migrations out of Jamaica, and in launching fundamental changes within Jamaica itself. The island in the 1950s had a growing population of two million, already more than its agriculture alone could support. Under English rule it was economically dominated by sugar and coffee plantations. In the post-slavery period bananas, often grown by small farmers, became important alongside bauxite mining by international companies. Universal adult suffrage came in 1944 and full independence in 1962. The early post-independence years were relatively prosperous, with significant economic growth up to the mid-1970s, to which both mining and now also tourism contributed. Nevertheless there was also considerable social dissatisfaction, partly because it was estimated that only half the population was fully at work, but also because Jamaica remained socially stratified along class–colour lines, with wealth and power still overwhelmingly in the hands of a small social elite of Jamaican white or light-skinned families.[10] Even the judges of the annual beauty contests for Miss Jamaica invariably chose a near-white contestant. Education beyond the minimum age had to be paid for, and was mainly the privilege of better-off families. Hence for the black or dark-skinned majority there was still little opportunity in Jamaica.

The 1970s proved a dramatic moment of change. Politically the message of black power — of which Marcus Garvey, himself a Jamaican migrant to the United States, was a lone but key pioneer in the 1930s — returned home, emboldened on the one hand by the successes of the American civil rights movement, and on the other by the growing strength of the Rastafarian movement in Jamaica. A populist government led by Michael Manley was twice elected in 1972 and 1976, and set about a modest land redistribution programme, and an expansion of free secondary education, creating a much broader path for black pupils into the professions. It also created a government Women's Bureau. However, perhaps the most important legacy of the Manley era was a new sense of empowerment and pride in the black majority, which encouraged a decline in colour prejudice socially, and thereby a further opening of work opportunities. But unfortunately, by contrast, Manley's strategy for creating an economic 'third way' failed disastrously, with the Jamaican economy collapsing in the unforgiving hands of the IMF. The economy contracted for the rest of the 1970s, and after Manley failed to secure re-election in 1980, it scarcely grew at all, despite the imposition of privatization, a massive devaluation and sharp cuts in living standards: thus fuelling the ambition for migration as the best hope for most Jamaicans for achieving better living standards.[11]

In the longer run, however, the Jamaican economy has recovered significantly. While the drift from the land has continued, tourism has continued to grow, bauxite mining exports remain important, and the income from migrants and returnees has become more and more significant. Jamaican society is still very unequal, but the visitor can feel the buzz of activity and see the signs of prosperity. The island is peppered with ambitious new houses, built by both locals and migrants, and the young have accepted the new communication technology with open arms. With one and a half million mobile phones, Jamaica has one of the highest proportions to landlines in the world.[12] The contribution of continuing migration to this economy remains crucial.

There have been two main phases in migration patterns since the 1940s, the period of living memory on which we focus in this book. Firstly, at least up until the 1970s, migrants tended to come from rural artisan or small farm families who had the resources to leave; subsequently, existing family connections in the host country, and also education, have become more important factors. Secondly, the main destination for the first post-war decades was Britain, but from the 1970s it switched to North America. Migrants to Britain came above all in the 1950s and 1960s.[13] With the increasing restrictiveness of British immigration policy and the converse opening up of the United States and Canada to West Indian migrants, North America became and has remained the main destination. However, some migrants try life in both continents; and because it is easier to join existing family, flows continue to all three destinations. In the past, while both women and men did migrate, it was easier for men to find opportunities; but especially because of declining demand for unskilled labour, it is now women who find it easier to get initial work.

The wave of migration to Britain was initiated by World War II, with the active recruitment, mainly of men but also of women, from the West Indian colonies in support of the war effort. While most servicemen and women returned after the war ended in 1945, some remained, and because there were many more black men than women, they often married white women — among them our interviewee Rufus Rawlings. The early post-war experience of West Indian migrants in London is vividly conveyed by Sam Selvon's novel *The Lonely Londoners*.[14] But the arrival of the *Empire Windrush* in 1948, packed with keen immigrants, proved a symbolic watershed. The scene shifted dramatically and the gender imbalance was rectified in the 1950s, when both London Transport and the new National Health hospitals were actively recruiting in the West Indies for both men and women staff. In the next few years many of those already in Britain also paid for other family members to follow them. By the 1961 census there were some 200,000, West Indians in England, already an unprecedentedly high figure, half from Jamaica, and more than half in London; and by 1971 numbers had more than doubled to over 500,000.[15]

The hostile political reaction to this influx resulted in the imposition of immigration controls on colonial British subjects, their right of free entry being removed by a series of key new legislation in 1962–71. As a result the growth of the West Indian community slowed drastically, with a current total of migrants and their descendants of approximately 600,000, now sustaining itself more through children born in Britain than from new migrants, while those new migrants who came were usually relatives of those who had already arrived.[16] Over time, too, the communities shifted from being mainly young migrants to mixed-age, with both children and grandparents present. Typically they maintained close contact with their kin both in Jamaica and North America. A particularly striking long-term change was that the rate of intermarriage with white partners, after dipping sharply in the 1960s and 70s, has now risen among young black men and women to a very high level. Of those young West Indian men who have partners, half are white.[17] This degree of interracial mixing represents a new radical demographic form of creolization.

Apart from immigration controls, migration to Britain had in any case become less economically attractive as the post-war boom was succeeded by the stop-go decades, and Britain faced the long-term crisis of ceasing to be one of the world's leading manufacturing nations. By this time in Jamaica people were saying, 'England bruck dung' (broke down). Certainly deindustrialization drastically cut demand for manual labour, for which most of the migrants had come, and this created serious unemployment problems especially for younger men. Nevertheless those who stayed in Britain mostly fared reasonably well.[18] The less fortunate have benefited from the welfare system, with subsidized council housing and free health services, while there has been significant upward mobility among both migrants and their children, and especially women.

Soon after Britain had begun to impose immigration controls, from the late 1960s both the United States and Canada opened up immigration, but mainly favouring those with educational qualifications and close relatives of earlier migrants. This is why Jamaican immigration to North America has not been primarily of manual workers, as it had been to Britain, but of migrants with higher aspirations. In the United States Jamaicans have an image as notably ambitious, both in work and education.

In North America the two foremost Jamaican communities have been firstly New York, and secondly and more recently Toronto. The North American Caribbean community has been estimated, including both legal and illegal immigrants and their children, as numbering up to one million in New York, of whom probably some 300,000 are Jamaican, and more definitely 150,000 Jamaicans in Toronto.[19] New York has experienced long periods of sustained economic growth, from which West Indian migrants have benefited: as in Britain, although clearly behind the white population and some other ethnic minorities, they do significantly better than others, such as Africans, Latinos, and African Americans. The Toronto community has been much less successful economically.[20] Culturally, on the other hand, these two North American communities developed in different historic contexts, which has given them strikingly different characteristics. Black immigration to Toronto only became significant from the 1970s, in a period in which multiculturalism had become a strong public aim in Canada. Jamaican immigration to New York, by contrast, has taken place in intermittent waves throughout the twentieth century, to a society which already has an existing and racially marginalized black minority, and in which for most of this period racism was institutionalized — at work, in politics and in private relations. As recently as the mid-1960s, black-white marriages were illegal in much of the United States. Moreover, despite the subsequent major changes in the 1960s, the black communities remain drastically segregated in terms of housing, and interracial marriage remains

— at scarcely one per cent of all marriages — extraordinarily rare. As we shall see (chapter six), many Jamaicans have found this segregated sociability particularly offensive. Nevertheless because their primary goal is economic, with most still thinking initially in terms of a successful return, it is above all to the United States — to New York, and now Florida too — with its thriving economy and high earnings, that Jamaican migrants today are still looking for the realization of their dreams.

How Much Do We Know?

How much is already known about these transnational families? Most of the information available to us is descriptive rather than statistical. There are absolutely no statistics concerning transnational families as such, since information is invariably drawn from separate national studies. Even the numbers of Jamaican migrants and their descendants living in particular destinations are approximate, especially in the United States with its higher numbers of recent illegal immigrants. Nor in terms of families are there any really satisfactory units of analysis, given that parenting and sexual relationships may often be not only conducted within but also between different households. The most interesting common finding which emerges from all the various national figures is that Jamaicans everywhere have for generations tended to marry late if at all, and also that they have a high rate of female-headed households, twice that in the white British or North American populations. But partly because West Indian migrants, especially women, also have a high rate of employment, this has not led to them being among the poorer immigrant groups in either Britain or the United States.

In terms of ethnographic and descriptive work, by far the richest is on the family in Jamaica itself, both historical and contemporary. Fortunately there were some notable and relatively sympathetic earlier studies, of which Edith Clarke's *My Mother Who Fathered Me*, and Raymond Smith's *Kinship and Class in the West Indies* are outstanding. During the last 15 years — and not by accident, precisely when for the first time divorce, single mothers and stepfamilies have become commonplace rather than exceptional in white American and British families — Caribbean family structures have begun to be interpreted more positively. Thus Jean Besson's *Martha Brae's Two Histories* is an important recent study of rural family and community, while Christine Barrow's *Family in the Caribbean* provides a very perceptive historical and contemporary overview of family through the region. There is also important new work on gender, including Verene Shepherd's *Women in Caribbean History*, Barrow's *Caribbean Portraits* and Barry Chevannes' *Learning to Be a Man*.[21]

In Britain the series of earlier community studies culminated in Sheila Patterson's classic account of the South London Caribbean community in Brixton in the 1960s, *Dark Strangers*. Subsequent work over the last 40 years has never had this broad canvas, but includes valuable studies by Nancy Foner and Sandra Wallman in London, and by Ken Pryce in Bristol, as well as many other insights from the wider literature on migrants.[22]

In the United States most research on 'the black family' has focused on black American families rather than the much smaller immigrant West Indian communities. Classic and highly controversial landmarks include work by Franklin Frazier, Gutman and the notoriously pejorative Moynihan Report.[23] It was assumed by many that all black families effectively belonged to a single ethnic culture. In Canada, where earlier black migrants were less salient, the situation was different. Thus we have a full study of the Caribbean community in Toronto, including a substantial section on family life, in Frances Henry's, *The Caribbean Diaspora in Toronto: Learning to Live with Racism*. There is now also a growing literature on West Indians in New York, pioneered by Nancy Foner and Constance Sutton, and including most recently Mary C. Waters', *Black Identities: West Indian Immigrant Dreams and American Realities*. The family life of early Jamaican migrants to New York is beautifully captured by Paule Marshall's novel *Brown Girl, Brownstones*. In addition, Christine Ho's *Saltwater Trinnies*, on Trinidadians in Los Angeles, and Peggy Levitt's *The Transnational Villagers* on Spanish-speaking Dominican migrants to Boston, provide very interesting parallels to the New York West Indian experience.[24]

There are an increasing number of studies examining a diversity of migrations which have resulted from the recent blossoming of interest in the transnational family on both sides of the Atlantic. There is a rare forerunner in Tamara Hareven's account of the resilience of Quebec families who sent migrant workers to the New England textile mills. More recent American work has included Sherri Grasmuck and Patricia Pessar's impressively designed project on Dominican migration to New York, *Between Two Islands*, and other research for example on transnational motherhood, Hong Kong global businessmen and Mexican migrants and their families. A particularly promising innovation has been the work of Linda Basch, Nina Glick Schiller and their colleagues, using comparisons of cultural, business or political transnational developments drawn from a range of different migrant groups (including to New York from the Philippines and the Eastern Caribbean) to lay the foundations for a sharper conceptual approach to transnational migration, including 'the family as a transnational relationship'. Also worth special mention is a personal contribution, Edward Said's memoir *Out of Place*, an autobiographical account of the ambiguities in growing up in a Christian Palestinian family which straddled Lebanon and Egypt, did business between Cairo and the United States, and insisted on the best American education for their son.[25]

There have been some parallel studies by European researchers. However, on the other hand, with British research on the Caribbean family the emergence of this new perspective has been particularly linked to a broader growth of interest in transnational and hybrid cultures. In particular, Paul Gilroy has demonstrated the transnational creativity of Caribbean culture in *The Black Atlantic: Modernity and Double Consciousness*, while in his *Global Diasporas* Robin Cohen has explored a wide range of 'travelling cultures' and their transnational connectedness over long periods. He includes among them the Chinese and Lebanese merchant diasporas, Jewish and Sikh faith diasporas, Armenian and African 'victim diasporas', and 'Caribbean peoples as a cultural diaspora'.[26]

Nevertheless, apart from our own study in this book, there has been no transnational study of migrant Caribbean families which encompasses their connections and exchanges of help across the whole transcontinental Atlantic triangle. Thus for our concerns, the most important research project on the transnational family is on migrants between the West Indies and Britain, carried out by Harry Goulbourne and Mary Chamberlain. The preliminary findings of this have been very rewarding, especially

Goulbourne's key article seeing the Jamaican transnational family as a progressive modern form.[27]

Mary Chamberlain has been exceptional as a Caribbean historian in her persistent use of the oral history method. In the Spanish-speaking Caribbean there was the pioneering anthropological life story work of Sidney Mintz's *Worker in the Cane* (1960) in Puerto Rico, and also of Oscar Lewis's later work in Cuba and Puerto Rico, which included interviewing Puerto Ricans from the same families in New York — but without exploring their transnational links. By contrast, there has been little significant life story or oral history work in the English-speaking West Indies. In Jamaica itself the most important pioneer, Erna Brodber, has subsequently become a notably successful novelist.[28] This gap has not been filled by the testimonies typically published by local community projects as in Britain and North America.

The most important exception is therefore Chamberlain's work, focusing mainly on migration between Barbados and Britain. Especially in her book *Narratives of Exile and Return* she has used her interviews with Barbadians to show how family stories and myths could influence decisions to migrate and to return. She interprets their stories essentially as cultural narratives. She vividly demonstrates how the high rate of emigration from Barbados, as from the rest of the Caribbean, is sustained not only by economic needs but also by a local culture in which migration is intrinsically valued, with old men telling stories to the young so that they felt that the experience of 'travelling' was an essential part of growing up. She has made a particularly original contribution by showing how migration cultures can vary not only between societies, but also between families in the same society, and how the intergenerational transmission of these cultures influences the migration decisions of family members. Thus while one family takes as its transgenerational theme the 'love to travel', in another family migration is rather a story of successive failures, and hence of forced returns; while in a third family, the migration theme is of setbacks and betrayals — being abandoned, or robbed of an inheritance — which are successfully overcome, again in each generation. She shows with rich illustrations how these family influences affected both men and women in their decisions to leave home, and also whether or not to return.[29]

Jamaican Transnational Families: Our Project

Our own aim is to understand more clearly, through an in-depth view of a small number of migrant Jamaican families, both their sources of strength and resilience, and also their points of loss and pain. Our research is based on life story interviews with 45 families. With each family we have interviewed up to four — and sometimes more — members in the different continents, and we also draw on participant observation at many family occasions. We are primarily concerned with the recent past and present, but the life stories which we have collected also yield fascinating double insights, not only on the past itself, but also on how movement to another country leads to new views by migrants of their family and community of origin.

We have each come to this project from very different directions. Elaine is an anthropologist, herself Jamaican, one among many migrants from a poor rural village in western Jamaica, and she belongs to a transnational family with kin in Jamaica, the USA, Canada and England. This is Paul's first work on Caribbean families, but it principally uses the oral history/ life story method which he has pioneered for over thirty years and argued for in *The Voice of the Past*. He first used transgenerational family oral histories for a project with Daniel Bertaux on families and social mobility in Britain and France. He has had a longstanding interest in complex families, recently publishing a life story sample-based study of British stepfamilies.[30]

The picture which emerged from that stepfamily study was not only of much real grief, but also of resilience: most of these stepfamilies worked reasonably well, and more than this, they showed an unexpectedly high rate of upward occupational mobility. From this and other evidence it would seem that complex families generate success stories as well as social work cases: risers, as well as fallers. With the transnational families we have again wanted to understand better the workings of such complicated families forms. We see this as potentially helpful, not only to those who work with them as cases, but also more positively because we may be able to learn from their ways of handling difficult family issues and transitions which have been part of Caribbean family life for generations. Equally important, we see the accounts which these families have given us of their experiences, both in Jamaica and also in the United States, Canada and Britain, as providing a rich and crucial descriptive thread for the social history of all four countries in our time.

While there is no practicable quantitative sample base for a transnational study, unlike most other oral histories of migrants we have adhered to a rough sample frame and sought a balance in terms of gender, age and occupations. The interviewees range in age from their thirties to their eighties. Altogether we have recorded 106 interviewees, of whom half are women and half are men. Of these, 36 were in Britain, 22 in the United States, 13 in Canada and 35 in Jamaica. We interviewed some second generation members in our transnational families, so that our study is not only transnational, but also transgenerational. The interviews include some family members in Jamaica who had never migrated, and also (to provide a contrast) five Jamaicans who had no active contact with transnational kin, so that taking into account the second generation born abroad, only 70 of our interviewees had themselves migrated. In terms of occupations, in the whole group we have a rough balance between those in non-manual occupations on the one hand, and those in manual work or unemployed on the other. In Britain half the interviewees are over 55, but in North America, where the main migration movement came later, most are younger. We found the interviewees mostly through different networks — families, clubs, associations — but also a small number were people we originally met at random in the street in Jamaica, London or New York.

We have combined these recorded interviews with participant observation both in Jamaica and the countries of destination, sharing everyday living and joining in mealtimes, casual talk and church services, and also at special occasions such as funerals, parties and migrant reunions.

Except for two interviewees who specifically asked for their own names to be used, we have used pseudonyms throughout in order to maintain confidentiality. Each interviewee was asked after the interview to sign a consent form, permitting us to use the material for our project, and also after the completion of the project to archive it as a resource for future research. For this book we have also included four interviews conducted by Harry Goulbourne in a much earlier oral history project with Paul

Thompson.[31] Apart from the four recorded by Goulbourne and one other interview, we have carried out all the interviews ourselves. For roughly half of the interviews both of us were present, while the remainder were recorded separately by Elaine or Paul. Given our very different social images, Elaine a younger black Jamaican-Canadian woman and Paul an older white Englishman, whoever led the interview could have had a significant influence in shaping the testimonies, and we looked carefully to see how far this was so. The really important difference seemed to be in the setting up of the interview, which Elaine was able to achieve much more easily and quickly than Paul. In the interviews, on the other hand, it seems that the importance of these differences in social position quickly faded. We both followed the same life story format which we had worked out together, and although Elaine's style is a little more conversational, there are no obvious differences in the broad content of the interviews. There is, however, some difference with the Goulbourne interviews, which used an earlier interview guide and were less focused on family and more on work and politics. With our own interviews, not only is the broad coverage the same, but we equally often recorded men and women who used many *patois* phrases; and we were each as often told about 'outside' children, or illegal activities, or experiences of racism. The really striking differences are much more between the interviewees themselves. Thus some would give brief responses, while others would articulate their memories at length or shape some of their story according to their religious beliefs — which could be with either of us. We have also been able to compare our recorded material with many informal conversations with migrant Jamaicans, visiting families, travelling round Jamaica in route taxis and so on. All this gives us confidence in its quality as evidence.

How far can we rely on the evidence of oral history? The familiar process by which memory is reshaped from the standpoint of the present was long assumed by historians to be a fundamental defect in oral sources, and a reason for avoiding them wherever possible. Since the late 1970s, however, it has been increasingly recognized that this very process in itself can give a second dimension to the value of oral testimony as evidence, enabling not only the conveying of past facts but also of the evolution of consciousness over time.[32] We have used this 'subjective' or 'narrative' perspective especially when interpreting childhood memories of family, community and environment in Jamaica, in which migrants explore their ancestral roots, or contrast the lost worlds of their childhood with the places to which they have travelled.

In this book, however, we are equally concerned with the accounts of direct experience which the interviews convey. They are full of information on, for example, family members and contact with them, work experience, childrearing, migration chains, housing and so on, which are known to be much more objectively reliable as evidence. Indeed interestingly, in some instances, as with the older women migrants who feel themselves bereft of family, a single interview may be equally vivid both subjectively and factually, so that we can see the contradictions within their own evidence between factual information and more subjective feeling, which highlights the importance of the emotional dimension.

Clearly the evidence of oral testimonies has a different importance depending on the field. No historian would want to use them as a starting point for a history of Jamaican local or national politics. A file of the *Daily Gleaner* would obviously be much more fruitful. None of these interviewees had a strong earlier interest in political issues, and only a few even recall talk among their parents of Manley and other politicians. For this kind of historical field much more specialized interviewees would be essential, with local and national political activists.

For family and for migration, on the other hand, oral testimony is a prime source. There is effectively no other documentation at all of ordinary family relationships. The raw material of important earlier studies such as Edith Clarke's *My Mother Who Fathered Me* does not seem to have been archived. Family land was typically handed down orally rather than through legal documents. Even demographic records are impaired by the prevalence of outside children and unrecorded fathers. Interestingly this can also be a difficulty with modern genealogical family tracing, because some family members may not wish to recognize other kin born outside of couple relationships. Thus moving from oral memory to a documented family tree can become problematic. We recall two instances of this: once a dispute in a grandmother's kitchen with her children, about how many grandchildren she had, because she refused to count an outside grandchild;

and another time, looking at a newly-drawn family tree, with a child again asking after a familiar relative, 'Why is X not shown there?' In this kind of situation the oral will prove fuller than the documentary evidence. And more broadly, there is thus no other way in which we can now explore twentieth century Jamaican kinship patterns, parent–child and couple relationships.

Similarly, for migration the main documentary source, the official statistics of migration, provide at best a context, and at that a dubious one, for inevitably they do not include illegal immigrants. Equally important, the documentation of migration is from the country of origin or of destination, with the two ends unconnected. It is only through life story evidence that we can unearth the processes of migration, the dreams and information and paying for tickets before the passage, the help from kin and friends in getting work and lodging on arrival, and the long-term outcome: whether of successful establishment, a career, sustaining a transnational family, or a story of discrimination and despondency, or a choice to return to the homeland.

We must emphasize that myth is intrinsic to history itself. These transnational families have their own myths, in terms both of ancestry and of ambition, and some of them are creating new myths out of their own histories. But still more important we believe is the power of oral history in giving voice to ordinary men and women, conveying their experience of work and migration and family, of religion and education, and their own interpretations of this lived experience. We also see the history of beliefs and dreams and life meanings being of fundamental significance. For it is these living forces, which can be tapped by oral testimony alone, rather than the dry bones of statistics, which generate and sustain the constantly evolving processes of both family and migration.

THREE

Jamaica: Recapturing Family Memories

Family stories and memories, and particularly memories of childhood, have the power to take us back into lost social worlds of the past: lost worlds, because these private worlds have left few traces in other documents of the time, so that living memory is the only way of recapturing them. Indeed, because of this lack of documents a convincing history of the family relationships of Jamaicans — or of ordinary people in any country in the world — before the last hundred years is effectively impossible. But memories of the family are not just clues into how the past really was. The reshaping of memories over time and the gaps in what is retold are deeply influenced by personal and social attitudes and contexts, so that memory is also a witness of changing consciousness. We shall use these childhood memories in both ways here: to evoke a past, but also to note how far those who have stayed on in Jamaica, and migrants, revisiting Jamaica at best infrequently and influenced by later experiences of migration and living abroad, recall the past differently.

We focus on four themes. Firstly, in this chapter the development of family stories of origin; and memories of childhood itself, of love and of hardship within the family. Then in the next chapter, two further themes: memories of lost community, in terms of harmony or conflict; and lastly, memories of the Jamaican environment, of land, water and fruits.

Family Stories and Myths of Origin

First, family stories and myths of origin. All those we interviewed had stories to tell about their families. However, typically these went back no further than grandparents, and often when a father had not been present in childhood the memory was on one side of the family only. In only a third of the families were stories of origin recounted which went back to earlier generations. Some indeed made their lack of interest clear: as Stuart Campbell, brought up in a rural skilled working-class family and now an accountant in the USA, put it:

> I don't know much really. I wasn't too curious really about going too far back. I mean, as far as I'm concerned there were more important things. You're brought up in poor families... So spending the time researching family history and all that wasn't important to me at all. I just want to go to college and get out.

But there were certainly other families, albeit a minority, in which stories and myths of origin were handed down, and in these often the interviewee mentioned there was either family storytelling at gatherings, or there was a grandmother, who along with Anancy stories 'would tell us a lot of stories about family'.[1]

Equally striking, there were clear class differences between those families which had myths of origin and those which did not. The families split broadly into three groups, according to the social position of the interviewees' parents' social standing: a lower class, where parents were unskilled and either landless or with no more than a vegetable patch; a peasant class, possessing some land and usually in skilled occupations; and a middle class, either substantial farmers or in professional occupations. We were not told family stories of origin in any one of the lower class families; but by contrast, we heard them from over a third of the peasant and skilled class families, and from nearly all of the middle class families whose members we interviewed.

One might expect that the reason for myths of origin being more prevalent among peasant families was partly functional, because of the need to pass down a precise oral memory of the transmission of 'family land' from earlier generations: particularly given the rules for its transmission in Jamaica, and the normal reliance on oral rather than documentary evidence of title. Rights to family land are held in common by every descendent of its first ancestral owner, whether male or female or legitimate or outside children. Moreover such land commonly has an added significance for family memory, as the place where family members have been buried. Jean Besson's research on seven older rural communities found that in each there were at least some families with oral traditions of ancestry back to the slave period.[2] Nevertheless, although those whom we recorded, whether migrants or staying in Jamaica, were well aware of their family land, often giving precise detail of its size and who held it at present, and although for some migrants their rights to it were an important part of their own identity and their hopes for building a house to enable a future return to Jamaica, not a single one could trace the landholding back beyond their grandparents — let alone to origins in the era of slavery and liberation. How do we explain this silence in their family oral traditions?

Since with those families who do recount stories of earlier origin, their stories or myths do not seem to convey any practical function in terms of claims to land or possessions, we need to consider what they mean to the families at a more symbolic level in terms of their social standing — in terms both of race and class. We also need to remember the social context in which these family traditions were generated, which was *before* the 1970s and the transforming impact of Michael Manley's reform campaign and the black power movement on Jamaican culture and society. Despite Emancipation from slavery, up to the mid-twentieth century Jamaica had continued to be a colour-stratified society run by a largely white or light-skinned creole elite. Social class and skin colour were largely coterminous, with whites at the top and blacks at the bottom, and in between a large mixed-race group, at least a quarter of the population, but very varied between darker and lighter, including within the same family, so that such differences could give one brother much better social chances than another. It was not only skin colour which counted: 'kinky' hair, thick lips and flat noses were also considered 'bad'. In this colour-class society fine judgements therefore had to be made. As Fernando Henriques, himself an elite Jamaican, but relatively dark-skinned, put it:

A person might exhibit European-like features, but his hair might be more negroid than European. In such a case, his colour status in the society would be determined by the texture of his skin. This individual would rank above a person of similar complexion with "good" hair, but whose features were more African.

And underlying all this prejudice was the past. The fair-skinned regarded blackness with 'abhorrence' above all because 'blackness was the badge of slavery'.[3]

Such long-standing attitudes had, moreover, become deeply internalized at all social levels. In many different ways Jamaicans could be found trying to make themselves seem fairer. Parents would dream of their children marrying a fairer partner, so as to 'lighten up' their offspring. Pregnant women would avoid eating chocolate or drinking coffee, in the hope that this would result in lighter babies. The few well-to-do black families would employ white servants to emphasize their own rank. As the old Jamaican proverb had it, 'Every John Crow tink him pickney white': every black vulture thinks his offspring is white.

The family stories which we have recorded seem to be strongly shaped by these attitudes. Every one of them is about mixed race origin, a mixing which is often celebrated in itself. Olive Carstairs, now in Canada, takes a contemporary pleasure in the stories she has heard of her unusually complex multicultural heritage, and is hoping to make a genealogical tree of her origins: 'On my dad's side, there is African and there's Indian. And on my mum's side there is white. I guess there is also African there some way back.' Two families also mention ancestors who were Chinese or Syrian traders. But there is almost always a connection with a white ancestor, usually a plantation owner or overseer: particularly English and Scottish, but also of Welsh, Jewish, Dutch, Portuguese or French Huguenot origins. Thus Hyancinth Beck, now a New York clinic administrator, recalls her grandmother's stories: 'My grandmother on my father's side, her father was English.... He was one of those people who owns an estate with slaves.' Often too the story is directly linked with skin colour, with ancestors who were 'fairish, more European': 'She was from the Scottish side ... fair-skinned.'

Family stories of this kind are well-known aspects of Jamaican culture at all social levels. Thus when Jack Alexander collected genealogies among the middle classes in the 1960s he reported that they had a common 'myth of origin' of descent from the union of a white master and a black slave, although they knew very little about the black side: 'I will never know, where the various families I'm comprised of come from.... My parents accentuated the white side. Well, we all know it's a healthy mixture — the fact that we know we're so mixed up.'[4] The popular equivalent to such celebrating of mixed origin may be found, for example, in a dialect poem of Louise Bennett[5] on the 'Back to Africa' movement:

> Back to Africa Miss Matty?
> Yuh noh know wha yuh dah-sey?
> Yuh haffe come from some weh fus,
> Before yuh go back deh?
>
> Me know sey dat yuh great great great
> Gramma was African
> But Matty, doan yuh great great great
> Grampa was Englishman?
>
> Den yuh great granmada fada
> By yuh fada side was Jew?
> An yuh grampa by yuh mada side
> Was Frenchie parley-vous!
>
> But de balance o' yuh family
> Yuh whole generation
> Oonoo all bawn dung a Bun grung
> Oonoo all is Jamaican!

Translated as

> Back to Africa, Miss Matty?
> You don't know what you are saying?
> You have to come from somewhere first,
> Before you go back there?

I know they say your great great great
Grandma was African
But Matty, wasn't your great great great
Grandpa an Englishman?

Then your great-grandmother's father
On your father's side was a Jew?
And your grandpa on your mother's side
Was French-speaking!

But the balance of your family,
Your whole generation,
You were all born in the backwoods
You're all Jamaicans!

Thus among our own interviews it is very striking that, in contrast to the frequent mention of white ancestry, not one has a story of descent from a black slave; yet in each of these families such black ancestors were likely to have been the largest group. On the other hand, however, four families do recount with special pride their descent not only from white but also from black ancestors who were free, one African and the other two Maroons. Stephanie Gladstone, now in Canada, daughter of a doctor, spoke of an African who 'came over from some area in Nigeria and was never actually a slave ... and he owned quite a big piece of land'. This means that blackness can also be recounted proudly: David McNeep, a retired London railwayman, described a Maroon ancestor as 'a nice Samba lady, used to comb all her hair and it would reach her in her back'. Similarly, Brigette Umber, now in New York, whose father was a skilled construction worker, told of her descent from the Maroons:

we're mixed with Scottish and Maroon.... But I'm a full-blooded Maroon, because I have it on both sides. My mother's parents, their grandparents are Maroon. My father's parents, their grandparents are Maroon. So I'm a full-blooded Maroon. It's important to me. It's lovely to know that I'm from a very strong vibrant family line!

This pride in *free* black descent suggests a vital clue towards understanding why most Jamaican black slave ancestors have been totally forgotten. There are some cultures for which past sufferings have become embedded in current identities: for example, the impact of the potato famine on the Irish, or the Holocaust on the Jews, or indeed, for African-Americans, especially from the old South, slavery times. The Jamaican mood has been totally different. The everyday greeting is, 'walk good'; and Jamaicans do mostly walk with their heads high, and joke and smile, and fight hard for their rights too. They are rightly proud of how they resisted slavery, rebelling again and again, and how the Jamaican Maroons in the 1730s were the first escaped slaves to defeat the army of a European colonial power, and win their independence by a treaty which still stands. And again, those Jamaicans and other West Indians who have migrated to the United States have been much less prepared to accept discrimination than American-born blacks, and have provided many of the leaders of the black power movement, from Marcus Garvey to Stokely Carmichael, Shirley Chisholm and the Trinidadian George Padmore. Lastly, Jamaicans are well aware and proud too that since independence their small nation has generated a highly creative new black culture, which has proved a powerful influence worldwide. This culture includes both Rastafarianism and the broader movement in popular music, of which Bob Marley has become the symbol. And it is no accident that one of Marley's best-known lyrics is 'Redemption Songs':

> These songs of freedom, is all I ever had,
> Redemption songs:
> Emancipate yourselves from mental slavery,
> None but ourselves can free our minds.

Almost all Jamaicans know very well that their black ancestors were slaves, but outside professional historians, few discuss this. A folk storyteller like Louise Bennett does not tell slave stories. A collection of women's oral autobiographies put together by the theatre group SISTREN has only one family slavery story, and that was a story of escape, 'how di slaves rebel and run way'. Proverbs are another very vital oral tradition, and again the very few which refer to slavery are about escaping from it: 'Bush, bush no have no whip.'[6] When we interviewed Selassie Jordan, a travelling Rastafarian streetseller in New York, he said that he was merely 'reborn' in 1977: but about his original birth it was 'hard to tell you right now, because I'm still suffering from amnesia of the slave trade and all those things, you know?' To put it briefly, Jamaican culture has sought to free Jamaican minds by observing a silence over the humiliations of living under slavery.

This interpretation helps to explain, we believe, why unlike ourselves Jean Besson has been able to trace oral traditions of much longer black ancestry among at least some families in seven communities in north-central Jamaica. Two of her communities are in fact of Maroon origin, and their traditions go back to the rebel leaders Colonel Cudgoe and Nanny (Jamaica's equivalent to Joan of Arc) who were buried here in the mid-eighteenth century. In the other five communities there are no traditions from the slave period itself, but some of the freed slaves who first acquired the land are remembered. However, these villages were the fruit of a high-profile free settlement campaign by the English Baptist preacher William Knibb, key leader of the missionary freedom movement, who organized the purchase by subscription from bankrupt plantation owners of much of the land himself. Knibb's whole family were involved, and at Emancipation his son 'leaped for joy', sketching 'a British ship in full sail, with the word "liberty" on her flag, chasing two slavers, [while] on the pendant was written, "slavery must fall"'. Knibb himself celebrated by ceremonially burying slave irons, collars and whips in his churchyard in nearby Falmouth, and he was later buried there beside them.[7] By contrast, in other more typical villages, family land originated from squatting on waste land, or was donated by plantation owners, or even simply continued the provision grounds from which slaves in Jamaica had been expected to supply their own food. We suggest that the highly politicized origins of Besson's communities made it much more likely for their founders to be remembered in local oral tradition, not because they had been slaves but because of how they ensured future freedom for themselves and their families.

With our own interviews, given the linking of colour and class in Jamaican society, it is not surprising that these family myths of origin invariably imply descent, not only from a white ancestor, but also from a superior social stratum. Stephanie Gladstone traces one side of her ancestors, 'the Wensums, back to East Anglia and the Norman invasion of England.' She claims the English ancestral line, but portrays the Wensums as if with a Jamaicanized sexuality: 'old man Wensum was quite prolific, both inside and outside the home.… There are a lot of Wensums in Jamaica.' Another woman, Dana Howard, now an accountant in Florida, brought up in a farm family, spoke of descent from Sir Nicholas Laws, 'our first colonial governor'. Other ancestors are simply plantation owners, or professionals: as Rose Lyle, a retired London nurse whose father was a tailor, put it, 'in our family we have, even on my father's side, we have a lot of doctors'.

In two or three families these stories of superior origin are linked with a story of lost inheritance, which partly explains the family's humbler present situation. Dick Woodward's father was a hill village tailor, but on his mother's side there was a romantic twofold family myth. For his grandfather was black, of Maroon descent, but cut off from the Maroon community because of his marriage to Dick's storytelling grandmother, who was 'white to look at'. Dick was told 'she was from a very rich family.' However, the fortune had been lost because her brother, the heir, 'was conned out of his family [inheritance] — the family, the other side, stole most of the property. He didn't have much of an education, and they conned him out of it'.

In Rose Lyle's family there are two different stories of lost inheritances. One was from a rich British relative who had earned a fortune in Jamaica, but Rose's cousin's claims could not be substantiated because 'the name is spelt wrongly, they said "no": they couldn't get that money, because of that. So that was it. That was it! They know for a fact that it is there, but … they didn't get it'. So the cousin stayed a bus driver. The other story was told by Rose's sister, Marisa Keat, who is a retired dressmaker in Kingston: this was of how her great-grandmother, Sarah Beckford, whose father had been a great plantation owner, had kept a secret heirloom in 'a little trinket box … and she's locked it up, nobody's to interfere with that box. And you know what they did? When she died, they buried the box beside her in the grave'. Marisa still thinks the heirloom should be recovered: 'they want to dig it up. Because Mother Beckford's grave, it was in the family land, in the family burial ground.'

Whether about white or black forbears, only rarely do the stories as told to us portray an ancestor as a strong individual personality. Stephanie Gladstone's family have passed down the rare proud black image of a grandfather's aunt, 'a very dark woman', dressed entirely in black, riding on a big black horse. There are also two white men who are recalled with some generosity. Sandrine Porto, a care worker in New York, and her father Lloyd, still a carpenter in Jamaica, described their descent from a Portuguese overseer, a plantation 'bacra', 'a busha on the sugar estate', who took as his woman a 'domestic helper', 'a lovely girl', who was 'really from the slave line'. But this Porto acknowledged his outside child as his son, and ensured that he in turn became a plantation manager. Rose Lyle told the story of a great-grandparent, Henry Vigne, a Frenchman who owned an estate, who rescued and married Sarah Beckford, the daughter of a big sugar plantation owner, who had got pregnant by a local farmer and was disowned by her own family. Henry Vigne was in Spanish Town on business one day, and he spotted her: 'and she was sitting there, and she was crying. He stopped, and he asked her what was wrong, and she explain everything, and so — she nobody to go to, and what to do? So he said, "All right, come with me." And he took her up to this place, [his farm] called Desire', where they settled and married for life.

Rose's sister Marisa in Jamaica gave a further twist to this story, a telling element of conflicting race feelings within the family. Sarah Beckford was herself an outside child, and while her father acknowledged her, he 'didn't want any Jamaican negro to grow up his child', so she was taken to England for her education. But when Sarah came back to Jamaica she was so eager to rediscover her origins that she escaped from the Beckford plantation to Spanish Town, and from there found the village where her mother came from, and got pregnant by a local man there. At this point the Beckfords gave up hope for her, and she was found by Henry Vigne. But Sarah in turn tried to educate her daughter, Rose and Marisa's grandmother, whose ancestry was mainly black, in plantation manners. Marisa remembers asking her as a child, puzzled, how it was that 'You're a nigger like we, but you don't talk patois like we.'

While all but one of these stories comes directly from oral traditions within the family itself, there are also hints in more than one interview of a possible new future direction for family myths. This is retrospective genealogical research in order to recreate lost family stories. Already in several of our families there are enthusiastic family historians: migrants or their children recording interviews with older family members, one Jamaican writing an autobiography, another constructing a huge family tree on a piece of linen — 'and she wrote all the relatives, all over Canada and America [and England], everywhere they were'. In principle this might become a way of retracing lines of descent which have been lost in family memories, including descent from black slaves on the plantations.

It is clear that some migrants have become aware of the popularity of genealogical research in both North America and Britain as a way of rediscovering family origins, and the influence of Alex Haley's *Roots* (1976) as an encouragement to tracing origins back to Africa. One of our interviewees is Leonard Selkirk, who comes from a skilled and smallholding family and is now an educationist in Britain, and has been drafting a booklet on genealogical research, intended for British Jamaicans. This lists possible archival sources both in Britain and Jamaica. He sees family tracing specifically in terms of migration, as a way of helping his own children 'to feel connected' to their Jamaican heritage, providing precise knowledge of the family patterns:

> not just "hearsay dat one deh a yuh family". A family trace became real and provided that essential bond of ensuring connectedness.... This for me was the legacy I could bequeath to the future: a sense of history and a sense of belonging. No matter where we are in the world, the family must transcend the physical and geographical boundaries that can act as a barrier to maintaining contact. Our children, in turn, must be given the chance to extend and expand on the start we provide. This for me is the legacy of true cultural reproduction and transmission. This provided a powerful drive to undertaking a family trace.

There are, however, special difficulties in family tracing in Jamaica precisely due to the family land system, which rarely leaves documents of the process of intergenerational transmission. This is not so throughout the English-speaking West Indies: for instance, in British Guiana, where land transactions were based on Roman-Dutch law, there were regular surveys of land holdings from Emancipation onwards, and we have met contemporary Guyanese who do have precisely-documented accounts of their ancestry back to slavery. In the Jamaican context Leonard's own investigations are impressively thorough. He had to start from scratch, because neither of his parents knew their family stories. Leonard has produced an elaborate computerized family tree, and shown that one side of his own family can be traced back to a part of the island where Arawak Indians may have survived, and that another side may have been descended from a Scot called by his mother's maiden name, a Jacobite who was transported to Jamaica in a ship in 1747 immediately after the routing of the Jacobite rebels in the battle of Culloden Moor. He has also carried out oral history recordings with his grandparents' generation. The details which have emerged are fascinating.

Equally remarkable, however, is that one can almost see the creation of new 'research-based' family myths here in process, for while neither of the links to the Arawak Indians nor the 1747 ship can be more than possibilities, with other family members whom we have met they have already become certainties — new oral traditions. Moreover, they have been rephrased so that the ship becomes a 'slave ship', with all the resonances of black roots, although it was a white Scotsman who was transported. It was in fact the mythical version of the story which we first encountered ourselves, from another relative at a public meeting in North America. It may well be that with succeeding Jamaican generations, the combination of new family history research with a growing pride in black ancestry will result in a much more general shift of emphasis in the family stories of ancestry and origin towards the re-evaluation and rediscovery of slave forbears.

Love and Discipline

We turn now from family myths and stories of remoter ancestors, handed down by earlier generations, to direct memories rooted in personal experience: children's memories of grandparents and parents. In our interviews just over a hundred significant parental figures are sufficiently portrayed in this respect, including some 25 grandparents, 30 fathers and 40 mothers. How did these adults try to convey love and caring and to instill discipline? As a whole the gentler and more communicative approaches to childrearing favoured in Britain and North America, and now a strong influence in Jamaica too, contrast sharply with the strict severity and lack of discussion which marked so many Jamaican childhoods in the past.[8] This could provoke reflection, and sometimes an outright rejection of the parental model, when these children grew up to be parents themselves. Equally important, there were many exceptions to the severe stereotype: most notably from grandmothers, but less expectedly, equally often from fathers.

Grandfathers appear least often as significant figures, usually at the margin. None of them played a disciplinary role, leaving that to the women, and there was one remembered because he 'would shield us' from chastisement. Rose Lyle remembers how her mother's father, a large farmer, would now and then ride up to their house, and 'we used to rush out, and there he sit on his horse, and he'd got something for everyone'. Spurgeon White grew up with a grandfather, another farmer, who he admired for his generosity to neighbours, but found hard to talk to: 'My grandfather never really have no communication ... I couldn't see all his emotions.' But there were also four grandfathers who were remembered as easy to talk to, including one who was a storyteller, a farm worker, for Robert Austin 'my favourite granddad': 'we just look forward to especially night time, because he would tell us many stories.' Nevertheless, only three seem to have been central figures for their grandchildren's young lives.

Leonard Selkirk lived close to his mother's parents, and then with them briefly as a boy after his parents had migrated to England. For him his small farmer grandfather, tall, white-haired and dark-skinned, was a 'powerful' influence. Descended from the Maroons, he had traditional knowledge from living close to nature. 'He had this remarkable skill to detect poisonous and non-poisonous mushrooms. He had the ability to walk into a nest of bees, extract from them the honeycomb, and they wouldn't trouble him at all.' He had equally striking social skills, which for Leonard made him an important model: 'a person who could stand up to anything, who would always be able to relate to anyone — young, old, anyone at all.' 'For me, he was a great hero, a great figure.' Leonard was with his grandfather when he was dying, and he remembers weeping: 'the last great pain of my childhood.'

Jack Constable, retired London engineer, grew up with an unusually influential grandfather, a powerful model for both his son and grandson. He was a successful farmer and beekeeper, and a local agricultural leader, with a large old house close to the town of Black River. Jack grew up with his parents and grandparents together, and he describes his grandfather as a 'lovely personality', who was against harshness to children. He said, 'The best thing is to sit the child down, and tell the child what the child is doing wrong, and give it some form of punishment, and make sure that you mean what you say, and don't go back on it.' This approach has been transmitted down the generations in the Constable family. 'He had a lot of influence regarding discipline, mannerism, one's attitude. It spilt over to our parents as well ... I was only once hit by my dad. Once in my life.' Jack has followed the same model with his own children, and he also shared caring for them when young. His white English wife Sophie describes how Jack always got up for them at night, bottlefed, changed nappies, and looked after them on weekends to give her a break: 'He was much better at it than me! Jack's got much more patience.'

It is, nevertheless, most of all with Sean Ismay, now a Toronto truck loader, that we sense the most intense emotional bonding to a grandfather. He tells of how he was a love-child, chosen by his farming grandfather at birth. His teenage mother had gone to Kingston and returned home to the country concealing her pregnancy. But Sean's grandfather, emerging from the rum shop, heard a child's cries and realized it was his child.

> So he picked me up, and he left his food, and took me right over to the bush, and I've been living with them ever since ... I guess the look in his eyes, when he was holding me.... They knew he was in love with me.... He know there was no way that my mum could raise me, right?... He fell in love, and he took me.

So Sean spent his first ten years, until rejoining his mother in Canada, with his grandparents as 'the apple of their eye': and 'I used to follow my grandfather everywhere.'

With grandmothers, by contrast, there was quite often a very special relationship: they are recalled as an 'angel' or a 'saint', 'wonderful', 'sweet old grandma', 'caring, warm', 'giving', 'really there for me'. Rickie Constable, now a professional in New York and London, vividly recalls his feeling of physical closeness with his Jamaican grandmother: 'Oh God, I remember her eyes, you know how some people get the blue ring around their eyes when they get old? I liked her voice, and I loved, always loved her smell! She used to smell sweet, like corn.' Some children called their grandmother simply as 'momma': 'my mother never got "mother" title from me.' But all these grandmothers were the disciplinarians in their households. Many were also hard-worked, and although some would talk, most had little time to talk with a child: 'You were put in your place.' Nevertheless they were usually gentler than younger parents, 'never with a heavy hand', 'can be strict at times, but was a nice balance': some striking or whipping, but nearly half of them not hitting the child at all. Gene Trelissick, now a New York social worker, remembers how her Port Antonio great-grandmother would whip her: 'She would! Yeah, and she'd finish whipping you, and she'd tell you, "Oh, I love you, and that's the reason why I whip you!"'

These grandmothers were loved and admired partly because they had taken care of the child, but also because most of them were still working in the fields and the bush, often taking the child with them, and because of the values which they instilled. 'She teach us things': above all, tolerance and generosity to others. Robert Austin's grandmother, a village higgler, would take in people and give them food, 'even considered mad and crazy, from the street. She would give everything away, and have nothing. That's how she is. It was really great to be around her, because of her personality'. For Connie Dixon too, her grandmother, a field and road labourer, was her biggest influence: 'In her generosity, her kindness, her non-judgemental attitude, her humbleness.... Basic survival mentality, you don't need much to survive. I learnt that from her.... She never complained, she never envied anybody.'

For all these reasons, even if strict and not very communicative, a grandmother was often a child's closest adult. Additionally, quite often, even though they were still working, these older women were not well, 'very sick', suffering from fits, or going blind, and their very frailty tugged at the child's heart. Connie remembered, 'I always thought somebody needed to take care of her, so I didn't want to leave her.' Charlene Summers, a hotel cleaner, vowed not to travel while her grandmother was alive: 'I made a promise, I made a pledge in my heart, I won't leave her. I get the opportunity of leaving here to foreign, to be in England, to America, even to Germany, and I said, "No".' Jacob Richards grew up in a farm family where he was known as a child as 'Miss Annie's lantern'. He used to share a bedroom with his grandmother, Miss Annie: 'She'd get up, and the minute she stirred, I'd be stirred, because I just slept in her room.' They would go out early together to work in the fields, and 'wherever she goes, I was in front of her … I don't know if it's the fact that I was there and she relied on me, or I relied on her, but I looked after her that way, yeah'. He felt very close to her, 'almost as one'.

There were of course many more grandparents who were unremembered, whether due to death, distance, or family breaches, but nobody spoke of this as an issue. When we turn to parents it was likely to matter much more. In chapter seven, we shall consider the fathers who left their children without supporting them, and also substitute parents, aunts and stepparents, who are remembered both positively and negatively. Here we look just at the parents who in one way or another were present in their children's lives, beginning with the fathers.

Jamaican fathers have been heavily criticized for a long time.[9] Our life stories give us clear enough depictions of some 30 fathers, and show how many of them gave crucial emotional and communicative support to their children. Typically they played the soft parental role while the mother was the disciplinarian: for while most mothers are portrayed as strict, spankers or hitters, half of these fathers never hit their child at all, and only three were severe punishers. The recurrent image of a father is of a man who was 'easy-going', 'mild', 'kind-hearted' and 'quiet'. 'A loving and kind and gentle man', Joyce Leroy recalls of her father, a Kingston tailor: 'My father would talk to you until you can't take any more. He would not spank you'. Certainly there were some fathers who were not talkers, described as 'very reserved', 'not one much for emotions and feelings'. Winnie Busfield, who would go to visit her father in the country, regretted that 'you didn't really know your Jamaican father. Maybe this generation is doing it, but they wouldn't sit you down and have a conversation, so you don't really know them. They'll just provide for the home'. But despite this negative stereotype, fathers were in fact more often remembered as 'easier to talk to' than mothers: 'we talk a lot', 'any problem I could discuss with him', 'my father was the person we all go to'. With a few fathers there was deeper debate: one was a farmer who was also a mathematician; Selassie Jordan's father, a technician and — like his son — a rasta, enjoyed discussions, so that 'he would, if you come up wid a question, like to reason about it'; while Celia Mackay, recalled how her father, an estate chauffeur, 'used to read a lot, sit, and he'd tell us bedtime stories at night'.

There were some other daughters who loved their fathers to the point of idealization, with almost — as one put it — 'a romantic notion about him': describing him as 'a very special man', 'a sweet man, very kind, loving, adorable', 'the greatest father there is'. Altogether almost a third of our migrants describe relationships with their fathers which were 'very close', 'we bonded'. Hyacinth Campbell and her brother 'loved him more than our mother, because of the quiet-natured person that he was'. Such closeness can be summed up in Sandrine Porto's relationship with her hardworking father, who was a fisherman by night in a dug-out canoe, and a carpenter by day. 'He would go to sea at 4:30, and he would come back to get ready by eight o'clock, ready to go off to work.' At weekends he was making furniture in his workshop. But when he did come home, he was affectionate and easygoing. He left discipline to his sterner wife: 'he was never the dad who would hit. And if she's mad about something, we would … stay away and just hope for dadda to come through the gate, "Please come home now!"' Similarly, when the children wanted a treat they went to him. 'Oh, very easy. My father was the person we all go to.… For example, like school trips … we wouldn't tell mum, it's dad'. For Sandrine, 'he was the greatest, he *is* the greatest person ever. He was the best father.'

Not all relationships with fathers were of this kind. Interestingly, in some middle class families parental roles were reversed, so that the father was the disciplinarian, and the mother gentler, even 'huggy, smoothy'. But provided the discipline was no more than spanking, such middle class fathers could be equally admired. Harry Davidson was struck regularly by his father, a Kingston warehouse manager, but Harry felt they were 'close',

'I look up to him all my life', partly because his father was also communicative: 'He was the one I always spoke to when I had a question about anything.'

Lastly, in two working-class families, by contrast, the punishing was much more harsh, to the point which would now be considered abuse. Patsy Clark felt ambivalent about her butcher and bus-driver father. 'He was a really hard worker, and I think that was a good influence.' But he had a short temper, and a savage streak too. 'He beat, he loved to beat people, and throw things at you, and then he ask questions at you.' Winston Lloyd, however, describes his father, a Kingston labourer, as 'a rough man to me' but 'a good dad', although certainly in his household 'life was hard.... He used like that wire you use for the light, straighten me up, give me some whipping, yeah'. There was also constant friction with a stepmother. At the age of 13 Winston sought refuge with his uncle in Mobay: 'I ran away.' Such tough disciplinarian fathers were, however, very much the exception among those remembered in these Jamaican families: much more often the fathers were recalled as gentle, communicative, and close to their children.

With mothers by contrast the whole range tends much more towards harshness. A quarter of all the mothers were described as hard disciplinarians, 'crazy strict', 'a prison guard', regularly flogging and beating with a belt or strap. 'She beat first and ask questions later.' Such mothers were often — but not always — struggling to run large families with five or more children, and they believed that 'if you'll whip them over the head, they'll listen to you'. One daughter of a teacher, 'an awful disciplinarian,' confided, 'I hated my mother for years.' One son, belted regularly, still finds it hard to kiss his mother. They also resented their mothers failure to talk with them. For example, daughters were not warned of the onset of menstruation. 'My mum, probably, would be the last person that I would confide anything,' a son declared: 'It's like talking to a wall.' Stuart and Hyacinth Campbell, son and daughter of a village building worker, reflect on their harsh and uncommunicative mother:

She loved to beat.... If we forgot one chore, it would be a whopping, you would never escape it. If we had to fill the drum with water, and she comes home and it's half of it, we would get a whopping for it.... She doesn't talk to us ... I grew up with everything bottled up inside ... I didn't like my mother, to be honest.... We didn't know a mother's love.... Today, you'll probably call it child abuse.

On the other hand, at the opposite extreme, another quarter of mothers who are portrayed as 'gentle', 'quiet', 'always smiling', 'tender and loving'. Occasionally this is linked with material generosity and giving to others: 'she will have the last and give it to you, and then she'll do without.' Occasionally these were families with few children, and in some homes the mother's role was also easier because the father was responsible for discipline. These mothers were also communicative: 'we could talk to her', 'we talk', 'I ain't scared to say anything to her.' In contrast to the more controversial harsh memories, descriptions of gentler mothers tend to be brief. Sometimes they seem to have become idealized, as 'a very special lady, the greatest mum there is', or with the mother's role as moral teacher linked to an almost perfect character: 'a blessed lady'; 'an angel, a saint, a woman with enormous strength of character'; 'she was a saint, she taught me everything I know.'

Nevertheless, most memories of mothers are more complex, lying in a variety of ways between these extremes; of disciplinarians, yet who did convey a strong sense of caring — 'old-fashioned, strict. Yeah, she's loving.' Some mothers did express this caring through talking and listening to their children — 'easy to talk to', 'if you're having problems, she'll listen'; but most through practical caring, cooking and baking and sewing — 'She would sew clothes for us, she would make our uniforms for school.' They are typically described as strict, even a few as 'a little bit rough sometimes', but also as 'very dedicated' mothers, 'there as a mother', 'very close', 'very very caring. She cares about all of us'. Thus memories of punishment by these mothers are often qualified by a justifying phrase — 'It's not anything like child abuse, just a tap with the hands', or 'She would beat, but of course, the Bible says, "Spare the rod and spoil the child"'; or linked to a note of praise — 'She's strong, a disciplinarian, she's a loving mother.'

With several children, the strictness itself is described as a manifestation of their mother's caring. For Selvin Green as a child, 'There was always a set time for everything: ... a certain time to go to play, a certain time to go and sweep the yard, and a certain time to go to bed.' With Sandrine Porto's mother, a fisherman's wife, 'the house must be spotless. We have to move all the furniture where we're cleaning, and clean under everything and everything.' Owen Callaghan's mother, a Kingston waiter's wife, on seeing her son had failed to wash up the supper, resorted to direct action. 'She saw the dishes in the sink, the next minute — the dishes were in my bed! ... The old people, the way they choose to do things is very effective!'

In retrospect, controlling and caring can be seen as two sides of the same coin, and with some of these mothers it was also linked to a leading role in the family as a whole: 'the leader', 'strong-willed, strong-headed', 'bossy', 'the backbone of the family'. We must be careful not to assume such exceptionally powerful mothers as typical, but nevertheless they do bring home the complexity which typifies so many of these portraits of Jamaican mothers. For even when resented for some of their sternness, these strong mothers usually became close and admired parents. Thus Rickie Constable's mother was a teacher during his early childhood in Jamaica, although when she came to the United States her qualifications were not recognized and initially she had to work as a cleaner. She is 'a community person', interested in politics, a deacon and Sunday School teacher in her church, concerned about manners, clothes, respect and public service. Rickie, after saying 'my mum did not spare the rod', and also that she is 'not easy to talk to, my mum talks *at* me, she doesn't talk *with* me', equally emphasizes how 'she's very dedicated to her children, very very involved in our lives, very very caring', that her influence on him has been 'huge'. He sums up, 'My mother's still my hero.'

Looking at all these descriptions of parents and grandparents as a whole, they are by their nature accounts from standpoints later in life, and often the ways in which they are phrased, particularly with the harshest parents and with the strict but caring mothers, are influenced by changing attitudes to childrearing. In over a dozen families there are also more explicit reflections on the relevance of past ways for the present. As one mother still in Jamaica puts it: 'There are similarities in there, but with the changes of time, things can't remain the same. Now that I'm an adult and I look back at things with my parents, I realise you can't grow your children that way. Because different time, yeah.' Two families — one being Jack Constable's, who we have already encountered — take a special pleasure in their own unusual transgenerational traditions of gentleness. In only two families is the direction of change criticized: here two men, now fathers themselves, regret the stricter ways they knew as children in Jamaica: 'You need to straighten the plant when young'; 'I might have let the kids down by being too soft on them.' All the others see change as being decidedly for the better.

So with the other families the emphasis is on positive change. Those still in Jamaica favoured a slower pace of change. Thus Hyacinth Campbell, herself now teaching in Jamaica, the daughter of a very harsh mother, describes herself as 'strict too', but more restrained and more communicative: 'I would talk to them, and when they were younger, I would beat, but not as much … I set rules in my house for them, even now. Like in the week, six o'clock our television is turned off until the weekend. I put education first. On weekends, they are free.'

For migrants, now living in societies which disapproved of harsh disciplining of children, the need for change could seem more urgent. Not all of course. Celine Parris, London-born, gives a chilling picture of her relationship with her father, a taciturn mechanic.

> He was more like the grandfather who you didn't really know. I was always afraid of him. He had that authority about him. He had yellow eyes with red veins, and when he'd shout and then roll around the eyes, as a little child, you're like "Uhhh!"… And he used to have false teeth, and he used to take them out, and then walk around with his gums showing.
>
> I used to get beaten with the buckle, or the leather belt…. My dad was definitely a belt man…. Now, really and truly, it's classed as child abuse, you know!

But for many more, perhaps for most parents, a shift away from such severe discipline was one basic aim. Thus Patsy Clark, now a nurse in America, has 'tried to teach them [the children] stuff, and tried not to holler at them, or beat them for everything'. Similarly Niam McNeep, now a cook in Canada, told us, 'The child I grow, I wouldn't really whop.... It's just like a free mother with them'; and Pearl Selkirk, a London factory worker, 'I've done it differently, I never beat them! They never got a beating!' Olive Carstairs, a Canadian assembly line worker, also aimed to become more emotionally expressive.

> Growing up, as a West Indian family, hugging wasn't, wasn't there.... We weren't comfortable, we didn't do that as a family.... It's now that I've gotten older and my parents are now older, when I go down to see them I give them a hug and a kiss to say hello or goodbye, and I try to reinforce that in my kids. I say, "Well, here's your grandmother, go and give your grandmother a kiss".

Making such radical changes in ways of being took a lot of determination in the midst of adjusting to the practicalities of a different society and culture. Ted Oliver, now a Canadian shipper and truck driver, who is deeply concerned for his children's progress, spending much time talking with them, but struggling to avoid the disciplinary means he learnt as a child, speaks for many other migrants: 'Sometimes you can't change your roots! ... Yeah, it's really a mind-working thing! It's a challenge, yeah. It's not easy to grow kids.'

Especially ambitious, Vivia Perrin, by then a London nurse, with her husband decided 'we should try the opposite of what happened to us', replacing severe discipline with encouragement, and putting their emphasis above all on communication. The focus of this was a weekly family 'round table'.

> No matter what it is, we sit, Sunday afternoon, after lunch, before we go to the park, we will sit and discuss what's going to happen, who's doing what in the week, who's going dancing, who's going to pick up.... This is how we've been running the family. We would have this round table, and we would make sure everybody agree before we leave the table.

Such changes were remarkable achievements. They were won by these migrants only through courage, in a context which could be confusing, and always was a struggle.

FOUR

Jamaica: Communities on the Land

Community and Class

For many Jamaicans, memories of childhood and family are inextricably linked with memories of community. In fact for many young people growing up in rural Jamaica, even today too, the local community is so full of relatives, close or distant cousins, that they could spend several days walking and visiting between one household and another. Those with closer kin living nearby could most likely eat or sleep under more than one roof. Community and extended family were thus intertwined. Most communities had a mixture of families and included migrants from other parts of the island, but the overlap between family and community can be a powerful image in memory. Moreover, in extreme instances, in some small rural settlements they really were synonymous. Spurgeon White remembers a childhood in a mountain village in St. Catherine, where he estimates that 95 per cent of the people were his relatives. 'That village was just one family village. At Christmas, all of them would come around sometime, we all eat at about four different houses. Just all my family, and all grandkids. The school was full of us.'

Many remembered the supportiveness which these tight village communities could provide. 'Everybody knew everybody,' said Pearl Selkirk. 'Everybody knew everybody's business, before you even know your own business! ... And they're caring. If you have sickness or anything like that, everybody's there. Somebody died, everybody's there. They're like that. It's a good district.' However, for both men and women the most telling test of the community support where they lived often came with a crucial turning point later in life, and especially with difficult moments after migration. Some men reflected on how in a life crisis abroad, about work or relationships, they depended for support on one close individual, rather than the network of friends they had had in Jamaica. For women a similar moment could be their experience of childbirth. Thus Sarah Chisholm contrasted experiences of childbearing in Jamaica and North America. Now an administrator in Toronto, she came from a poor rural background in Jamaica, where, after three days in hospital:

> I went home, I had a sister, a mother, two nieces, those two nieces are with me now, and the neighbours, and the community, that would come by, who would wash the clothing for the child, who would want to take him for a walk. It was so different.... Here it's a different story. You have the child all on your own.

For bringing up older children the importance of the community in Jamaica, and the role of neighbours in disciplining misbehaviour, was reiterated by both men and women, migrants and stayers: citing the words of the proverb, 'It takes a village to raise a child.' Selvin Green, now a London factory worker, who had earlier taken his children back to Jamaica for eight years, recalled how there, strictness was 'in the air, it's everywhere. If you going down the street, someone is going to be seeing you down there, and tell it to your parents — you are protected by the whole community.... And you must say, "Good morning", you must not misbehave on the street'. Bill Fox, brought up in a Manchester hill village, confirmed that 'for any misdeeds, a child could be punished out of the street.... You cannot go home and complain.... A neighbour scold you on the street, and when they see the parents, they tell the parents what happen.' Stella Wadham recalled how

> if grandma don't catch you, uncle is going to catch you, or a aunt is going to catch you. But it was more of a community environment.

When I was growing up, like my grandmother's friends, we could not pass them in the street, we had to say "Good morning Miss –", and we had to call them by their name. And if we passed them, whether by accident, or you just don't feel like saying hello to them, they could chastise you out there, in the road.

Harry Davidson, brought up in Kingston and now a sales representative in Florida, maintained that 'we never disrespected anybody for that reason, because we knew they had every right to slap us and put us in place'. He thinks that childrearing in America is 'a lot more difficult, ... because you have to pay for it, day care, at the early stages, and mostly because you don't have as much family around'.

In Jamaican villages there was also a form of help which the men of the community would give together, known in some places as 'morning sport'. This would be for tasks which were difficult for one household alone, such as clearing a field, lopping a big tree, putting on a house roof, or moving a family's whole house to another site. On such occasions, the women would provide a meal. 'There is no payment involved, because it meant that you would do the same, when it was necessary, for others.' Migrant men abroad could not summon help in this way: like their women, they had to do the best they could on their own.

On the other hand, it is sometimes clear that these contrasts are based more on feeling than on what really happens. Thus two older women, who had come to London in the mid to late 1950s and worked as hospital nurses' aids, both described themselves as cut off from their families. But the first, despite complaining about her lack of family contact — 'I don't keep in touch' — revealed a transatlantic network of some 40 kin, and on the second session of the interview two of her sons were in her flat. Similarly the second, who also suggested that she was isolated — 'I don't have no family here' — turned out to again have a large family tree, with her six children all living within five miles, and two sons regularly driving buses down her own street. Both are now older Londoners, clear that they have no intention of returning to Jamaica, so that perhaps the lack of family contact which they express is more for the relatives from their earlier years in Jamaica: few still living, yet still symbols of their own lost youth.

While many memories of community are posed as a contrast favourable to Jamaica, this does not mean that migrants recall Jamaican society as egalitarian. It was in fact far from egalitarian, and this is how most remember it. They portray it clearly as stratified by social class, and indeed Stephanie Gladstone was brought up in her professional family by a mother who was 'very class conscious'. Better off families were also more likely to be concerned about inheritance, and so take a restrictive attitude towards outside children. For example, Clover and Trudie Brown's grandfather had a 100-acre sugar and banana farm, 'so the family were, in those time, the upper class, people who have land, they were the big house in the district'. But their grandmother was one of his house servants, not his wife. As a result the girls rarely saw their grandfather's family: 'We weren't that close to him', 'not very close, because — well, my father was born out of wedlock'. So although their father was brought up on the farm, he was raised as an inferior. When the other children were off to school, 'he was the one that was up in the mountain working, have to wake up early, five o'clock, to go and feed the cows, and [fetch] the wood.... He was neglected'.

Similarly Stuart Campbell, from the perspective of his poor rural childhood family, while maintaining that 'people in the community, in general, tend to look after each other', also described the contrast between the poorest people, surviving from fish or gifts of yam and breadfruit, and families which were considered better off because they had land, or a good job with the Parish Council, or a shop or a bar: 'they had material things'. Dick Woodward, brought up in a Clarendon hill village, similarly noted the social gradations in his community. He lived for a time with an uncle who had 'a lot' of land, a 30-acre farm with two horses, two donkeys, cows, and a bull which served the region; and he allowed various poor families, unrelated but 'seen as family,' to build huts on his land and grow food for themselves, being expected in return to work for him in season. Dick also felt that migrants and their children were seen as advantaged. 'My parents would send parcels of clothes.... The fact that you could wear things which were different from other kids, also marked you off.' He had an uncle who had returned from Cuba with enough money to stop working and buy a 'huge' two-storey house: 'He would swear in Spanish! And he never did any work himself. He was always sitting on his verandah, holding court.'

Dick was also aware of the presence of two wealthier families, large farmers and landowners, light-skinned, to whom his own family 'looked up,' although they had much less social contact, except perhaps at the village cricket. 'Whereas with us, as kids, I learnt to ride bareback' on a horse, these were 'people who rode on horseback all the time.... You thought he and his horse was always wonderful! Formally upright, with a hat, hard hat, and his bridle'. In the towns a superior class could also be seen at worship, for there was a noticeable class grading of the church congregations too. Thus Winnie Busfield, a small farmer's daughter, felt that she was not always kindly greeted by the congregation after her five mile walk to church, although she still enjoyed the adventure into another social world:

> The Presbyterian church in Lucea town, very big church, them days, they look on you — just the posh children would go, and you love to be there, because there you were with the MPs children! And the doctor's children.... You put on your best clothes, and you put on your shoes. Oh that was lovely! But long walk.

Memories of childhood homes also bring out marked social distinctions. There were a few privileged families with large houses. Jack Constable grew up with his beekeeping farmer grandfather in a large farmhouse near Black River, in which all three generations slept in traditional style, 'because on the whole side of the house, there was this long room, but it was only partitioned off by curtains'. Harry Davidson had a more modern urban childhood in a seven-bedroom Kingston house, including a patio, TV room and 'helper's quarters'. The older generation in such well off 'light brown' families usually had live-in maids to keep their homes tidy: Marcia Trelissick, later a London dressmaker, recalls how 'they spoil me', 'the only thing I was given to do was to make the bed'. Her husband later told her, 'You were grown up in a cocoon!' Most romantic was Anna Gladstone's memory of an elite childhood in a big old house by the sea in Portland, a castle 'right on the cliff, overlooking the bay. We used to see the boats coming in, loading bananas, and we had a little walk down to the beach, down there, with a big rock'.

At the other end of the spectrum, Connie Dixon started as a country child in Hanover living with her grandmother in a two-room thatch house with a dirt floor, with wattle walls. 'She would wattle it herself with bamboo wattles, and the roof was [sugar] cane thatch. And even that, she would weave the thatch herself, and then she'd have a man hoist it up on the roof.' Inside there was a wooden bed with a straw mattress, two stools and a table, a small food cupboard, one picture of Jesus, and bare floor without mats. They cooked and washed outside, and for a clock, just 'look at the sun'. By the time Connie was a teenager, however, the house had been rebuilt with money from an uncle in America as a two-room board house.

Selassie Jordan grew up in a one-room board house in August Town, Kingston: 'it was one bed there. Me and me brother, mother and father share one bed.... So basically, very poor home. But rich wid culture, rich wid love.' Winston Lloyd, still in Jamaica as a taxi driver, was also a town child. He observed how money could affect housing when he went in his teens to live with an uncle who was a baggage handler at Mobay airport. They lived on the edge of a very poor neighbourhood: the houses, 'they just like old board box, zinc, just about anything they can find. But my uncle he live on the edge of the gully at that time, and he was working at the airport and making a little money, selling some weed and stuff. So he built this nice wooden house, board house. So he was doing good'.

Many remembered the importance of these social distinctions in housing, whether in town or country. Sarah Chisholm, who was in secretarial work before migrating to Canada, described how in Lucea town, ''if you're born or live in a thatch house, you're considered very very poor. Into a board house, well, you're just one step up. Into a wall house, my God, you have money!' Joyce Leroy noted the same grading in her Kingston neighbourhood, although with its four rooms and verandah her family had a relatively good home: 'we live in a board house, but all around us was all brick houses, so we were the poorer ones, we were the poor set.'

In deep country, very similarly, Josephine Buxton described the mountain village of her childhood as divided between families with board houses and zinc roofs like her own, and the poorest, whose 'houses were made of just rough wood cut from the field, to make the post, and bamboos for the wattling' of the walls, filled in with mud: more vulnerable to storms, and also, being landless squatters, more likely to be forced to move. But equally she recalls even such forced house moving in a positive community frame as 'a kind of celebration too. On Friday night they would be moving houses. Many people gathered to help, to lift the house, which was only put on joists, so it is lifted up and planted at the place where they're going to put it'.

Above all in the countryside, clearly observed inequalities could be mitigated by mutual aid, giving practical meaning to local community. Here children were not only taught to respect the older generation, but taught by the older generation to give help to neighbours in need. Stella Wadham recalls her Portland grandmother would be cooking, 'and she's telling me, "Miss Maud is sick, and you have to carry dinner for her." Or she need water, and you have to carry it.' Stella is trying to hand down the same values to her own daughter:

> I'd rather have a cardboard box on the corner of the street, and all my friends will come there, and we hang out and chat, than have a big house and have everybody passing and skin their face up and down and say, "She thinks she's all that. So I don't want to go there". Those are things I learnt from her. You don't have to have a lot. You don't have to wait until you hit the lotto, to share.... Whatever you cook, you can share it with somebody.... So those things I remember of my grandmother.

There are parallel contrasts in memories when recounting attitudes to race. In Sarah Chisholm's view, 'it's not only black and white in a family in Jamaica, or in the islands, being prejudiced is rampant. Because if you have a family where you have children who are darker than others, you tend to favour the lighter skin, the lighter complexion children over the darker ones. And comparing now with wall house and wood house, that's exactly how it is'. Such favouritism could make for bitter memories. Alice Wadham, an office cleaner in Kingston, grew up cut off from her better-off father and grandparents, who did not recognize her.

I never really had much, nothing to do with them, because it's like, my mother was your complexion [dark], and my father was a little lighter than her. And they [her father's family] say I wasn't his. So he didn't care about me. Until his mother died. At that time I was about 9 or 10, and he wanted me. And it didn't go as well with my mother, my mother say, "No! You didn't recognize her at an early stage, so you get the hell out!" So I didn't really have nothing to do with that side.

Those who came from the poorest families — who in fact must have experienced the effects of Jamaican race stratification most directly — mention colour least often. By contrast, there is a clear undercurrent of colour consciousness in Jamaica in the interviews from one middle class and one skilled family, with recollections introducing family members in terms of skin tone: 'she as very fair', 'she was quite light-skinned, yeah — she was lighter-skinned than I am, and she had grey eyes'; 'she was just dark, she was darker'; 'a very dark woman'. Interestingly, it is one of these interviewees, Rose Lyle, who came from a better off Jamaican farm and business family, and later came to London as a hospital worker, perhaps because higher aspirations were possible for her, who most strongly recalls suffering herself from direct racial discrimination as a child in Jamaica. On the one hand she remembers being mocked by other schoolchildren as 'red', and on the other being deliberately pushed out the running for a scholarship by a teacher who instead put forward and coached a white English girl. 'I've never forgotten that thing, that's lived with me ever since.... Every time I think of it, my blood boils!'

Probably the most pervasive sensitivity to the significance of colour was in the lives of elite families in the decades before Jamaican independence from colonial rule. This 'fair-skinned' local elite, the outcome of three centuries of sexual liaisons between the white colonists and the black underclass, had been deliberately used by the British colonial administrators as their lieutenants, with privileges given for their loyalty. But never explicitly, by custom rather than by law, there was always a glass ceiling above which they could not rise. Anna Gladstone, whose father was a senior civil servant and whose brothers became lawyers, remembers the restrictions on job opportunities in the 1930s.

> There were not many jobs open to Jamaican coloured in my days.... There were girls with clerical jobs, but there was restriction. For instance, there were no coloured girls employed in any of the banks.... Jobs were open to do clerical jobs, work in stores, sales girls, and if you're a bit educated, you could join the Civil Service.

These restrictions were not by rule, simply 'informally known'; but they were one reason why Anna jumped at the chance of war service in Britain. There were also places where she knew she would not be accepted, including the smart Myrtle Bank Hotel on the Kingston waterfront, 'which was very exclusive, only white people could go there. We were not allowed. There was colour distinction'. Her own mother worked at the hotel as a caterer, but 'because she was light-skinned, she had brown hair and a light skin, so she was accepted, and she worked there'. Anna reflected on her family's social position, and the intersections between race and class:

> When you are the middle class, you cut across both sections — those down below and those a little above.... You're in the middle. So you had very poor people, but we had to have servants who would help out my mother, and that was very different. No, there were certain places like the Myrtle Bank, you didn't go there. We went to where we knew we could go. We went to the movies, we went to Hope [Botanical] Gardens, and we had our own lives.

Down the generations, Anna's private family life has in fact been a striking rejection of the colour conventions to which in public in her youth they conformed. Even then through her father's work with the Post Office, they met 'many people from overseas, ... so we were quite accustomed to meeting people of all races when we were small'. Anna herself met and married a dark-skinned Jamaican while in Britain. Her daughters, who have lived in Britain and North America, speak with pride of their multicultural social lives, and in their turn most of her children and grandchildren are in mixed marriages. Meanwhile the social world in which Anna grew up has vanished with the changes in Jamaica, leaving memories which now seem more quaint than harsh.

By contrast it is less easy for many others, mainly among the older migrants, to forget incidents of open prejudice which they experienced in coming to Britain and North America: being refused promotion at work, being turned away when seeking housing, being abused by hospital patients, white partners being taken for prostitutes, or even being asked by church ministers not to join a congregation. These experiences clearly provided a new frame through which to think of social divisions back in Jamaica. However, this might result in a rethinking in two different directions: a more critical perspective on Jamaica, or an idealization.

The more critical perspective is the view that migrating made them for the first time aware of racism, so that they could now see in retrospect that there was racism in Jamaica too. For example, why were all the high school teachers white? As Nelson Pinnock, brought up in a poor rural family, who became a factory welder, put it,

> When I come to Canada I really learn about racism. And then when I look into it, Jamaica, they have more racism more than North America, for you have some people out there, if their skin is browner than you, then they feel they're better than you.... These black activists talking, they don't speak for me. [He tells them] Jamaica wasn't much different. Over there is society, here [in Canada] is colour.

Others take a very different view. Ted Oliver, Canadian truck driver and shipper, maintains that in Jamaica, 'where I grow, I never see a racial motive. The only time I really learn about racial … was when I came here.... Like people see you, call you names'. Harry Davidson maintains that 'in Jamaica there was never a discussion about racism … I first experienced racism when I moved to New York'. He describes his mixed neighbourhood in Kingston as socially integrated, 'close-knit' — 'when I was growing up, everybody helped everybody else'; 'all the kids were brought up by everybody'. But when Harry maintains that this mutual helping was not affected by differences in skin colour, this might have been less the reality of social relationships in Kingston then than the predominant focus on class in public discussion. For Harry clearly was very conscious of skin colour, and indeed uses it to denote his neighbourhood's social composition. 'Mixed neighbourhood: black, white, all different colours on the street.'

Nevertheless, those who have had white friends or family members in Jamaica, and then encounter the social wall between blacks and whites in the United States, especially tend to idealize Jamaican attitudes to race. Dana Howard, from a farming family, maintains, 'I did not know prejudice until I came to the United States. My father's family is very mixed … a black and white integrated family, and there is no difference in races there. It's just now that you come to the States, it's like, "Wow! There is a difference of races in here!"' And similarly Sandrine Porto, from a skilled family on the western Jamaican coast, experienced working as a domestic in New York for white families who never entertain black people in their homes, remembers Jamaica as a non-racist society:

> A big, big big difference.… Because we were brought up in Jamaica … [One] side of my family is, they look white. But nobody see them as different!… And in Jamaica, there are so many white people, we never see them as different. Tourists started coming and all these hippies.… But we didn't know that there were white people who didn't like us!… Did we have racism in our vocabulary? It was never there. We didn't know there were people who hate black, because you are black. But now I'm here and I realize that.

It is of course true, as we shall see later in chapter six, that the kinds of racism which migrants were to encounter were often very different from experiences of prejudice in Jamaica. But the idealization of earlier memories about race in Jamaica in some of these testimonies also bears witness to the need for migrants, finding themselves minorities in white countries, to find a powerful moral basis on which to rest their fight for equal rights. So these were memories for the future, to live by.

Land and Environment

Perhaps because we did not deliberately ask for memories of the environment, where clear descriptions occur in our life stories, they are almost always linked with activity. For some this was for play. Thus Connie

Dixon, from a rural landless family, recalls how unlike most local girls she was keen on swimming, jumping into the sea from the cliffs. 'I would also go to the morass, into the woods where it's really swampy, and catch fish with the boys.' Trudie Brown, who today has a shop in Negril, spent part of her childhood on a very isolated farm in the Trelawny woods, where with her brothers and sisters she had fun 'exploring the bush there', picking wild fruit, and swimming in the Martha Brae river: 'one of the great things is the river that was there … and the water was always cold! It was cold! A big river.' Afterwards, 'we missed it a lot'.

More often it is the farmed land which is remembered. Some talked about their family holdings: how family land had been exchanged for new plots in exchanges with a bauxite mining company, or developers on Negril beach — or how it is still held today, split between a cluster of relatives. Jacob Richards's family land in St Elizabeth comes from his mother's side. His maternal grandfather had the whole of the land, but —

> as each member of the family grows up, the land gets split between them. They grow up, and then their children take on. It's a little hamlet, I'd say about twenty or thirty houses, all related.... When I was born, I was given an acre, and that's there. The only thing that marks it is a coconut tree with my name on it! But I, personally, don't want to go an live there. If I want to sell it, I'll have to sell it to someone in the family. You've either got to be related or married to the Stents to get there.

Jacob's father, who preceded him as a migrant to England, was given five acres of the land when he married, and now he has returned, 'he farms it, he grows yams, sweet potatoes, sweet cassava.... He still goes down there now, gets up in the morning, goes down early, before it gets too hot.' Trudie Brown's family have over 100 acres of family land in Westmoreland, but it is now divided between over a hundred relatives. The land was in two main sections. The first was where the family members mostly lived, like a little village by itself.... And then there is another part, like mountain, bushy-like, where people do most of their growing provision, they plant and grow ... [My father] went to the bush in the morning, on his donkey, and late evening, you'd see him coming down with the donkey.... He was a bushman. When we were much smaller, he plant a lot of vegetables. Because my mother, she spend a lot of time selling in the Montego Bay market.

Carl Watts, still farming in the central hill country, also talks about crops and livestock and how to sell them. He has been an environmental progressive, setting up two of his own water retention systems: 'Ye dry on the mountain. So you get rain today, tomorrow you just dry, yessah.... So we have to make our own water catchment.' Similarly, Josephine Buxton, brought up in a family of smallholders, who lived up mule tracks — 'right up to the Blue Mountain, near the Blue Mountain peak is at my right hand, so I'm a real country girl' — focused more on the productive side of the yard, chickens and mangoes and water. 'If we have to carry water from the spring, then you make sure the water is carried in Saturday evening, and full up the drum. And the woods are being chopped.'

More commonly, there are more domestic memories of fruit on the family land or nearby. Winnie Busfield grew up in a 'crowded' family house, but there were 'fruit trees in the yard, so we were free to have fruits.... In the country there were plenty of fruits as well so food was no problem. You could always find something, that part of Jamaica'. 'You have to love it', Morris Derby, another migrant to Britain says of the land: 'we, as boys, it was a pleasure to go and you pick an orange, or pick a water coconut and eat.' Spurgeon White, lumber yardsman in the United States, describes the abundance of food which came from the family land shared between his parents and his generous-minded grandfather.

He had land with a lot of breadfruit, coconut, pears, cocoa, everything.... He raise pigs and we always kill a pig at Christmas, and spice it up.... Him have so much fruit like breadfruit and mangoes and bananas and coconuts, a lot of very good fruit. People come, during season time, come all over and pick up things. He was that kind of man.

Some children were also taken out to family plots in the bush, and given their first lessons in growing crops. Morris Derby, now a porter in London, recalls how as a boy aged seven, 'my grandfather take me to the field. And I dug that hole, and he showed me how to put in a banana. And he said, "That one is yours". I remember watching that banana grows up until it shoot'. His grandfather sold it, giving his grandmother the money but saying, 'This is his one.' Clive Henry, today a tourist guide in Jamaica but still actively growing food for his family, was given a similar lesson in self-support by his grandmother, a higgler who used to sell fruit to tourists in Mobay.

> Now my granny used to have like two grung [grounds], now we have to follow her and go bush, and move to grung. Even me have fe me little grung too, different. Where me plant sweet yam, and affo blue yam and nigger yam and dark St Vincents and alum yam.... When she was having her bigger farm, I was having my little farm different from her.... I used to grow my own, I used to have my fork, my machete and a hoe.... When you live in Jamaica as a Jamaican, you have to have a machete, a fork and a hoe, so you can grow a little food on your own.

Most Jamaican migrants who came from country backgrounds were doomed to spend their lives working in cities. Even coming to Kingston as a teenager, surrounded by crowded yards of houses, Stella Wadham felt unable to identify with her new context:

> We're used to picking ackees from the tree, and you have your yam, and you have your eggs from the chickens ... [In Kingston] I didn't have the river, I didn't have the trees just out there.... And that was one of the things I found even harder to deal with when I just came to New York, because I couldn't relate to it.... You live in the same building with somebody, and you don't even know them. I am used to chatting across the fence for a teaspoon of sugar, or some salt, or ... the pot is already on the fire — you call over the fence, "Oh, I'm making dumpling and its soft! Can I have a cup of flour?"

In their new homelands, a few migrants sought out countryside, but for many more there was an abiding sense of loss, lingering in their consciousness and helping to sustain their dreams of return. Selvin Green is a welder in an inner London computer parts factory. Born into a skilled family with little land, he was brought up by his grandmother in the beautiful mountain countryside of eastern Jamaica. However, when as a teenager he moved into Kingston, he was delighted to turn his back on the country, seeing the city as an escape from a monotonous fate: 'Oh, it was great! When I was in Kingston, one is like you're in heaven! Yes, it was great! Because I'm always at work ... because I didn't want to work in the fields, in the cane fields ... I hate that ... Kingston is the big bright lights, and everything is there.'

When Selvin was 24 he travelled again, joining his mother who had gone ahead to London, getting chilblains that first grim English winter. 'It was cold. Man, it was so cold.' But by this time he was in a new phase of life, married with children, and he soon decided to move out of the metropolis to a smaller town to give his children a better chance and all of the family 'fresh air'. Selvin is back in London now. But in the interim he has also spent eight years back working in Jamaica, and he is longing to retire there. 'Oh yes! Oh very yes! I'm just rearing to go! Oh yes, I will go. If I'm not dead, I'm gone.'

Perhaps most striking is the lyrical way in which he now speaks of a countryside which once, as a teenager, he had been so glad to escape. When he speaks of the Jamaican landscape, it is now in terms of observing rather than doing, as an environmentally sensitive townsman, rather than as a practical farmer or smallholder. He speaks of returning to 'my home' with the passion of a nature-lover. What draws him so powerfully is —

> The lifestyle, the place, the beauty. The simplicity of life. I want to go out the back and pick a lettuce, just off the real land grown on. I want to pick orange. I want to hear the birds. I want to see the coconuts, I want to hear the wind blow between it.... I want to see the bees fly up to the flowers, and I want to stand there, because I used to do that, and look at it taking the nectar from the flowers, you know?

Cos I used to do that. I used to watch, I used to get disciplined for it. When I'm going down to the stream to get water.... That's like you see a bird fly in the tree, and it make a sound, a whistle: when you look, you see another one fly, come along, and some communication going on between those two bird. These are the things I like.

In Selvin's memories, as in so many memories of childhood, acute observation is intertwined with nostalgia and even with myth. But myth is intrinsic to history itself, and is in itself one of the driving forces of change. So these memories of lost Jamaican childhoods give us not only many vivid glimpses of how the past was experienced in everyday life, but also, in the rediscovery of black ancestry, or in the belief in community and sharing, or in the tangible beauty of the island, visions for the future.

FIVE

Staying or Leaving

In 1967, when Leonard Selkirk left his hill farm village of Five Mile in St. Catherine with his brother and sister to fly to Britain to join his parents, the peak of the post-war migration boom from Jamaica to Britain was already past. Nevertheless, Leonard remembers how the whole village still seemed lit up by migration enthusiasm. Leonard's parents had gone ahead five years earlier, leaving their three children with their grandparents, but always intending that one day they too would follow. By 1967 the children sensed that their time to travel would come soon, feeling 'excitement, but still not knowing what it meant', and pestering their grandmother, 'When are we going to go foreign?' But it was in June, when Leonard's close cousin Robbie, who lived next door in the same yard, left for Britain, that for the first time Leonard, now an eight-year-old, got a sense of what migration really meant. In the yard, alongside pigs and chickens and cocoa and tobacco, under a big coconut tree there was a big patch of cho cho (a watery vegetable, like cucumber). 'Robbie, he just loved planting, so he planted this cho cho patch, and it grew and grew, it's all over the place.' And when he was leaving —

> the truck came to the front, to the gate, and everybody was piling on to the truck, and the last thing Robbie said.... Everybody piled into the truck and we couldn't go. And I remember Aunt Carrie was saying, "No", she was holding us back saying, "No, it's not your turn yet." But we didn't realize the enormity of what was

going on, until Robbie said, "Look after my cho cho patch!" Then you realized he wasn't just going up the road! ... When he went, you know, when people are leaving on a big truck, ... you know they're not coming back.

Leonard and his siblings followed within three months, in the same truck, full of other cousins who were also travelling and friends. 'It was still exciting because it was an adventure, but then we're also scared.' And as they walked across the tarmac to the big BOAC plane, 'you could see everybody waving, and it's like the whole of Five Mile, it's like the whole of Five Mile was up there! They weren't just shouting for us, but you just felt it was the whole of Five Mile, because you know that two truckloads of people come down. And it was a fun day out for most people'.

For the Selkirk family the switch from hill farming on small plots to wage-earning in British cities, where there were plenty of jobs in factories and public services, certainly made economic sense. The migration wave of the 1950s and 1960s to Britain was probably the most intense in Jamaica's history, but it was just one in a whole succession of migration surges, each initially opened up by work opportunities: earlier to the mines in Venezuela, constructing the Panama Canal, for farm work in Cuba or the American South, and subsequently for jobs in New York and Canada. But these waves of migration, going right back to the creation of Jamaican society in the slavery era, along with the return from abroad of successful migrants, have also built up a migration culture which in itself pushes young people towards migration. 'Travelling' is widely seen, not just as a way of earning better, but as an important broadening experience, a path to adult maturity.

In fact it was only a minority of Jamaicans who migrated. What reasons can we find for why some chose to migrate, and some to stay? With such a social push and economic pull, it is easiest to suggest why the migrants left, than why others stayed. In addition, our own interviews were designed to focus on the migrants, so that we have 27 accounts from Jamaicans who never migrated, in contrast to 70 from migrants. Furthermore a migration that did happen is much more likely to be well remembered than not having chances to migrate, or a decision not to go. Nevertheless there are some revealing clues in these life stories.

Firstly, looking at the interviews as a whole, there seem to be two important differences between those who left and those who stayed: social resources, and age. Up until the 1950s there were more men among the migrants, but in the long run there were as many women as men among both migrants and stayers. And in most families, among the siblings there was typically a mixture of stayers and migrants: in only five families did all the siblings, or all but one, migrate. But there were significant class differences. For although the interviews show how migrants and non-migrants both came from a broad spread of social backgrounds, mostly in the countryside, those with little or no land were twice as common among stayers as among migrants. Nearly two-thirds of the migrants came from small farm and artisan families, and large farm and professional families were also over represented among migrants. Migration required some resources: cash to travel, and to survive on arrival, and it was also helped by networks of kin and friends abroad — all of which the poorest families were least likely to have. 'Most of them [leaving] were self-sufficient', observed Patrick James, who came from rural St. Thomas to England in 1956. 'They have big house and all, you see, they sell it to come away.... Everybody say, "Why are these men leaving to go to England to work, they have a plantation [some land to grow crops], they have a couple of cows — they wasn't so badly off." No, they weren't poor people from where I'm from.'

There was also a second key point, which distinguished migrants from the overall Jamaican population: their age. For migrants were overwhelmingly either children rejoining their parents, or young adults. Only five migrants first travelled at over the age of 32. So that men or women who did not travel with their parents, nor seized the chance to migrate when young, usually spent the rest of their lives in Jamaica.

Of those who stayed in Jamaica, some said they had wanted to travel, but had never had a good contact abroad, or had failed to get a visa. A few still hoped their chance might come. 'Yes, if I get an opportunity,' said a dressmaker; while two men hold onto lingering hopes of international success in music. 'I could make lyrics down the line. Yeah man!' Clive Henry, a tourist guide, sees migration as essential to the realization of his dream of becoming a landscape gardener:

The dream I have, I don't think I can stay in Jamaica to dream. I figure I have to go somewhere in the US or Canada, to get some of my landscape work done. So I could make some money for doing what I want to do.... Landscape work, like, say you have a nice home, you want to change the flowers, you want to take up the grass, you want to put in some bigger tree.... So I can say, "Well we need two truckload of soil, or two ton of soil, for your garden, keep it more flourish." So all of those dream there for me. Yeah man.

Others had felt that they had good enough work already: 'Teaching is my first love'; 'I was doing my minicabbing back home, I was quite comfortable, have a nice home, I didn't want to [migrate].' It is noticeable that when a family had a moderate or large farm, one or two of the brothers typically remained in Jamaica to work it. But those who stayed most commonly expressed some form of commitment to Jamaica or its people as their reason for staying. This could be in a general form: 'My roots is here', 'I feel at home here', 'I love Jamaica'. 'I travelled a lot [to visit relatives], but I love Jamaica', commented Edley Keat, Kingston bus driver, 'and I made up my mind to stay here, regardless of how this country was, I must survive where I was born. Here I grow and here I lived and here I die'. 'Each country need to develop, right?' asked Morris Derby, who only finally migrated to England in middle age: 'I feel every man is supposed to make their living in one country.' In a similar spirit, Jack Rawlings, still a working smallholder in his seventies, was content to stay rather than follow his brother abroad, because 'me a Jamaican, Jamaica me country, me must love Jamaica more than the other man country.... Why me no fe love Jamaica, when a fe me country?'

Others spoke of powerful particular commitments: of reluctance to leave their children or the older generations in the family. Sid Constable, truck driver, remembered how 'the old people was alive and I couldn't — everybody else went away now, so I decide it's my duty to them'. And indeed, older people certainly could grieve for the loss of the young: when Dahlia Noble set off as a teenager from her Hanover village for England in 1961, 'the elderly people, a lot of them cried when I was leaving.... People who were poor, I used to go around them a lot, and quite a few people cried'. Rose Lyle recalled how her father had migrated to the United States, and after two years 'he wanted my mother to move over there, and she decide she wasn't going, because she wasn't leaving her parents'. Commitment to children was still stronger. One father decided for his children, 'until they can fend for them own, I never leave them'; while a mother remembered how when her son was small, 'I used to consider going abroad, and I'd say something to him about it, he'll say that I should not leave him'. Another mother explained how she delayed following her husband abroad for ten years, in order to see her children through their education in Jamaica. Howard Beck, shopkeeper's son turned farmer, summed up his various reasons against migrating: 'I decided that I was not going to go. My wife was a teacher, and we decided that I wasn't going to go. I think it was very important for me to be here for my children. And I don't think everybody should go either. Somebody need to stay here to hold the fort, keep the base firm.'

The tug between opportunity and commitment is especially well expressed by two men who both did eventually migrate to North America, in the late 1970s and 1980s. Ted Oliver grew up with his farming grandmother as part of a large family of cousins, with migration clearly a possibility from his earliest years. He had cousins in England, and his mother had migrated first to Kingston when Ted was three, and then on to Canada 'for a better job offer'. His reaction to her leaving was strikingly positive: 'Well, it's kind of happiness too, because, "Our mum went to Canada" — it was the thing in those days, right? People travelling, right? People used to migrate to England, and then Canada was the next part.' Nevertheless, when Ted's mother sent for him to come to Canada with his sister at 14, he refused to go. '"I don't wanna come", right? Because I'm having so much time with my grandma, I can't leave here. Because we're just so close.' So his sister went, and Ted stayed another five years with his grandmother. Then his mother tried again: 'Oh come! Come! Canada is so nice. You come and be with your sister.' This time Ted's grandmother encouraged him to go. 'My grandma say, "Go. You'd better go!"' So Ted finally migrated. But he came to Canada more in grief than in hope, and he says that it took him three years to get over the loss of his family and friends in Jamaica.

Robert Austin suffered from very similar ambivalences. Brought up by his grandparents in the Jamaican countryside, he had a sister in Canada and other kin in Miami and in England, and from early on had thought of migration: 'it was at the back of my head… I would always pray, and ask the Lord to help me to have the experience of another country.' But he hesitated because of his widowed grandfather's need of him. When in 1989 he was given a tourist visa as part of an athletics team, he told the dairyman who employed him he would be returning: '"Of course! I do have my job to come to, plus my granddad." And he [the dairyman] was like, "You fool! You crazy man! What are you coming back for?"' But Robert was still determined to return, until the very last moment, when he had a similar conversation with his Miami relatives. 'Tuesday morning, I dressed and everything, waiting, with my things packed, but they keep quizzing me, asking me, "You really wanna go back down? Your granddad, he has gotta live his life [but]…" It was sad for me to think that. I say, "You know what? I have no choice."' But his cousins prevailed: they made sure that Robert missed his plane. So in the end he did stay — initially as an illegal immigrant, feeling guilty about abandoning his athletics team and his friends as well as his grandfather. He remembers the first phase of his new life as being especially 'tough', because his migration was 'a sudden thing' and he had not prepared for it: 'It was really strange, and sad. Because every day is like, I think what I would be doing — I would be with my friends, and I would be playing cricket, doing soccer. And I really did miss my granddad, I really did miss him so. I mean, it take me about two years to get over it. Two long years.'

Men's Stories and Women's Stories

Both Ted and Robert tell the story of their own migration in subtle ways, conveying the complexity of feelings and influences underlying their own decisions. They do not project themselves as independent actors, solely responsible for their own fates. This was not what earlier oral history work had led us to expect. We had anticipated finding men more often as active storytellers, speaking from the 'I', making autonomous and often sudden decisions to migrate, inspired by zest for adventure, and proud of their success abroad. Women, by contrast, even when they did migrate independently, would be much less likely to portray themselves as autonomous agents, but instead typically describe their migration in a family context, narrating their story in terms of family decisions, as 'we' rather than 'I'.[1] So we were interested to see how far the narratives of our Jamaican migrants were similarly shaped by gender? Do men and women tell different kinds of stories of migration? Do men more often present themselves as autonomous migrants?

We have not found any indication of such marked gender storytelling patterns. There is no gender difference in terms of the grammatical use of 'I' or 'we' in our Jamaican narratives, nor in general, as to whether or not the interviewees' self-presentation was as an active and autonomous migrant. We have divided our stories between those who presented themselves as independently 'autonomous', and those who describe their migration as brought about by their family — usually their parents or a spouse — who we shall contrast as presenting themselves as 'family' migrants. We decided to count more than once those migrants whose migrations, for example as a child and as an adult, were of opposite character (one migration 'autonomous', the other 'family'), or who as adults made separate migrations to different countries, which gives us altogether 73 migration accounts.

Using these broad divisions, we found that of the adult interviewees, just over half described themselves as the active agent of their own migration, while the remainder presented themselves as migrating through the agency of others. Although there certainly were examples from our interviews which seemed to support strong gender differences, looked at as a whole we found the 'autonomous' and 'family' narratives were both equally often from women as from men.

If we look for examples of women presenting themselves as 'family' migrants, there are indeed several. Thus Josephine Buxton, despite being a notably active churchwoman and working mother, who became a London nursing assistant, presents herself almost as a victim. There was no tradition of travelling in her family: 'No. None of them. I think my grandmother, she was surprised when she saw an aeroplane! On the morning when she saw it, she say, "Oh, it looks like a coffin in the sky!" And my grandmother, she's never been in a motor car.' But in 1960 Josephine followed her husband, who had gone to England four years earlier to earn. 'He came here, he said he have to get some money to help look after the children then, because we had quite a lot of children' — six — and 'everybody was coming to England to make a bit of money, to help themselves'. None of her family were then in England — and still, 'sometimes I wonder, with so many of us West Indian together, and there are no brother, no sister, nobody that concern me'. So Josephine wanted to return:

> But when you come to England, that is where a catch is. The simple reason is that you put away the things you used to live by to come, and then you can't put back enough to get out, to go back home, and to start living. So some of us have to stay.
> And then I couldn't get home, then I had to send for the children, then the children come on.

Joy Beck, now a medical visitor, also explained how it was not her own choice to come to New York in her late twenties. She was depressed, 'pining away' after her mother's death, and in the hope of rescuing her 'it was my sisters who made that decision for me'. Joyce Leroy was similarly brought to England at 19 to 'get a factory work' by her eldest sister. This sister paid for the ticket, which had originally been bought for another sister who would not come, so Joyce was sent instead as a last-minute substitute: '*But did you want to go to England?* No. I didn't. Because I was immature.' Her father encouraged her: 'You go and do something for yourself. See the world. Go, learn something. Make something of yourself.' But Joyce felt she was being pushed out, 'it's like they, they just want to get rid of me. That's how I felt. I cried — many nights, just lying there, in England. Just to think of it.' In Joyce's case it does seem that age was a factor in her 'reluctant' first migration. For interestingly, when only eight years older she decided to follow a group of friends who had gone to New York, leaving her own daughter for two years with another friend.

There were, however, as many men who explained their migration in very similar 'family' terms. Thus Selvin Green was 24 when he joined his mother and aunts in England at the instance of his cousin Lola, who found where there was work for him and paid his shipping fare. 'I was here in Jamaica carrying on, and Lola think, "Well, it's best for Selvin to go to England, because he's a builder, and there's so much good building going on here". And she says, "Oh, come along." And she just paid the money. And I came.'

Similarly, Harry Davidson, although belonging to a migrant family — 'pretty well everyone had gone' — and working in a minor administrative role for Air Jamaica, so that he had briefly visited England, Canada and the USA, had not thought of migrating himself: 'I was content being right there in Jamaica.' But Harry's wife-to-be was a Jamaican graduate and both of his sisters had got degrees in the USA, and finally, aged 27, he decided to follow their path. His younger sister Keetie in New York 'was the one that really made it happen'. She helped him choose a college and handle the paperwork. 'She [had] moved to New York, she made the move to go to school. And while she was in school she was always encouraging me to come and do school. And I think after hearing it for so many times it hit me and I realized I needed to do something.'

Len Dickens went to the United States in 1945–47 as a post-war temporary factory worker living in camps. After returning to Jamaica, he 'had the spirit of travelling again', and wanted to return to complete his technical training. But in 1955 he was persuaded by his mother to go instead to England: 'My mother was saying, "Everybody is trying, you can try too!" I say, "Well, I don't like England." I never know the place, but my imagination of what it is, I just didn't have this thing. But I say, "OK. I'll go." So I went.'

Len stayed in England, as a factory worker and an active trade unionist, an outspoken man who was not afraid to write protest letters to the Queen. It is therefore interesting to hear his view of the migration move of his own girlfriend, which on the face of it would seem a classic 'family' move by a woman in the wake of a man. By 1960, he recalled —

I had a girlfriend at home, and she been harassing me and she want to come to England. My mother after me again. What did we want most to do was to get married, you see, and I was frightened of this thing, you know? I couldn't really dig for it. I was just frightened, I didn't want to marry her. You try to please parents. So I say OK. I sent somebody over for her.

Len, at the time of his interview which was recorded by Harry Goulbourne in the 1970s, by then the father of two children and contemplating remarriage, still presents himself as the victim of migration demands made by women, even if this time he paid the ticket.

If we turn now to those presenting themselves as self-activated travellers, there are certainly plenty of men among them. Linton Black, for example, who in 1968 was the first in his family to migrate, describes himself as fulfilling his own dreams of 'travelling' and working abroad: 'That was always my dream to go to America. America was my first choice if I had to go, and that's where I went.' Patrick James came to England in 1956 in a boat with 500 other migrants, hoping to earn for his wife and children: 'I wanted to earn and I wanted to travel ... I wanted to see what life abroad is like.' But there are more striking examples in some of the interviews with women of surprisingly 'male' narratives.

Sarah Chisholm, for example, left Jamaica at the age of 24 to become a domestic worker in Canada, unaware that she had a half-sister already there, and she describes her migration as a purely personal decision, primarily for fun: 'Yes, I was always fascinated in going abroad. I'm not sure about to live or work, but just going on the aeroplane.' Rose Lyle went to England aged 28 in a very similar spirit, joining a boyfriend and becoming a nursing auxiliary, despite her father's opposition: 'he loved to have his girls with him all the time.... My father didn't want me to come. And I thought, "well, I've had enough of Jamaica, so let's see what the other side is like!" So I came here.... He didn't want me to come, but I did come.'

Lola Woods provides a double example. After leaving school she tried working in a fruit canning factory in Kingston, but gave up after a fortnight — 'couldn't work with them people, that wasn't my style' — and tried instead to earn her living as a dance promoter. But then, aged 17, she got into difficulties when she and the dance hall proprietor fall out! The owner of the place! And I said, "To hell with this. I'm going to England." And that's why I went to England'. In England she found good work and grew new roots. But after 20 years she felt the urge to make another step forward. Leaving her two daughters with her own mother, Lola migrated to New York in 1970 to join a former workfriend. This friend, 'She came to America, to some man she have, and it never work out. So I think she was lonely. And then because we were good friends, she wanted company.... And she buy my ticket.' Lola found America more difficult than she expected — 'it was rough at first' — and as for leaving her children, 'Oh my God! That nearly killed me.' But her friend urged her, 'she said, "Don't give up", so I fight it out'. Lola, after a third move, is today retired in Florida.

She was one of many Jamaican mothers who were prepared to leave her children, either temporarily or for their whole childhood, in the care of grandparents or other kin in order to seek out higher earnings. Celia Mackay describes how in her late thirties, although already a hotel manager in Negril, she chose to leave her three children to work in New York: 'I decided I could come ... I was willing to take my chances.' She recalls that her decision was opposed by many of her friends. Other women also met opposition from kin. Sandrine Porto, a single mother who left two children in the hope of earning more in New York, again leaving a similar good job in the mid-1990s, recalled how 'my father was mad when I decide I was to leave my job and come [to New York]. He was crazy ... "You have a good job, a secure job, so much opportunity, you're travelling all around" ... But I said, "If I leave my daughters, my daughters are old enough, they're not babies." I leave them and come.' Despite the pain of separation, she too has stayed on in New York.

In short, among our Jamaican migrants there are no clear gender patterns in the narratives, such as we had anticipated. But does the evidence of the interviews suggest that in reality women less often migrated autonomously than men? Can we say that women tend to primarily move through family and men through work, as earlier oral historians have suggested?

These questions are closely linked, but distinct. Of our 73 migration accounts, over half are described as for family reasons. Of these 'family' migrants, the largest group were the 17 children, clearly not yet able to make their own independent choices — although certainly sometimes feeling strongly, whether finding 'it was exciting at the time, packing up and leaving', or conversely, like Rodney Scott, who shuttled between a great-grandmother in London and a grandmother in Florida, feeling himself 'like a ping-pong ball, backwards and forwards, backwards and forwards'. But putting these child migrants aside, migrations for family reasons and for work (or travel or study) were closely similar between men and women.

Most of the 26 adult 'family' migrants were rejoining parents or a partner, their motives expressed partly as emotional but also as looking 'for a better life'. Some such migrants were very eager to go, attracted by better economic opportunities, and deliberately using their family connections to go — 'I like to live comfortable'; 'mostly economics, it's hard to make an honest living in Jamaica'; while others went very reluctantly. Winnie Busfield, who went as a young mother to rejoin her husband in England, confessed, 'You know, many people say, "I went to England to do this and that." If you ask me, I don't know what I went for. He just said, "Come", and I went!'

There were two young women who were sent away by their families to kin abroad in order to rescue them from dangers of violence. It is also interesting that sometimes for a man or a woman a later migration was for negative emotional reasons, to leave a marriage. Indeed Roy York's mother and father deliberately decided to emigrate in different directions, one to the United States and the other to Britain, as a form of separation: 'so that's where the breaking up start'.

Lastly, there were four men and one woman who were brought abroad by their families explicitly in order to work, or in two cases, to study. Russell Peel was in his late twenties, a well-established cabdriver with a fleet of three cars, 'I was quite comfortable'. But his aunt in England fixed his college course, and bought his plane ticket, and Russell's mother encouraged him, '"Go and see the other side of the world." So I said, "all right, no problem. Let me try."'

With the remaining 30 migrations, by contrast, the migrants said that they had themselves decided to migrate to work, to travel or in one case to study. They recount this explicitly. David McNeep explained, 'Jamaica is a poor country and you hear about England, you can get a few pence more, you come to look fi it.' Or as Clover Brown put it, 'I decided it was time for me to relocate.' Contrary to what earlier oral historians had led us to expect, these 'autonomous' migrants were also as often women as men.

Migration Agents and Global Vision

Interestingly, the moving forces described in all these migration stories are the migrant, other family members and friends. Official migration recruitment agencies have only a shadowy background presence. In fact they were very important for migration to Britain in the 1940s and 1950s, first as part of recruitment for the armed forces, and then for public service work. The post-war migration boom gathered force precisely because it was encouraged by this official recruitment, which made the migration process itself relatively easy, in contrast the more individual or family-led migrations to Britain and North America from the mid-1960s onwards. Our earliest migrants, Rufus Rawlings and Anna Gladstone, both came to Britain through wartime service in 1943–45. Don Bartley first travelled briefly to America as a factory worker in 1945, housed in a camp, and subsequently several others were recruited for temporary farm labour and housed similarly: when Linton Black came in 1968 his ticket was paid and his farm job waiting — although he soon eloped from it.

Migrants were well aware of these official agencies as well as other possibilities from gathering and comparing news from different destinations: 'Some sent back saying they were earning good money and all these things, some sent back and say things was bad,' Patrick James remembered. 'I wasn't interested in going back to the States — always read about this colour problem and I didn't like it.' But there was mixed news from Britain too. One man came back 'very sad, … and he advise me not to go, he say things are not good over there and you are not doing too bad over here'. Another man by contrast had been in the RAF, 'and he speak well about the treatment he got'.

But as important as these official recruitment agencies undoubtedly were, they are simply indicated as context in migration stories: the main narrative remains personal. Thus Anna Gladstone, a Kingston civil servant's daughter, was recruited for the ATS in 1943: 'we were the very first lot of girls ever recruited from the Caribbean.' But the story she tells is of a migration which was certainly her own choice.

> Yes — much to my parents — they didn't want you to go.... My father told me a lot about [England], which I had not realized before.... I said, "It doesn't matter what you say, I'm going." So I was determined.... We were all excited about joining, taking part in the war. I just felt that it was a big drama taking place in that part of the world, and we wanted to be part of it. Didn't think about the dangers of being bombed. We said, "You can be killed anywhere".

In a rather similar way, there are very few among either men or women who explicitly 'narrate' themselves as determining the migration moves of others. Two exceptions were both husbands. Don Bartley, who had gone ahead to England in 1953 and got work as a gas stoker, recalls, 'We were really married over a long period of time, and I think it's just impossible for her to be over there and me here, so I decide to take her over.' Edley Keat, who stayed as a bus driver in Jamaica, also talked in a similarly assertive style: 'I marry here and I told my wife, that any day she go abroad we separate, because I not following her. So if she go abroad to migrate, she would be on her own.'

However, much more often the agents of migration within families only become clear through a closer look at the evidence in the interviews, including sometimes those with another member of the family. Altogether of our 73 migration accounts, over half, 26 adult and 17 child migrations, are described as happening through the agency of others. But through the interviews we can identify which members of the family were the agents for these 'non-autonomous' migrations.

Thus among the children rejoining their families, we find that six were joining couples, and the rest lone parents or kin, so that we could estimate that the agents involved here were 8 men and 17 women. With the adult 'family' migrants, there were eight women and three men following their partners. But very strikingly, all of the other 15 migrated at the instance of women: most by their mothers, but also sisters, an aunt and a female cousin.

Thus altogether, putting together the evidence for all the migrations, whether 'autonomous' or 'family', we can say that of all the agents they yield, 32 are men and 49 are women. So women are definitely more represented than men among the activators of migration.

This is a remarkable outcome. How might we explain it? One possibility would be Jamaican family structures, with the high proportion of households headed by women. It would not be surprising to find women less often playing the key role as promoters of migration in intact couple-headed families than in female-led families, with the men either missing or treated as less central to the family. However, our interviews have not shown any differences in migration processes between these two types of family.

Indeed some of the most active female migration agents were the wives of men who were successful earners and respected in their families, while others succeeded with little male support. These are women who organized a whole succession of family migrations: multiple migration agents. We have not been told of any man who played this role, but ten instances were described in the interviews of women who were multiple migration planners.

Thus Lola Woods was a good migration organizer, from a family in which men have remained marginal. She not only orchestrated her cousin and her children in successive moves to London and New York, but also persuaded groups of friends to follow her each time, and again most recently to migration in Florida. She lives there deep in a suburban pinewood, but her neighbours seem to be mainly also West Indians.

Another multiple migration planner was Cathleen, the eldest sister of Donetta Macfarlane, who by contrast had been married for over 40 years. She had herself gone to England at the age of 15 in 1953, sent for by a friend. After bringing over Donetta, Cathleen next sent for her second sister, and then paid for her fourth sister to go to Canada (who in turn sent for her brother and fifth and sixth sisters). Cathleen had also bought a ticket to bring another sister to England, but when this sister declined, she sent for an aunt in her place.

Equally striking was Olive Carstairs's mother, who had been a postmistress in Jamaica, and so well placed to understand what was happening. By the late 1950s she was married with four children, and despite having three brothers in England, 'she decided, OK, well, she's going to the States to see what it's like'. She left her children with their father and a maid, came back after a year to Jamaica, and 'this is where she decided, "OK, well, I'll try Canada"'. This time she left her husband and children with her grandparents, 'and then, I think a year after, she sent for my dad', and finally for the children. Here is a married woman, whose husband was in a respectable non-manual job and a father close to his children, yet it is she who is described as taking all the initiative and making all the decisions.

In two other families of similar multiple migration planners, men have been a presence, but not continuously. Here these women are recognized as multi-purpose anchor figures for the family. Sarah Chisholm's niece Andrea explains how 'she [Sarah] just wanted everyone to be together.... She is like the mother of everyone in the family. So everyone turns to her'. Nelson Pinnock spoke very similarly of his Aunt Edna, who 'took my mum here [to Canada], and then, you know, cause me to be here. So she, you have to say, she was the father of the whole family'.

Thus the strikingly active role of Jamaican women in migration processes does not appear to derive directly from particular variations in family structures. Our interviews suggest that women are the most active migration agents, whether they belong to 'intact' couple-headed families or to female-led families. Their role is rooted in the wider gender culture and economy of Jamaica.

It is clear that these multiple migration agents were highly successful in maintaining their familial and other information networks. It could be that women migrants in general write letters or phone more frequently than men: our evidence is insufficient to guess at this. Our interviews show, however, that men were as likely to remain in contact with home as were women, and also to send back money and gifts. Moreover, because men have always been likely to earn more, they may well have sent back more money than women migrants, and particularly than the high proportion of women who are now drastically underpaid illegal immigrants to America and Europe. On the other hand, it is women who overwhelmingly take on the role of caregiver for the children of migrating mothers.

We have also found that as migrants, Jamaican women modify their identities in ways which are similar to those of men. As we shall see in chapter six, the chief differences in identity depend on the country to which they migrate. It is striking, however, that the most eloquent expression of a transnational identity, with a vision of his children as world citizens, came from Arnold Houghton, whose mother was another multiple migration planner. Although his parents were a strong married couple, Arnold saw his father, in Jamaica a lorry driver and chauffeur, as much less expressive, not the family leader. His mother was another postmistress, which meant she knew much more what was happening in terms of migration:

> the counsellor for a lot of people in the community, she knew everybody. She knew who was getting money from abroad, she knew who to give the money to and who not to give it to — some of the husbands, or some of the kids, when the cheques came.... So she had her relationships with her people that way, and they treated her special. They would bring the best mango, the best banana, the best fruit from their farms, for her.... She ran the show there.

It was just the same in the family:

> She was always the leader, and he, basically, toed the line.... He'll do what he can. He'll work hard to get there, but he's not the one to take up a *global picture* of things, and say, "Okay, we have to make this drastic move". So he wasn't in favour of her leaving. No, he wasn't. But she was the one that was able to see that, "Hey, we've got to make a major move", and do something drastic.

Arnold's mother left for Canada alone in 1972. Four years later, working as a caregiver for the elderly, she felt well enough established for her husband, six of her children and one granddaughter to rejoin her there: as Arnold's sister Verity put it, 'We left Jamaica in May 1976, and it was like everybody, the whole family.'

In one other family, who at the time we began interviewing were busily planning a transatlantic family reunion, bringing kin from Britain, Canada and the United Sates to celebrate their common roots in Jamaica, we again found this concept of the need to have a 'global' view. Dana Howard is a successful accountant practising in Florida. She set on her migration path when she left home for school in Kingston at the age of 12, and then at 24 on to America. Her parents were again a strong and hard-working married couple, who in this case stayed in Jamaica. Her father combined farming with informal maths teaching, and successfully 'steered' four of his daughters into accountancy, three of these migrating to work in America.

Nevertheless, Dana sees her mother as the more crucial influence, a woman with 'eyes in the back of her head', who 'knows what she wants'.

It was she who basically helped to plan our careers.... My mother's concept in raising us, was, she was not going to send us to school within our district where we lived, because this is such a small rural village. She wanted us to go to the city, go to the best schools, so that we could make the best of our lives when we grow up. And that was, I think, more so my mother's doing. *She's always been the person with a very global vision.*

The Strategic Role of Jamaican Women

How did this role of Jamaican women as the 'global' visionaries and strategists for their families arise? We would suggest that its roots are in centuries-old gender roles in Jamaica. As far back as the slave era, because they were able to use their 'provision grounds' to market the produce of their plots independently, women as much as men were the economic mediators between families and the wider society.[2] The strength that this gave them could sometimes even influence relationships between a black slave woman and a white plantation manager. Thus Thomas Thistlewood, overseer at Egypt plantation and later owner of a cattle farm, lived thirty years as common law man and wife with Phibbah, a black slave who was head of the Egypt kitchen. She was able not only to send him many gifts, such as fruits or turtles, but more remarkably, when Thistlewood was in financial difficulties sometimes it was Phibbah who bailed him out, lending him money over periods of months. Equally striking, they reversed the conventional symbolism of rings: it was Phibbah who 'gave me a gold ring, to keep for her sake'.[3]

We do not know of any historical sources which would help us to understand the changing gender balance in Jamaican families in the century after Emancipation.[4] How far, when out-migration from Jamaica gathered pace in the late nineteenth and early twentieth century, a time when more men migrated than women, did the power of Jamaican women in their families mean that they were also decision makers in migration? However, by the 1970s the anthropologist Nancy Foner certainly gained the impression from her work in rural Jamaica that women had been taking the lead as far back as could be remembered. She learnt that Jamaican women had been among the pioneers in migrating to work in Kingston, and then in the 1920s to Cuba, and now 'the present migration to the United States appears to be dominated by enterprising females.... Many women in the Jamaican village I studied left their families to take jobs in America; and women, rather than men, often sent for their children and husbands once they settled'.[5]

We have found hints, too, of an earlier humbler phrase which precedes that of *global vision*, which we would suggest provided the conceptual step towards it. This was the belief by Jamaican women that they should *tink and plan*. Thus one countrywoman who told her story to a Jamaican theatre group regretted her impulsive youth in these terms: 'In dem days, ah never tink and plan. Ah never know notten bout notten.'[6] A similar phrase was reported in an account of a small market town in the 1970s by Henrietta de Veer. One of the women she interviewed was 'Mrs F', who had been born of Jamaican parents in 1922 in Panama — then a major migration magnet — but had returned, and worked for nearly 40 years in a grapefruit canning factory. She was now living with a road labourer. Mrs F contrasted the family vision of men and women:

I feel that men should be interested so the children can go to a better school, get better teaching, like that. My opinion is that they're just not interested....

It's good for everybody to work and help themselves.... Together you make a better life.... You're keeping yourself, you're helping your husband. So when you're independent, it means anything you *plan* to do, anything, you know, when you have the money, you can get yourself into it.... I like to work and I had children and I went to work to help bring them up.... I am going to save my money so I can school my children good.

Mrs F saw herself as belonging to an older generation whose values, to her deep regret, were passing: 'We used to have a *plan* and take life serious.... They [young girls] don't have a *plan*.'[7] As our interviews cogently show, contrary to her fears, the younger generation of women did go on planning, with an equal determination.

Jamaicans in their New World

When we first went to New York to interview Jamaican migrants for our project, their stories in many ways echoed those we had already heard in Britain and Canada, but we were taken by surprise by one sharp difference. Almost unanimously, however materially successful, and often despite having taken American citizenship, they emphatically rejected the possibility that they had become Americans. As one woman put it, 'I'm not American. I have American citizenship, but I'm not an American. I'm a Jamaican'. This has also been the finding of recent American researchers.[1] While in both Britain and Canada, we found migrants more likely to describe themselves as having acquired a mixed identity, whether as 'Jamaican Canadian' or in more complex ways, migrants to the United States almost all saw themselves quite simply as Jamaicans. This is not what might be expected. There seems to be little difference in terms of overall black-white occupational inequalities between Britain, Canada and the United States: in each country the broad figures show twice as many blacks as whites unemployed, half as many as whites in professional jobs, and so on.[2] But in the United States wage rates are highest, and in addition, West Indians there are better educated and occupationally more successful than indigenous African Americans. Hence on a simple materialistic basis, Jamaicans in America should be more likely to identify with their new country. Why is this not so?

It is of course impossible to make more than suggestive comparisons, not only because of the number of our interviews, but also because our migrants reflect the historical changes in migration currents. Thus those who came from Jamaica to Britain nearly all arrived between the late 1940s and the early 1960s, before more restrictive immigration legislation was imposed. Later migrants most often went to the United States and Canada, which both switched to more open immigration policies from the early 1970s. Hence one reason why migrants to Britain are less likely to think of themselves as straightforwardly Jamaican could be because they have spent much more of their lives away from Jamaica. It is also important to remember that Jamaica itself changed over these decades. The older migrants had grown up in a Jamaican society in which race and class were very closely tied together; they expected whites to be at the top, and indeed could feel disconcerted when they were not. But the younger migrants were leaving a Jamaica which was becoming racially more open, and its black majority population more self-confident; and thus may have been more likely to feel surprise and anger at experiencing racial discrimination in North America[3] than the older generation had been in Britain. On the other hand, time does not help to explain the contrast in attitudes between migrants to Canada and the United States, which although parallel in time, is almost as different as between migrants to the United States and Britain. There must have been other factors also at play. What other possibilities are suggested by the experience of migration which were recounted to us? Let us consider three issues: firstly, culture shock on first arrival; secondly, the implications of the immigration process; and thirdly, different forms of racism. Lastly, we shall then return to the issue of identity.

Culture Shock

Strikingly few differences between destinations show up when we look at first impressions on arrival in the new country. The dashing of dreams by reality is a recurring story, whatever the period. Most migrants set out with high hopes. Thus Selvin Green recalls how 'we know everything about England from starting school. I walk along the road with a flag — red, white and blue. So everybody said the streets of London is paved with gold. And now they say, "you can come!" And we are going to the mother country'. Most also undertook elaborate preparations. They had to get proper photographs taken, go to Spanish Town to get their passports, and very often buy smart clothes for the journey: elaborate dresses, or tailor-made suits with jacket and tie. 'You had to travel in style'.

On arriving, the first unexpected shock was simply climatic, leaving the tropics for the cold north. Rufus Rawlings came to Britain by boat as an RAF volunteer in 1945: 'We landed on the Clyde. Imagine that! Imagine that! On a grey, March morning. Foggy! Coming from Jamaica! You want to go home right away!' Selvin Green remembers the snow, his chilblains, the windowsill outside used as a food fridge: 'Man, it was so cold!' These feelings are closely echoed by the younger migrants to North America. Andrea Sole remembers as a child emerging from her plane in Canada, and literally feeling a shiver of excitement at the clear air and the ice-sheathed ground: 'It looked like I was standing in a freezer'; Belle Dickens, coming as a student to Toronto, remembers similarly, 'I'm freezing! October! And I'm wearing sandals!' And when she came to New York, Gene Trelissick, whose friends had been saying, 'You're going to a better place,' complained, 'Nobody ever tells you that it snows, it gets cold, the streets are not lined with gold.'

Vivia Perrin had a particularly bad start when at the age of seven she left her grandparents to fly to London and rejoin her parents. 'Nobody bothered to think that it was in the middle of winter, in the heart of January.' They were dressed up with big summer hats, 'these pretty boleros, blue dresses, my sister and I, we looked like little dolls! ... And this one little grip between us. I've still got that grip today.' When they landed,

> there was this thing on the ground called "snow". Now me, in my white shoes and my white socks, had to step off the plane, walk right across the tarmac, and I thought I was going to die.... And it was the hostess who really saw our plight, ... we're so cold, and bless that hostess ... she went back on the plane and gave us some blankets to wrap ourselves in.

To make matters worse, due to an accident her family missed the children's coach at Victoria, where they were eventually found by a porter. Although in the end a very successful migrant, it took a long time for Vivia to put all this shock behind her. Her grandfather had told her, '"If you go and you don't like it, you come straight back." So from that moment, I hated it. Even if it was going to be nice, I hated it. I wanted to come back!' Vivia blamed her mother for it all. 'So for many many many years, I was, and I'm still, a little bit aloof from my mum ... I hated my mother for years, for bringing me to Britain.'

The signs of poverty, both among white people and in the degraded city environment, were indeed the second shock. Rufus was astonished, on reaching Britain, to 'see white men sweeping the streets, right? We couldn't believe'. Lola Woods thought Britain 'backward' when she saw housewives washing the street pavement in front of their houses, 'white people on their knees, scrubbing the streets'. Josephine Buxton, who had been living in a two-room village board house with a verandah, now found herself living with her husband in one room: 'a room was all you could have in those days. And I tell you, that was the bed, that was the cooker, that was everything in the room ... and no bathroom, and an outside toilet. That was some of the living that was a little bit lower than what we had left home.' Equally off-putting was the general grime of British cities, then still massively polluted by millions of coal fires. Instead of the 'lovely little cottages' which Chris Bartley had expected, she saw 'all these chimneys'. Rose Lyle was astonished that in London 'the buildings were so black and horrible' and she asked, '"Don't they ever clean them?" I thought it was the dirtiest place I'd ever seen in my life!'

Again there were parallels in the feelings of later migrants to the United States — although not to Canada. Stuart Campbell, now a New York accountant, remembered:

> One of the worst things in my life was actually coming here.... I was overwhelmed really, especially when I went to Manhattan. These wide, huge streets, these tall buildings. But to some extent, I was a little disappointed, because you hear stories of America, you didn't think they have potholes and broken down buildings .... There were also poor people here too, living real tough lives.

Similarly, Gene summed up New York as 'concrete jungle', while Selassie Jordan, Rasta street trader, calls it 'a garbage pan ... shitty dirty, man'. He fears its pollution is 'rubbing off pon me too', so that he needs to 'burn the devil off.... The devil easy fe get pon you but him hard fi come off'. Joy Beck, now a medical visitor in the city, at first felt very cramped by the tall blocks, and was surprised to find 'people were just sitting out there not doing anything ... I thought everybody had a job somewhere to go'. In Jamaica, observed Patsy Clark, 'we only always hear the good stuff, the bad things were never talked about'. Brigette Umber indeed felt so repelled and disillusioned when she arrived in New York as an eight-year-old child that she had to be sent home to Jamaica to recover from her depression:

> When I came, it was in the night. So at night, you saw all these beautiful lights, and then I'm like, "Wooow!" The morning, I got up, ran outside. I saw buildings, huge buildings. And I'm like, "So what happened to all the lights? Where's the beauty?" It's dirty. And then I see people was throwing things on the floor. And I'm like, "Man, I can't live here ... I wanna go home"...
>
> I'm depressed. I'm just sitting there, I wouldn't play with anyone, I wouldn't talk to anyone. I just had to go home.

Brigette in fact recovered fast, and two years later was back in New York. But the emotional costs of migration were very high for many others in each generation, particularly in terms of the feeling of loss and loneliness which it could bring. This was the third shock, and it came both from separation from loved ones, and from the more private culture which they now found. As Josephine Buxton put it, in England 'when a door is closed, you don't know the next person. And all like that: we used to, like, meet people on the way. Nobody saying "good morning" to anybody. The way of living wasn't too right for us'. Don Bartley had come thinking that 'this was England, the mother country', so that 'it must be disappointing' to find that people 'were far from being as friendly as I thought'. Arnold Houghton recalled the sense of disempowerment he felt on coming to Canada: 'I felt like I was part of something that was happening. All of a sudden you get torn from that role: you have to come into this role, where you're a nobody, you're a number, nobody knows you, and to boot, you're a minority on top of it! It wasn't a pretty feeling!' Linton Black, now a pensioner, still has something of this feeling of isolation after 30 years in the United States, with only a cousin nearby to turn to in difficulty: 'I have no friends, I keep telling you that.... It wouldn't be like that back home, it would be a family surrounding, as most of my family would be around me.... I wouldn't basically depend on one individual if something would have happened, if I was in Jamaica.'

Indeed for migrants of all ages, the realignment of close family relationships, both partings and reunions, continues to be a primary pain — on both sides. Children had to not only lose carers such as grandparents whom they loved and trusted, but readjust to parents who in the years apart had become strangers. At the airport Leonard Selkirk mistakenly rushed up and greeted an uncle whom he thought was his father. Dick Woodward recalled how when he 'saw my mother, the memory was there, but she wasn't the same person ... I was very very unhappy. Very very unhappy. I wanted to go back, partly because I missed my grandmother very much'. On the other side, Dana Howard remembers as a child finding her grandmother crying after seeing off her grandchildren at the airport: 'my grandmother was very very lonely ... so I said, "Don't cry, Aunt J", I'm going to stay with you.' And when Celia Mackay left her three children for New York, 'for about six months, I cried days, and I cried nights, "Did I do the right thing?" You know, "I miss my kids, I miss back home"'.

The strongest feelings of loss and loneliness were recalled, however, by those who came as teenage migrants. This was not so with the earliest migrants who came to Britain as wartime members of the armed forces. Rufus Rawlings remembered how 'in those days, once you had on a uniform, you're accepted. The trouble started, when you're not in uniform'. Anna Gladstone, who did administrative work in the ATS, remembers how she was invited for the weekend by middle class families, and brought breakfast in bed. 'We had lots of invitations. People would write in and invite us to different places.... People were very hospitable in those days, especially due to the fact that we had volunteered'. Hospitality offers were also organized by the West India Committee, who provided tea and snacks and newspapers at their Norfolk Street office. In the war years in Central London there was casual fun too: 'it was nice to bump into the RAF boys because they invited you to lunch.... All the forces, the Americans were there, and the Canadians, everybody who was taking part in the war. They were hard times, but there were also a lot of good fun times as well.'

It was much less easy for young people after the war, and some who went to each country recalled feelings of confusion and loneliness. Joyce Leroy came to England in the 1960s, working in various factories and lodging with an aunt. But she felt she 'had no friends in England. Remember, in those days, it was mostly men going to England, and older men'. She moved on later to New York. Verene Gladstone was also 'miserable' at her middle class London school in the 1970s. She disliked her school life intensely. 'I didn't have any friends.... It was just very lonely. I missed my friends. It was cold going home. I hated the bloody uniform. It was awful.' 'It was very lonesome', recalled Donetta Macfarlane of being a newly-arrived Jamaican teenager to Canada in 1972. 'It was lonely.... There was no one in my age group to talk to, they're either older or too young, right? So all I want to do is to go back home. I was miserable.' Ted Oliver expressed the feelings of loss and confusion of many migrants especially well. When he rejoined his mother in Canada as a teenager, he felt pulled apart. 'To me, seeing my mum again, it was like — joy. We hug, we kiss, we dance together, we do everything. So family life with my mum was great.' But he missed his family left behind in Jamaica too, and above all his friends. 'I was a very active person, so I'm with the boys all the time, and we have a cricket team, we used to go from village to village, I'm the one who's the Captain — so to leave all that wonderfulness, it's dumb, it's sadness.... It takes me around two, three years.'

In short, the culture shock of migration does not seem a likely source for contrasting migrant identities. The stories of encountering a new climate, a new urban environment and a new society on the one hand, and of emotional loss on the other, echo down the generations, wherever the migrants went.

The Immigration Process

Whatever their destination, as we have seen, over half of the migrants came to join kin: mostly parents or spouses who had gone ahead. Thus only a minority were affected by differences and changes in immigration processes, but for some of them this could shape their experiences. It is important to note that the realities — as opposed to the official rules — of immigration processes are not well documented, both because of the unknown proportion who enter improperly, and because of the political need of the authorities to present politically acceptable figures. But in a nutshell: up until the early 1960s migrants to Britain entered easily under an open system, whether or not they had work already fixed or already had family members in Britain. Many were deliberately encouraged to migrate to Britain through official recruitment policies in the West Indies, such as by London Transport. From the mid-1960s, however, just as Britain imposed more restrictive rules, both Canada and the United States became more open, dropping earlier racial quota policies, while nevertheless maintaining selective processes. Since then, all three countries have operated systems primarily based on either work qualifications or family reunification. But while in the late 1960s Linton Black could still enter the United States 'legally' as a farm labourer, the demand is now for much better-qualified workers: hence the easiest route for most Jamaicans is through a parent–child family connection. Even then, however, moving from being a visitor to becoming a resident with a public right to work is a complicated and difficult process.

As a result, the majority of those who came to the United States and also some to Canada had at some stage skipped the rules. Typically this was either through manipulating kinship or the form of visa, or both. Even Linton never intended to stay as a farm labourer. After only three weeks living in a fieldworkers' cabin in the American South, he escaped to the New York region, where after a month he found an American girlfriend, moved in with her and married her. 'I got married because that was the only way I could stay in the country.' They stayed together over ten years and had two children, but in retrospect he feels they had little in common, 'we wasn't on the same wavelength'. Similarly in the 1980s Patsy Clark came on a tourist visa to visit an uncle, disappeared to the west under a false name, and then regularized her position by marrying an American, with whom she still lives. Two other American migrants also came through spouses, from whom they fairly soon split. Two others similarly reached Canada. The most unusual was Winston Lloyd. He met his Canadian wife in a Jamaican beachside bar 'through my bigger brother. He was dealing with her sister, at the time'. Winston 'just reason for a while.... Thing work out and we start love each other'. After six months living together by the sea, 'di money run out', she went back to Canada, and a year later in 1988 they married 'up the beach at a pastor man yard' and he followed her. They were together, migrating between their two countries, for ten years.

Family likenesses could also be used. One woman was able to enter New York by pretending she was one of her cousins and using her papers: 'one of her cousin paper, passport and thing'. Much more often, however, our Jamaican migrants came in to visit family on tourist visas, and then immediately looked for ways of staying on.

There could be serious emotional consequences from this, for without official papers they could not respond to a crisis at home by a visit, for they would not have been readmitted as migrants on their return. Already lonely in an unhappy marriage, when Stella Wadham's grandmother died during her first two years in New York in the early 1990s, and she could not go to her funeral, Stella still feels that was the worst thing in her life: 'Stuck, no papers, and couldn't go home. And that was, like, totally devastating.... That killed me. I just wanted to go home.... Every time I hear a plane, I would weep'. But when she phoned, her family said, 'Your grandmother would not want to see you give up ... just throwing away everything you've spent the last years trying to do.'

In terms of work, the effects could be even more lasting, for being illegal has meant they have been confined to the informal sector, thus severely constraining any hopes of advancement.

For men, informal work opportunities are particularly unpromising. Thus Winston found that in provincial Canada 'the one work me get is farmwork', and the farmers were suspicious of him. He did no better after going back to school for a certificate. So he returned to dealing. 'You see fi survive.... Because, if you have a youth [child] and him want food, you have fe go to any measures.... And when me can't get work ... me have fi do something. So then you start deal drugs.'

In New York Selassie Jordan makes a more successful living as a street trader, selling tropical black soaps and creams, aloe and other Caribbean items, and taking American clothes back to sell in Kingston. 'I do almost everything on a small basis, because it is not like I have that much money. And I'm just a small, small man livin and livin around di system to tell you di truth. Living around the system. Refuse to comply with it.' In particular, he feels he cannot afford to pay a trading licence. 'I don't have a licence to hustle, to do panhandling. Cops come, they ticket me. Sometimes I just be straight up with judges, man: "You gotta leave poor people alone"…. Me get over two thousand tickets over a period of three year, and I haven't paid a cent.... By the time me fi go deal with it, yow Jamaica' — he is off back home.

More typically, men got paid manual jobs by evading the social security regulations. This meant that they were always vulnerable. Spurgeon White came in as a stowaway in a boat from The Bahamas in 1965, and he is still working as an illegal immigrant today. 'I get lost in the society here ... I didn't have no papers. I've been living in America all these years as a fugitive.' He has never been able to revisit Jamaica. He survived under an alias, using a false Social Security number: 'You just make up one! They didn't question you.' Robert Austin also had no papers, so he pretended to be one of his cousins. 'I worked in his name, so I would use his social security. Because at that time, they didn't really ask you to bring it, you just give them a number.' Eventually he came to realize that with several of 'the guys' who were stacking in the supermarket with him, 'it wasn't their real names they were working in either'. He was able to get a credit card, which he needed for a driving licence, with the help of an ex-girlfriend by putting both of their names on the card. Finally, after five years of these subterfuges, he found a way to get his papers. 'Well, my friend, his girlfriend decided to do it for me, and we had to do a marriage.... She didn't charge me a lot. So that's what I did. For the wrong reason.'

Nor is it easy for a woman who has arrived on a tourist visa to get regular work and stay. Joyce Leroy recalled how she talked a lawyer into finding a 'babyminding' job for her: 'Oh, you have to have guts! This is illegal, but you have to do it!' Nevertheless, women can find work much more easily as caregivers in families for children or older people. Through this kind of work they may in time gain their employer's support for an official 'green card', opening up wider job opportunities. However the implications for these women's chances of success through work are very restrictive.[4] For example Sandrine Porto had a senior managerial post in the hotel industry before she came to New York on a visiting visa in the mid-1990s. Since then she has worked unqualified in turn as a baby nurse, a nanny and a home caregiver for the elderly, much below her professional potential. Her downward mobility is in fact a direct consequence of the migration process itself. She still has ambitions, but feels trapped. She spells out why:

> This country is a little weird, in terms of they push you to get involved in illegal stuff. Because the legal route of getting to become an Alien Resident, it's so tough, that they really push people to do things that are not the proper way.
>
> I know lots of people who are getting married to people they never know, they never sleep with, but they pay them some money, and the marriage is just to become an Alien Resident here. Because that's the only way you can get opportunities.... The system is set up in such a way that most of the people who become a Resident Alien, go some illegal route.
>
> I'm not an Alien Resident.... All I can do now is work ... I don't have the opportunity, like, to get a loan or anything.... I want to go back to school [higher education]. I want to do something ... [but] when you start school they want to see all your papers.
>
> If you're here, and you honestly want to make a living, and you want to be a decent citizen, and you want to live and be in accordance with all the laws here, how do I do it? Because the immigration system is set up where there is no way.

The evidence of our interviews suggest how much more difficult it is to become identified with a new society whose arrival paths conspire to push you towards cheating, and to subjugate you socially.

Living with Racism

Experiences of racism have varied still more importantly over time and between places. It is also important to distinguish between personal experiences of racism, such as name-calling or direct rejections at work or in housing, and less visible forms of racism, embedded in the social structure and in institutional practices, of which many individuals were unaware. Both kinds of racism were at their peak in the 1950s both in Britain and North America, and in much of the United States at that time discrimination was legally enforced through segregation laws — one reason why migration to Britain then seemed more attractive. But despite the fact that migrants went later to North America, there are sharp differences between the three countries in the proportion of our interviewees who remember direct personal experiences of racism. Of migrants to both Britain and Canada, two-thirds had such direct memories of racism. By contrast, of those who went to the United States, nine out of every ten migrants recounted personally experiencing racism.

Surprisingly, those who felt that racism had not affected them personally included some who came to Britain in the 1950s and 1960s. Joyce Leroy seems surprised by this herself: 'Funny, I didn't. I had a lot of whites that likes me very much, so I didn't have a problem with that.' Dayton Cripps, who also came in the 1960s, said he too had never had trouble: 'England, right, it's a tolerant place, you come across the odd person who's not, you can ignore them, because most of the people are different.' From the start, there were also at least some streets where new black neighbours were made to feel welcome. Don Bartley certainly had some bad stories. At work he had to deal with an ignorant stoker who, 'when we finish work, we all stripped off and we bath together, so this bloke was looking' — excitedly thinking that he could spot how black men had tails. Don and his wife also at first suffered many housing difficulties, but when they eventually got a house in a white working-class district in south-east London, where they were the only black family, they remembered the neighbours' kindness to their infant son: 'It used to be quarrels and fuss who is to take him out in his pram', and on his first birthday, 'it was really warmth down that street'. It is also noticeable that those early migrants, including Don, who had experience of both Britain and the United States described American whites as 'much more aggressive'. Although that could cut either way: Lola Woods, who first went to England in 1948 and then on to America in 1970, said, 'I kind of prefer American way. Because if they don't like you, in England, they pretend. When I get there first, they pretend. Smile at you, and they hate your guts. Over here, you know just how you stay.'

Nevertheless, it was the older generation who came to Britain who had to deal with the most overt racism, which was at that time not legally restricted either in terms of work or housing discrimination, or in public comment. Selvin remembers how there was 'a lot of black and white talk'; Winnie Busfield recalled how 'you would walk the streets and the children would be calling you names'. But on the other hand they came from a Jamaica which was itself sharply stratified by colour, and some, had already directly experienced discrimination there, which in the memory could weigh still worse: as with Rose Lyle, whose blood still boils when she thinks of how she was cheated of her chances of a scholarship.

It was these older migrants to Britain who had to cope with the most open racism at work. For example, of four who worked as nurses, one remembers being constantly abused in the ward by a white nurse, another was pressurized into not taking a full training, while a third, Rose, who did retrain, came back to find she had lost her job. They also had to cope with racist patients, making comments such as, 'Black, go back to where you're from', or 'Don't touch me with your black hands'. Josephine Buxton, one of these nurses, started work in 1960 as an orderly on one of the wards of an old local London hospital. She was working with three other black orderlies, but also a white girl.

> There was a white girl there, she was blondie, nice blondie girl, long hair reach down here, and she was so fair. But boy, she was a troublemaker! She just come and hold you like that, and she hit you.... We turn this cheek, we turn the other cheek, I don't know

what we didn't do. And she used to beat us off. Every time they say, "You coming here to take away our job", all like that.... They do you this, and you passing and thinking of the little money you're going to get. Or if you don't get that, what you'll do. So most of the time we had borne all.... So we had lots of discrimination, which take time, die down, die down.

Perhaps the most effective of anti-racial measures in all three countries have been to make direct work discrimination illegal, so that few of the younger migrants had experienced it. It may have been a key to making upward social mobility more of a real possibility for them. We can see clearly in such instances how open racism kept most of the earlier Jamaican migrants to Britain in a subordinate position, and pushed them towards eventual integration at a lower class level.

In the 1960s even churches in Britain appeared to be openly racist.[5] Vivia Perrin's family had been active Wesleyan Methodists in Jamaica. When they came to Britain in 1957 —

we were put off, somewhere along the line, because of the racism thing. Not put off religion, but put off going to church.... Walk into a new church — you move into a new community, you go to church.... You sit in the back, you sit somewhere to be not so conspicuous. You go in and you sit there and you wait, and the church is filling up and filling up, and somebody will come and say, "Can't sit there. That's my seat." Not, "Hello, good morning, welcome. Can I sit with you?" "This is my seat." You move somewhere else, and somebody will tell you, "That's Miss Jones's seat, she's sat there for 40 years."

By contrast, when she returns to Jamaica, 'when I go home, I go home to a very loving, warm, church family.' Later on such off-putting comments had become unlikely: indeed, the churches in the big cities came to rely on migrants to provide the backbone of their congregations.

In Britain there was also an important change in housing discrimination, which was one of the commonest racist experiences of the earliest migrants. Chris Bartley recalled how 'sometimes people only want to see you come to the door, and they just open the door, if it's a flat you want, and they just slam the door in our face'. Selvin Green encountered one landlord who told him frankly, 'I don't deal with black people.' Josephine Buxton remembers how 'there could be, like, the advertisement at the corner shop … there is a room for rent at such a place, "Enquire within". And then, "No children. No blacks. No Irish. No dogs."' More often, the racist refusal was covert. Even middle-class Anna Gladstone, on finishing her war service, 'walked all over London, trying to get accommodation, and couldn't'. Rufus Rawlings recalled the frustration of first seeking lodgings as a black man: '"Hello, I see advertisement, 'Room for let'" "Yes, thank you." Right, and you go there. "Oh, oh!" when they see your face. "The room is — Oh, I went out and husband let the room." You know what I mean?'

Such housing discrimination has proved a phase in Britain not only because it became illegal. West Indian migrants have chosen not to cluster in all-black neighbourhoods, for beginning with some of the earliest, enough of them have decided to move away to buy houses or place children in better schools in mainly white districts. Indeed Rufus himself was driven by the difficulties in renting to buy a large house in a white neighbourhood of Islington, which he restored and filled with lodgers. This combination of legislative and self-push has meant that today our British migrants without exception all live in areas which are either multiracial or, with one-third of them, predominately white. This is equally true of our interviewees in Canada, where again West Indians have chosen a more dispersed pattern of living than other minorities.[6]

In the United States, by contrast, only one in every ten of our migrants lived in a mainly white area. For here an older housing pattern has continued. Up to the 1960s racial segregation in terms of public facilities was not only legal, but also legally enforced in a third of the country, along with the prohibition of mixed marriages. Earlier large-scale migration of American blacks from the south had resulted in the growth of segregated black neighbourhoods in the northern cities. This pattern has not been shaken by later anti-discrimination legislation, and in New York there have been incidents of the fire-bombing of the homes of West Indians who have moved into white neighbourhoods, and also of the estate offices who have sold to them.[7] Jamaicans thus have had little choice but to slot into this segregated housing pattern. With the exception of one high-earning professional, we found all of our New York migrants living in non-white neighbourhoods — in the Bronx half of them mixed black and Latino, and in Brooklyn the other half 100 per cent black. As the subway train heads towards the Jamaican heartland in Brooklyn, at a subway stop just beyond City Hall the last whites leave the train: for the subway is now crossing a territory where white people neither live nor work. This part of Brooklyn feels more like a South African black location than anywhere in Canada or Britain. And this segregation both helps to cut off migrants from the mainstream American white society, and sustains their feeling of resentment at marginalization and discrimination. Celia Mackay, for example, now a caregiver in New York, thought she knew about racism from the subtleties of Jamaican attitudes to skin colour:

> But coming to America is an entirely different story. An entirely different story. Coming to America, it's like a culture shock, because the things I see people do, because of the colour of your skin, seem to me stupid. If you are going to tell somebody, "You have your money, but you can't live in a certain area because you're black." "You cannot get a certain loan because you are black" ... to me it is outrageous. That is what you call racism. And to me, it is stupid.... When I think about it, it gets me really angry. Because as far as I'm concerned, we're all created as one.... You're getting a cut, and it's the same blood that comes out.

Segregation of housing, through separating whites and blacks, also leads to a subtly pervasive racism in sociability in the United States, of a kind which again we rarely found expressed by migrants to Britain or Canada. The earlier migrants to Britain certainly encountered difficulties in developing mixed relationships with whites, but in the longer run these difficulties were to be overcome.

The problems were worst for black men seeking white women partners. Rufus Rawlings felt of the women, 'lots were interested, but they was under pressure.... You would be considered a prostitute if you seen with a black man. Yeah, that was the thinking'.[8] But in 1950 he did find a white woman to marry, for life. His wife Ursula's family in Dublin also accepted him: her mother, on hearing the news that she was marrying a black man, 'wrote a letter back saying, "He could be green for all I care as long as he's a Catholic!"' Indeed, years later Ursula's mother was to die in Rufus's arms. Rufus and Ursula did stick together, despite severe harassment in their earlier years, including being evicted when their daughter was born because the landlord could not tolerate a mixed baby, and being shunned by friends and neighbours. As Ursula recalled, 'I just walked along with the pram, and that was it ... nobody would talk to you. Oh yeah, they put all swastika on me door, shit on me door. Yeah, when I wake up in the morning, "Get out you black bastards" would be written in black'.

Nevertheless, many of the early migrants did marry white women, partly because in the 1940s and 1950s there were considerably more black men than black women in the English cities, as Sam Selvon so vividly describes in *The Lonely Londoners*.[9] And even after the sex ratio had evened up, many Jamaicans remained keen for mixed social relationships. They set going a cumulative change in attitudes and practice which have transformed the culture of London and other large cities. As Dick Woodward put it, 'any part of London you walk, you'll see people of all generations, elderly white men pushing black babies around, elderly white women obviously with their grandkids. And that social change is part of the strength of both communities.' Today in Britain mixed West Indian-white couples have become commonplace, to the point that survey information now shows that younger British-born men of West Indian descent are as likely to live with white as with black women — a change which Rufus in the late 1940s could have hardly imagined.[10] This survey information fits with the migrants of all ages whom we interviewed, for in both Britain nearly a quarter and in Canada a third were in mixed marriages with white partners. In the United States, by contrast, if we exclude one who soon migrated on to Britain, there were none.

In both Britain and Canada this change was encouraged by the choice of many migrants to move into white areas. Thus Olive Carstairs moved to Toronto as a child where she 'grew up with a white crowd', so that she had no difficulty with the idea of mixed relationships. 'It wouldn't bother me, because it's there in the roots.' The change was also a consequence of the deliberate efforts of Jamaican migrants to engage socially with their new neighbours and workmates. Isabelle and Yolande Woods had been brought up in Britain to their Jamaican grandmother's injunction, 'You mix.' It was therefore a shock for them, when they later followed her to New York, to find mixing with whites seen as at best eccentric, and at the worst a target for abuse, with black American men shouting, 'Aren't we good enough for ya?' or 'You ought to be whipped', or throwing bottles. Both daughters eventually returned to England. Their mother Lola, who stayed on in America, reflects, 'People are people.... You can have nice white people, you have bitchy black people.... Some black people can't deal with white people. They just hate them.... I don't grow up that way.'

In the United States, even in the great metropolitan cities, mixed couples remain remarkably rare. Few said they even had white friends. Jamaicans in New York found this kind of segregated sociability doubly disturbing. Firstly, there are those who were proud of belonging to mixed-race families, or who previously had been used to white friends, sometimes 'lots', and feel their absence. We both asked Gene Trelissick whether she had white friends in Brooklyn. She replied, 'Not here. But in Jamaica, I had a whole bunch of white friends from Canada'— and others from Europe. But it was unlikely now. 'You hardly see white people around here. [To Paul:] You see why you look so strange! He does! No, it does look strange, seeing a white person around here.'

Secondly, those who were living-in helps for white families could see the segregation from the white side of the barrier. Sandrine Porto lived in with a white family who claimed to be 'anti-racist', but in two years, 'they have parties and things, and I've never seen a black person'; and when television showed 'things like black people being victimized, they'll walk away like they don't see it. Just because I'm there'. In a similar way, when Celia Mackay is pushing the elderly man she cares for in a wheelchair, she notices how his friends 'would actually come up to him and would totally ignore me, white friends. Totally ignore me. "And how are you keeping? How are they taking care of you?" ... as it I'm not there. I'm not there.... So I just, like, get up and walk away. It hurts because you are a human being, you know.'

Jamaicans in the United States, despite their relative income and educational successes by comparison both with black Americans and with Jamaicans in Britain, thus still live within patterns of housing and sociability which they feel deeply stigmatizing. We see these forms of discrimination, coming on top of the distortions imposed by the immigration system, as the most likely keys to their different sense of identity.

Maintaining or Shifting Identities

Again and again we heard from Jamaican migrants to the United States, whether or not they had taken American citizenship, that they still considered themselves Jamaican. Others — interestingly unaware that since 1995 dual citizenship has been allowed by the United States — expressed resentment that they could only get their full rights by becoming an American citizen, 'forcing you to give up your citizenship of the country you actually belong to. I don't think it's fair'. Nor do they want to be confused with 'African Americans'. As Gene Trelissick put it: 'I don't know where it came up with this African thing from all of a sudden. I really don't. You know, you could identify yourself as African African or whatever you want to identify yourself as, but I know, deep down ... anything else you wanna hyphenate or add to it, so be it, but I'm Jamaican all the way!'

Out of 20 Jamaicans who have settled for a substantial period in the United States, although half of them are already American citizens, only two took a different line. Both are middle class. One is Dana Howard, a successful accountant, who described herself as having a Jamaican identity, 'proud of my heritage', but through citizenship 'a proud American as well'. More borderline is Stella Wadham, New York caregiver, who described herself as 'American in the sense that there is a dream of the home and the education and the aspirations'; but 'in terms of totally leaving my culture behind, no ... I'm Jamaican. I can never give that up'. Also, but at the margins since he has never settled, is the very different vision of Selassie Jordan, who as a rasta dreams of return to his roots in Africa: 'me done visualize myself on the plains of Africa, hopefully Ethiopia.... I'm an African. We are African and we must think African ... I hate America.... Cause me have no future a Babylon, I have no future here, right here.' It is in this spirit that he eats African rather than American food, and keeps his dreadlocks.

Selassie's vision of 'cosmic travelling', as he calls it, is in a sense a form of anti-American transnationalism, re-seeking lost roots. In practice the most transnational of our migrants is Lola Woods, who has lived 31 years in the United States after 22 years in Britain, and now lives in Florida, but returns regularly to London. She again exclaims, 'I'm not American!' But interestingly, while she says she must be Jamaican — 'I have to, I was born there' — she feels her heart is tied to England. 'In England I feel comfortable.... It's like I've come home, when I go to England.'

In both Britain and in Canada there were certainly some of our migrants who continued to identify themselves simply as Jamaican: around a third in Britain, mostly older migrants, and a quarter in Canada. For example Winnie Busfield recalled, 'I never felt at home in England. To me, it was a place to work, and after working days, I would be out. It was not home. It was somebody else's country.' She has indeed returned to Jamaica on her retirement from hospital nursing. But she adds, 'I would never knock the English', particularly because the welfare system 'was there to serve everybody'. There was a brief phase when she was in acute difficulty: 'they gave me a home when I did not have a home. When I wasn't working, they provided money and food for my children, and my children could go to school.' Two others in a similar spirit mixed criticism with praise for the English spirit of legality: 'the most law-abiding people in the world'; 'no matter what you may be, if you break the law, they're gonna get at you. Back home, you have money, you can buy it out.'

In both countries, however, there were many more who spoke in mixed terms. In Canada, migrants typically described themselves in mixed 'Jamaican–Canadian' terms, some simply, 'in the middle somewhere', but others in complex ways. For example, Arnold Houghton, a Toronto financial professional, sees himself as 'more a Canadian', but 'there is Jamaican in me, in my kids. I also try to reach back to the African in us, the African heritage'. In Britain, similarly Marcia Trelissick, now retired from clerical work, explained that she was 'more connected to British, but to say I am completely British, I can't say that, because I think of Jamaica a lot'. Rickie Constable, a professional who migrated to America and then to Britain, explains that: 'I have roots in Jamaica. I've developed roots in the States, and then here, because of my migrating, so there's a feeling of being unsettled.' And while he feels 'I'm totally westernized', he is also aware that he is 'of African descent, and there's some Scottish and some native Jamaican Indian in there. And my grandmother is from Panama, from the African diaspora!'

For some, this sense of mixed belonging was primarily a recognition that time and experience had changed them, and that their children belonged to the new country. Rose Lyle observed that the friends she once had in Jamaica are now 'scattered all over the world.... I've lived here more years than I lived in Jamaica, where I was born. So what's the point in going back?' Two had tried returning to Jamaica and since come back again to England. Josephine Buxton expressed the complexity of such mixed feelings with the biblical resonances of a pastor's wife:

> I am like, I am like Moses, never forget that he was a Hebrew, even being brought up at the palace of the king.... I know that I am from Jamaica, I having so much of my old culture in me. I have adopted so many others of other country until, I think, I've lost much of my culture too. But there is the little bit that left there ... that I am a Jamaican.

In Britain there was also a small group of professionals who described themselves as primarily British. 'I'm British', Deborah Gladstone put it. 'I don't deny where I'm from, but I see myself as British now, and I think this is a multicultural society, and that everybody can contribute, and the richness and diversity is all part of this.' 'I'm British first,' said Vivia Perrin, 'I say "home", England!' Although now back in Jamaica, 'The pull of England will always be there'.

Lastly, there was another small cluster from mixed backgrounds, who thought in a variety of internationalist terms, focusing in different ways on the future: as a socialist, 'a man of the people', a humanist, 'perhaps a cosmopolitan', or a nascent global citizen. From Britain a businessman, Jacob Richards, described himself as having been 'as western as you can get' — although recently he had also become interested in his Jamaican heritage too. While from Canada, Arnold Houghton projected an optimistic view of a transnational future. 'I think the way the world is going … I don't see people living, or being born in one place, growing up, spending all their life in one place.… I see people moving around a lot more than they've done in the past, probably having dual residences, different times of the year, or different periods of their life.' He describes his hopes for his children: 'I'd like them to see not just Canada as some place where they can live and grow up and make it, but they should be able to see the whole world as some place where they can explore and grow and achieve.'

Behind Identities

The contrasting attitudes in the reshaping of migrant identities revealed by these testimonies have been shaped by many complex influences. All of these lives move between different societies at different points in historical time, and this makes comparison inevitably difficult and speculative.

There are certainly other perspectives from which our evidence could be examined. For example, it can be argued that the different earlier evolution of forms of ethnic identities in the three societies has provided different cultural opportunities for subsequent migrants: that there was less cultural space for mixed identities in the United States, because American society was already clearly organized around existing ethnic groups. But we are not persuaded by this argument, partly because Canada has historically been as ethnically divided as the United States, but also because new migration has itself helped to bring major changes in the handling of race and ethnicity in Britain and Canada. In these countries West Indians have themselves been crucial pioneers of cultural mixing and complex identities.[11]

A more revealing contrast, which almost certainly has influenced identity, was the different positions which West Indians found themselves in the hierarchy of immigrants in each country. Today in all three receiving countries there are now immigrant groups significantly poorer than West Indians. In Britain from the 1950s until the 1970s West Indians were the poorest non-white group, but in the United States there was already an American-born black underclass: hence there were advantages in not accepting an American black identity.

This point is reinforced by *Legacies*, a notable recent book by Alejandro Portes and Rubin Rumbaud about the whole ethnic range of immigrant families in Florida and California, and especially their second generation members. Their survey findings confirm Jamaicans as being notably hard-working, with the highest median family incomes of all Caribbean and Latin American migrants, and the highest school engagement of all immigrant groups. However, they also reported that Jamaicans were also more likely to feel racially discriminated against than other groups, and to respond to this by sustaining their original identity, based on Jamaican culture rather than skin colour. The book opens with the story of a second generation West Indian daughter who, having observed how positively white people responded to her mother's accent — 'Ah, you are Jamaican, hard-working people. Good English too' — is now 'taking lessons from her mother, seeking to regain an island accent'.[12]

Nevertheless, as this example itself shows, it is not just the social structure, but also how people feel about it, which shapes evolving identities. And our own interviews do suggest that in terms of personal experience the crucial factors in shaping evolving migrant identities may be more straightforward, and not so easily explained away. Thus on the one hand, significant material success is more likely to lead to a positive acceptance of new identities. So is simply living longer away. But on the other hand, a sense of belonging can as often be drastically impeded by experiences of discrimination and marginalization in the new country. So for our migrants to the United States, it was the cumulative experience of the immigration process, housing segregation, and the absence of mixed sociability, which brought the repeated cry: 'I'm not an American!'

SEVEN

Women and Men

Images of Women and Men

Growing up as children, it must have been easier for these Jamaicans to grasp the roles of women in the world than of men.[1] Women were the anchor figures in their homes. Roughly half grew up in households headed by women, typically a grandmother, from which men were absent, or played only transient or peripheral roles. Hence women had to take on the whole range of responsibilities, not only of caring for the home and children but also economic. Such women of necessity performed the male as well as the female roles in the family: as Eva McNeep said of her mother, 'to me she will always be my mother and father'. Yolande Woods spoke for many when she said that in her family in Jamaica, Britain and North America, women 'are the only thing that really [matters]. There's never been any real male role.... Men are really a sort of unspoken entity, phantom figures'.

More remarkably, in households headed by a couple — usually a mother and father, but sometimes grandparents, or parent and stepparent — the woman's role in the family typically overshadowed that of the man. There were three or four exceptions, households in which the man seems to have led, and there was just one mother who is portrayed as over-submissive: 'You can walk over her. She is a person who — somebody hit you on one cheek, turn the other one.' But much more typical were Greta Houghton's parents. She describes her father before they came to Canada as a hard-working shoemaker and small farmer, and when at home 'a very quiet person. Very quiet. Never talk much.... A peaceful person'. He left 'the planning of the home' to Greta's much more articulate mother, who was 'very ambitious'. She had no paid job — 'that was her job, cooking, taking care of the house; she could wash, she could iron' — but she earned extra money by cooking and washing for the local police. She raised six children of her own, an outside child by her husband, and two nieces, as well as temporarily caring for several children of distant relatives, 'who would have come in and asked her, a mother might be migrating to England, and ask her to let the children stay for a little while. So she did that too'. She had left school very young, but got her children to teach her to read and write properly so that she could send letters to her children abroad. She was also a respected public figure in the United Church, an office bearer, and a talented speaker. 'At church she prayed, she was fluent in her prayer.' Greta found her very easy to talk to, and a big influence: 'my character comes from, handed down from my mother.'

Many other mothers are similarly remembered, before and after migration, as 'the backbone of the family', 'determined', 'extremely strong', 'the leader of the family', 'in charge', 'headstrong', 'bossy', 'strong head', 'the one with a global vision'. As Belle Dickens summed it up, her mother 'was more or less the head of the household. She respected my father, but she was the one who said, "We're going to do that", and that gets done'. The activities and influences of such strong Jamaican women were in no way limited to traditional women's roles such as cooking and ironing. For example, Brigette Umber's mother 'did everything. My mother was a carpenter, my mother was a dressmaker, my mother was a nurse, my mother plumbed.... She can build, she paint the house. So I never had the concept of different roles, that male versus female thing'. We shall see in the next two chapters the energy with which Jamaican women threw themselves into work at all levels, and their crucial contributions to education and to religious life. We have also seen earlier how traditionally Jamaican women were expected to 'tink and plan' for their families, and in this role as leaders and strategic planners often became the crucial agents of family migration.

This leading role of Jamaican women in their families is likely, as we have earlier suggested, to be linked to their economic family role as higglers, selling farm produce for themselves and their neighbours in the nearby town markets, which can be traced right back to the slave era. It is therefore interesting that some of these strong mothers were themselves higglers; and also that their strategic role could survive migrating abroad. Thus for example in Dick Woodward's hill village family in Jamaica his mother, although semi-literate, was 'the person who ran the money entirely'. Through marketing she learnt to guess weights and to calculate sums. 'You could throw any amount of numbers at her for the conclusion, and within a matter of seconds, you would have them.' She was also an active Pentecostal, 'a brilliant speaker'. After the family migrated to London, she still kept her control of the family finances, although the decisions now needed were about buying and selling houses. 'My father was very cautious, he always left it to my mother to deal with.... She ran the family, in terms of investments.'

In contrast to the strong role models offered by women in these families, the images of fathers are much more muted. The clearest description of a man's role comes from Owen Callaghan, son of a Jamaican town waiter, who grew up partly within the home of a village uncle:

> At a very young age, you can see where certain foundations were laid.... Growing up, you look up to the older people, and also your relatives. Because as a child, you said, "One day I would like to do this." You see the men playing cricket, soccer, and at the same time, not only the games, but also being productive in the family, where Daddy go to work, or they chop wood, and they go to bush, they have ground that you planted food.... Their hands were coarse, rough, so you wanted yours like that.

Other images of fathers were more muted partly because so many of them were absent. But fathers were living with their children in over half of the households, and for those in the home it would seem that there were just two simple expectations: to provide for the family, by earning and growing food for them; and otherwise, not to disturb the family peace. Hence it would be a form of praise to sum up a Jamaican father as 'a good dad, hard-working'; or even to simply describe him in his role of going out to work. 'He would be the one who went to the bush in the morning, on his donkey, and late evening, you'd see him coming down with the donkey.' In the home, while some children did talk with their fathers, more typically the word often used to describe a good father was 'quiet', 'very quiet'.

This quietness, however, could be symptomatic of difficulties too. Owen Callaghan, who followed his parents to the United States, described his father: 'He's quiet.... The typical Jamaican man, where they would prefer to listen to their friends outside, as opposed to their wife and family.... He's married, physically, but mentally, he's still a bachelor.' Children might know less about these 'outside' interests, which were typically sport, drinking or womanizing, but they were a crucial part of the problematic role of men in their families. At the least, they implied lack of companionship for the wife, which could undermine a marriage, although many women would adapt to it. For example Hyancinth Campbell and her husband are a middle-class couple still in Jamaica. She describes him as 'very dedicated' to his work, but when at home as 'a very quiet person, very nice, not very talkative. He cannot stay in the house like I do. He gets bored easily'. Instead, for stimulus he likes to go to a bar 'to hang out with his friends.... He is a night person'. Hyancinth is not happy with this: 'Sometimes we have a clash there ... I think he should spend more time with his family.' But she has tried to adapt. 'After a while, I just learn to accept this ting, because that's how he is, and you don't really try to change people. You just have to learn to compromise.'

More seriously, such night activities and 'outside' interests led in a few cases to drunkenness, or violence, or more often to the man fathering outside children. Some women would then prefer to see the man go: David McNeep's wife even engineered his migration alone to England. Other women chose to ignore drunken episodes, or even took the child in and reared it as their own. Rickie Constable's grandfather had seventeen children, including seven 'for the woman next door', but she and his grandmother 'knew each other, and they raised each other's kids'. In short, the much lesser expectations of men's contributions to the family were matched by a considerable tolerance of their 'outside' displays of masculine vigour. Hence while the model of the 'strong woman' was clear, there were more diverse models among men, and more paths for becoming a man.[2]

Boys and Girls Growing Up

So how did such varying images of men and women and their roles relate to the activities of boys and girls as they grew into young men and women? We can consider this in terms, firstly of education; secondly of roles in the home; and lastly of leisure outside home.

Differences in educational expectations between families were generally related to their occupational level. As we shall see in chapter eight, professional families all supported their children, both boys and girls, through education, while children from working class families usually finished their schooling much earlier. There were, however, some families which made explicit distinctions, seeing education as much more important for giving girls earning power and independence than it was for boys.[3]

Thus Dana Howard's father was not only a farmer but also — very unusually — an informal maths teacher for local children. He insisted that his own daughters —

> must be educated enough to where we could take care of ourselves.... Every evening, he would be home with his family and he would teach us.... We sat at the dining table, and we would all have to do our homework. He would review everything that we do in school.... That's why all of his daughters have chosen a career in the accounting field, because that is where he steered us.

But the steering came equally strongly from Dana's mother, who believed that education was crucial 'especially for girls.... She basically helped us to plan our careers'. It was moreover supported by Dana's grandmother, also a 'very strong woman', telling her, 'You can do it'. Their strategy has indeed proved effective. Of their nine children, only two are in manual work — one working the family farm. The remaining two sons and five daughters are all in business or professional work, including two in the USA.

In a working class family Ted Oliver felt it was reasonable that he should go to fieldwork while his sister stayed at school. He believed a man did not need education in order to get work. He was continually taken out of school to help his grandmother on the land. 'You would have to sacrifice some way, for her to go sometimes, because what can she do [to earn after school]? So the girl will go to school more than the guys would go.' While Ted got work as a truck driver, his sister later was to go on to college and banking work.

While the direct expression of such attitudes is rare in the life stories, it is noticeable that in many families the boys went into farming or other manual jobs, while girls got clerical or professional work. In Britain the second generation girls have again had a higher success rate than their brothers, who are more likely to be in manual work or unemployed — and this reflects a similar marked gender contrast in education and work levels in the Caribbean British population as a whole — and also, indeed, in the white working class.[4] In the Caribbean, where the gender difference in education is still more striking, women now outnumber men at university by two to one. The life stories suggest that these modern differences are linked to the more long-standing images of women and men in Jamaican culture. On the one hand, Jamaicans have found it easy to accept the rising success of women in education and their move into professional work, for this seems an updating of the 'strong woman'. On the other hand, their view of masculinity is much more conservative and also less coherent, based on a combination of manual work, sport and mischief. With the shrinkage of manual jobs it is no longer easy, as Ted Oliver believed, for unqualified men to get work. Such an image of men has therefore become increasingly unhelpful, enticing men towards poor insecure work, unemployment or worse dangers.

Turning from school to home, there were certainly some homes where expectations of boys and girls were sharply divided, but there were others where they were not. 'We had very different rules for the two sexes in the house', Dana Howard recalled of her socially aspiring farm family. The girls were kept at home as teenagers, while the boys were allowed to wander. 'They wanted a more refined lifestyle for us.... You had to speak a certain way, you had to walk a certain way, you had to dress a certain way, while the boys were very relaxed, very loose, they could do whatever.' At the other end of the social spectrum Winston Lloyd describes his mother, a washerwoman and higgler, as if being a woman was defined by domestic roles: 'She was a woman…. She would do just about anything. She scrub the floor, she cook for people, she sell fruits, she wash.' He took domestic roles for women so much to his heart that when he discovered that his stepmother was not washing his father's clothes he took that as a serious 'form of disrespect', and told her, 'You don't let me come back over here and hear nothing like that. You got to have some respect'.

A more ambivalent picture was given by Owen Callaghan. 'Normally the girls would take care of some of the things in the kitchen, and the boys would take care of chopping the wood', he recalled of his neighbours. But his own mother, 'from an early age, taught my brother and I how to cook, clean, iron, the laundry, everything'. And there were other boys taught to help in this way. Sean Ismay, now in Canada, grew up with his grandparents in a rural Jamaican houseful of children where similarly everybody was expected to turn their hand to anything. 'All of us, all the kids that grew up there, we all were taught, ok, there was not a male–female difference, you know what I mean? *There was not gender role?* Exactly. And I grew up that way. Like right now, I cook, my wife cooks, right? … We're the ones that was polishing the floor, taking care of the house.'

In terms of leisure, on the other hand, there were much sharper differences, with many more boys free to roam at play than girls. There were rare exceptions: for example, Connie Dixon describes herself in adolescence as a tomboy. 'I would hang around with the boys, and I'd go down to the seaside, and would jump off the cliffs like the boys were doing.' Unlike the other girls, she learnt to swim and fish — for which she was soundly belted by her grandmother. But the boys were allowed without question to swim, explore the woods and the bush, fish, climb trees, play makeshift cricket and soccer, and watch the adult scene. They would also have fun making toys like carts and wheels from odds and ends. As Owen Callaghan remembers —

You were more creative, you would make your own kite. Here [in New York], if they want a kite, they go to the store…. When we make the kites, we make the outline of it, and then we go to the store, we buy the paper, and we use a flour, we mix it up, and that's paste, and we put the paper on it, and it glues it down. So when we hoist the kite up now, it was a little friendly rivalry — where we put razor blades at the end of it, the tail, to cut other people's string.... You'll play the same games in the school too, they're mischievous.

As they grew older, the mischief became more adult. They began to be interested in alcohol, music, dancing, and girls. For parties, they would club together to buy a quarter rum and share it. Several became enthusiasts for music. Carl Watts, who now runs gigs on his hill farm, grew up in a musical family. His Uncle Wellington played the fife, and other uncles played the banjo and guitar: 'they form a little band, yeah, me grew up fi hear that, afore me catch much height, yessah. Yeah, them old days them form a band and go round like play band at parties, like wedding reception.... Mento music, not reggae music, mento.' Lloyd Porto, fisherman and carpenter, taught himself to sing as a crooner to charm the women at dances: 'I was a good singer.'

It was above all at parties and dances, and also picnics that adolescent boys and girls, young men and women, came together for leisure fun. 'We'd go partying', Lola Woods remembered of her Kingston youth, dancing into the small hours. Anna Gladstone recalled of her middle class youth in the same city, 'lots of parties, and moonlight picnics, going to the beach.... You had a gramophone. Sometimes we'd have house parties.... We had a piano, a saxophone and a drum and a piano, a combo, we'd dance too ... foxtrot, whatever was popular, and waltzes'. A generation later Belle Dickens learnt the piano for dancing, 'and I danced all over Kingston'. And in the same spirit, in her village Joan Bower, west coast roadside fruitseller, lights up as she tells of her youth. 'Lord have mercy on me! I used to go, I'll go to parties. There was a shop up here, we used to call it "The Soon Come" Yeah man! I used to be there almost every night, dancing! I love to dance, I love music. I love to dance, yes, until this day, at this age, I love music. I'm a good dancer too!'

There were, however, many girls who could not share these pleasures, indeed more recalled being barred from dances than going to them. This was sometimes because their parents disapproved of dancing on religious grounds, but particularly because they wanted to protect their daughters from the dangers of dancing into the night and the threat of early pregnancies. But typically parents gave no advice on sexual behaviour. 'You don't even know nothing about meeting boys and nothing about courtship,' recalled Winnie Busfield, who was to become herself a teenage mother before migrating to England. 'It was all done in ignorance. You have no teaching on it and you have no training and no discussion, it's just done in ignorance.... I was a lovely looking teenager, I have no problem with boys! ... It gives me lots of problems!'

So protective parents were most likely to respond with bans. Joy Beck, a village shopkeeper's daughter, remembers how 'my father, as a teenager, he look at us and he say, "If you do it, I know. And if I know, you are dead". So got to stay away from boys'. Pearl Selkirk's higgler mother made a distinction. 'Anything to do with church, you're welcome'. Thus a church concert, 'oh yes, you're welcome to go to that, but when it come to the boogie, no way! No, no. Mum wasn't into that one'. Sarah Chisholm's cookshop mother imposed a much broader ban. 'That was put on the table, "No boyfriends" ... I was a good girl, not one!' She was not told anything about sex. 'My mother told me, "Don't play with boys." She didn't tell me why, just I don't play with boys.... Of course you dare not ask why. You just accept it.' Most severe of all was Stella Wadham's mother, Kingston office cleaner, who was determined not to allow a second daughter to become a teenage mother. 'I never went to fetes, I never went to barbecues, I didn't went to any school functions, because of my mother, it was like prison — "She got pregnant, you're not getting pregnant". So I paid for that.' Stella regrets, 'I was not allowed any teenage life', but many other teenage Jamaican girls were similarly restricted — as well as others who refused to be so constrained.

Young People in Danger

So what happened when young women and men got into difficulties? The transnational extended family system of Jamaican migrants is at its strongest in supporting children and the old, and can respond effectively to their crises. With children, for example, who are emotionally unsettled, or doing poorly at school, it can enable a shift of context through a move to another family household or to another country. For example, Brigette Umber was desperately unhappy after migrating with her parents to New York at the age of 8: 'I hated it. I hated it. It was the most awful experience of my life!… The schooling, the kids, the language, their behaviour. It was very depressing … I was so depressed, she [mother] had to send me back home.' Brigette returned to her sisters in Jamaica for another two years, after which she rejoined her parents in New York, this time successfully.

Less often, this same kind of help could be given to a young adult. Frankie Mackay spent his middle childhood in the countryside living with his mother and an uncle, but when he was 18 he 'ran into a little problem', and so was sent to live with an elder brother in Kingston. More dramatically, Isabelle Woods had migrated from Britain to New York at 15, following her mother, and at 18 was living with a man whom she discovered was a gunman, and who was then imprisoned. Her mother immediately paid for her return ticket to London and her English friends: 'Look, I've got some money together. You're too young to go off your head, to have a nervous breakdown, so take this money and go home,' she said. 'I know you'll be safe there.' Isabelle flew back the next day, and the strategy worked: she is today a successful professional worker.

For young women, however, much the commonest source of danger for their future was to become an unsupported single mother. For them, the extended family system and its values were doubly effective. Firstly, because it was so normal for both men and women to have children with more than one partner, a single mother was unlikely to be shunned by men. Secondly, grandmothers or other women in the family were typically willing to provide support in childcare, or to take the child wholly into their care, thus enabling the young mother to win economic independence through migration and work. Mothering was seen as central to being a woman, and the ease with which women could take on such new childrearing responsibilities, thereby prolonging their phase of motherhood, is striking, and indeed could be undertaken with positive enthusiasm. Thus Judith Bowes, whose grandparents ran a rural bus, explains that her young mother could have managed, but her grandmother asked to take on 'me and my brother, and she love us dearly. She wanted us, so we go to her. My mother give her to us'. In the same spirit, when Eva McNeep became a teenage 'single mother', she gave her first son to her mother to bring up. Although her mother was running the family restaurant singlehanded, she accepted this without any upset. 'I never really grow him, just my mum…. She take him when he was three months old. My mum was like the one who really look about him…. She never quarreled with me.' Her mother also accepted a second child. It was only when a third child was on the way that she showed any disapproval, 'that's the time she start to get mad'. More unusually, Spurgeon White's 'diehard Catholic' mother, a hospital worker, even took on the child, by another man, of Spurgeon's girlfriend who had died, and later on also took two of Spurgeon's own children, thus raising three for him altogether in Kingston, while Spurgeon moved on to the United States. Among our migrants half of the eight teenage mothers were helped in this way by their mothers or grandmothers. Two others were also helped at work — in teaching and child care — by employers who were accepting of their needs as young mothers. It is partly because of the continuation of such family support that migrant Caribbean women in Britain are able to have a higher participation in the workforce than do British-born white women.

The situation is much more difficult for young black men, partly because there is less effective help available for them from their families. Their difficulties are not only personal, but also arise from prejudices in the wider culture, in that boys in general perform less well at school than girls, and partly because of this, as well as racially-based apprehensions among employers, it is less easy for them to get work than for young black women. But their families can do nothing about these fundamental problems. Worse still, it could be argued this structural employment situation is made harsher, because their families are so female-led, that it is difficult for a young man who is not an earner to hold a respected role in the family — for example as a caregiver or house-husband. A young man out of work thus has to choose between the values of a family which is unable to offer him a role, and the values of his peers — the common masculinity of all ethnic working class groups: a rejection of education, and an admiration for physical prowess, including sport, sexuality, and fighting. Nor, alternatively, is it practically possible for the family to exercise the harsh discipline, which is the traditional remedy for disobedient children, on the small minority of tough young male kin who become involved in drug dealing, guns and violence.

In this context of such male cultures it is misleading to assume that a stronger paternal role should be helpful. Indeed in one family with three sons, all now in Canada and two doing well, it is Earl, the son who was brought up with his father, who became an 'aggressive kid' in Kingston and has ended as an unemployed 'street person'. His brother commented that 'with the father, you're under less rules and regulations. Growing up back home, the men let you do more, and he was going out and doing big people things.… He got used to that … got all the bad habits'. The problem here, as we shall see again, was not with the presence or absence of a father, but with the kind of masculinity which the boy took on.[5]

Four of our interviewees, two in Jamaica and two in Britain, have become part of this deviant male sub-culture. Again with at least three of them this does not appear to arise from difficulties in family relationships, such as splits between parents, but on the contrary, from strong models of masculinity within their families which have proved misleading. Selassie Jordan's parents were both rastas when he was a child in Jamaica, and he remains especially close to his mother in New York. His most difficult phase seems to have been after she migrated ahead of him, leaving Selassie with his father in Kingston, and the boys 'explore a lot, explore with guns, badness, all type of things'. Although still frequently into minor troubles with the police, Selassie has now become a peace-loving transnational rasta small trader.

Sid and Crichton Bell grew up in London with their mother in a secure home. Their father Dan was a regular visitor, a strict disciplinarian and a powerful influence. He pushed them with their education, at which both did well, if not well enough to satisfy Dan. 'He really did push us', and later on, 'because he hasn't got a rocket scientist, and he hasn't got a lawyer, hasn't got a doctor, and the time he spent with us, I think he's disappointed'. Indeed, although both work regularly they clearly have jobs below their capabilities. But the boys also learnt from their father to steal, for Dan was a regular small trickster, 'himself crooked'. He worked on the railways, and always kept two wallets, one for his employer and the other for himself.

If that train came in from wherever, and you'd be flashing your passes, like, "No, that one needs 60p on that one" — "Sorry, that one finished three stops ago, and you have to pay an extra £1.20." So what he did, he'd collect the money off that train, and put it to the side. When everyone's gone, that goes into his pocket. You see the next train come, the station can have that. You see the next train come, that's going into his pocket.

With a father like this as a model of manhood, and a half brother already in trouble for trying to smuggle 'the green stuff' from Jamaica, it is not surprising that Sid and Crichton were drawn towards similar paths. When Crichton became an adolescent:

> his male testosterone was kicking in, and he started to behave a little bit badly at school, and started to get into the wrong company. Mum had to keep going to school.... Truanting. Going to Brixton, hanging out with people, and before you knew it, he started doing little burglaries here and there.... And when he came back in, he'd be coming in with a portable TV, marble chess sets, all kinds of bits and pieces. So it just got from bad to worse, till he got caught one day.

Sid followed, beginning with pilfering and then drug dealing. But when both brothers were caught and sent to prison, their father was annoyed not at what they had done, but because they had been foolish enough to be found out. 'He said it was unnecessary, didn't need to get into trouble.' Dan refused to read his son's letters from prison. 'He's so hurt by his son going to Her Majesty's Institution.... "You should have been smart enough not to go there." Because he never got caught.'

Winston Lloyd, by contrast, is different, because he certainly did have a very unsettled childhood. He moved between his grandmother, who was loving, and his mother, whom he feels 'disrespected me.' At six he was sent to live in Kingston with his confrontational father, 'a rough man', and his equally rough stepmother, but ran away from them to a childless neighbour when he was 13. But Winston also took to his family model: his paternal grandfather, 'a rough guy.… He was like a vicious man. Now, I think, in this life, I think I live on his spirit'. This grandfather was a gambler and a womanizer, violent and frequently in jail. 'Sometimes if I get really upset, is like I become like a different person. And they say is just like my grandfather used to operate.'

Life has indeed proved hard for Winston. He has had a combination of jobs. He has supplemented these by growing and selling weed, and for his drug dealing and fights with the police he has been imprisoned: 'Me go a jail man, whole heap of times.' He married a white Canadian woman, but that did not work out, and he has lost contact with their child. More recently, he has turned over a new leaf following a semi-religious vision and conversion, and is working as a driver. And interestingly, he is trying to realize family life as he believes it should be, rather than as he experienced it when younger. He is a very caring father to his two younger children. And above all, loyal to his mother's deathbed call, he has remained in close and supportive contact with his six siblings (of whom one is a junior manager in Canada): 'My mother left me to look over all of them. So I have to keep check. Yeah, she hold my hand and told me on her dying bed.'

Fathers Beyond the Home

Such troubled pasts mark the extreme and fortunately exceptional extent of male 'mischief'. However, a much more common display of masculine misbehaviour was to get young women pregnant and then abandon them without giving any support to the new mother. We should emphasize that abandonment was *not* the most typical behaviour of Jamaican fathers. In fact over half of our migrants did grow up with their own father in the home, and also — leaving aside those who had died — nearly half of the fathers who lived outside the home were in regular contact and providing some support for their child. Some indeed had often moved or migrated in order to seek better work. Nevertheless a quarter of our migrants had no contact and no support from their fathers. One of the roots of such behaviour was again in the prevalent traditional images of masculinity.

'That is what Jamaican men do —manufacture children,' said Edley Keat, Kingston bus driver, who had 12 children altogether from five women.

For becoming a father was traditionally seen as a proof of virility as much as a pathway to parenthood.[6] Thus while some of our younger migrants may boast of the number of their girlfriends, they do not seem to need children to prove their masculinity, in contrast to some of the older men. Three of our migrant generation's fathers or grandfathers had over fifteen children, and four — although only one a migrant — had a dozen or more children themselves. Such men were exceptional, but they saw themselves as symbols of this kind of masculinity, for as they talk they take evident pride in having begotten so many children. Some do not know who many of these children are. 'Yes, man, I had a woman down there, I got children too,' smallholder Jack Rawlings told us. 'In all me get seventeen. Some wha me no know, and [some] me know.' As a roving mason, 'me in an out of parish man ... licking a shot,' said Neil Knight, 'Me know when me shot them. And me left them there.' A travelling worker was certainly especially exposed to such temptations. As Morris Derby put it, 'I used to drive a bus, and this true thing about bus work, what you achieve from bus work, bad stomach and kids! First thing, you don't get to eat on time, and at all time you have the women around you, so as a man, where do you go?' For men such as these, the task of parenthood effectively ended with conception, so that their masculinity was the total reverse of that of the caring feminine mother.

Whether or not such attitudes to having children were traditional among men, they meant that close relationships with their children were usually impossible. 'I just know the name,' said Robert Austin, now in New York. 'I try to question my mum ... and she start breaking down in tears.' Some of these fathers — rightly or wrongly — refused to accept the child as theirs. Just before leaving for Canada, Sean Ismay remembers going with an uncle to the factory where his unsupportive father worked as a foreman, hoping to speak to him, but he refused to come out of the security fence. Many children continued into adulthood to feel resentment at the failure of their fathers to recognize and support them. 'I want to know how a man can have his kids and he don't care about them,' asked Morris Derby, whose father had migrated to England and became a car worker:

I don't check for him that much. Because his treatment wasn't that of a father, because you must look out for your offspring, which he never do. Sending the money, come and such, was that all? ... You must always look how to give [your kids] a start, which he never do for me, and he never do for my two sister.... Yeah, he marry up here [England], but I don't wanna see him.

Probably a more typical attitude was acceptance of the situation, with a degree of forgiveness — 'we didn't have no grievance against him' — but a rather marginal relationship if contact was renewed. Nelson Pinnock, welder in Canada, has been intermittently in touch with his migrant father in England since becoming a father himself. 'We do all right. I don't have anything against him, just as well — I always said he must know why he didn't turn back and pay me any mind when he leave.... We didn't have much in common to talk about really.' Ted Oliver, Canadian truck driver, who did say he missed having a father, 'it was a very sad point', found him again as a teenager, but was disappointed: 'he's not a person who really relate to us.' 'I wouldn't say I missed having a father, because I didn't know what a father was in the first place,' reflected Gene Trelissick, whose father had migrated to England to work for the Post Office. 'I didn't have any care in this world about a father ... I didn't have a world view of, "Well, okay, I have a father out there somewhere, and I wonder if he loves me?" No. Cause I had all the love in the world in my house.' Gene does now occasionally visit him, partly to give him contact with her children, but 'we just can't connect', and she tells him, 'You were never in my life at no time.' Similarly Yolande and Isabelle Woods did not miss having their unsupportive father living with them in London, and being twins saw their rare contacts with him as funny rather than serious. 'It was really funny how he just didn't know us. I used to be always the gregarious one when he used to visit, very sporadically, when we were very young. And when we were older now, my sister was very chatty, and he completely mixed us up!'

Against these unsupportive non-resident fathers must be set others, in each generation, who did continue to care for their children. One remarkable earlier instance was Rickie Constable's grandfather, who ran a lime marl quarry near Black River, and had seventeen children, but 'he took care of his kids.... He sent all his kids to school. Even on his gravestone, it said, "Father of his flock"'. More modestly, Sandrine Porto's separated carpenter father in Negril would visit his children every evening, just as today from New York Stuart Campbell phones his children nightly. Some children went to visit their fathers regularly, such as Stella Wadham, who went weekly to her shopkeeper father in Kingston. She describes him as 'easy to talk to ... very mild temper, really easy-going', and she says, 'we bonded: I never lived with him, but it was close enough.' There are similarly committed fathers among the younger generation too. Jacob Richards, a salesman in England, saw his children one weekday as well as weekends and was always 'very close to them'. Frankie Mackay, a maintenance supervisor in Jamaica, has a son and daughter by different mothers, and is proud of being a responsible father.

> I am the only one doing all the spending. Both mom, they don't work, so I make sure I take that responsibility for taking care of the kids.... The best thing for me right now, I have two kids, and I am taking care of them, and I am very grateful for that. I think that makes me feel happy, and I feel free in my heart.

Becoming Couples

While for some of our migrants, their parents were models to follow, for others they were examples of what not to do. This applied to parenting and it also applied to marriage. Thus in terms of parenting, Robert Austin wants to be the opposite of his absent unidentified father.

> I didn't get an opportunity, as a youngster growing up, to be around my father for him to show me things, that I see other people's dads did.... So just to be there, to come home in the evening, and to see my son growing up, that's something that I'm looking forward to. That I never had, and wish I did.

Similarly, in terms of couple relationships, some repeated the patterns of their parents, while others strove to strike out afresh.

Even for those who stayed in Jamaica, whatever was said about roles in public it seems that in private roles have been changing, with more than half of Jamaican men helping in the household cooking, cleaning and shopping today.[7] But migration itself imposed special stresses and demands for adaptability in couple relationships. Quite often a husband or wife would go ahead, which sometimes resulted in separations of as long as ten years before being reunited, or instead in one of them finding another partner. Others were pushed by immigration restrictions into marriages with people they had hardly got to know. Dahlia Noble came to England as a teenager in the early 1960s, for a marriage which had been arranged by a friend:

> What happened is, a friend of mine migrated here. And he was a friend of my husband, you see. We used to go to the same church. He came over here, and he introduced me to my husband. I never knew him. I only saw a photograph of him. Yes. So that's how I actually got here. He sent for me. He got — just by photographs! Just by photographs!

Dahlia got married at the age of 18, and is still with her husband. 'I just fell in line and started doing everything. And started working, and until now, I'm carrying on!'

Dahlia's parents had separated, but it is striking that those of our migrants who have stayed with their first main partners — roughly one in three — had more often grown up with parents who were living as couples. There could also be continuities in terms of difficult relationships, including in one instance a repeat of violence across the generations. Thus Vita Paterson grew up with a strict stepfather, 'a very big bully in the area.... And what did I get from him? Nothing more than beating'. But then as a young woman she was sent for by a man from her district who was a factory worker in England, decided to go partly to get out of home, and married him, only to find that he too was abusive, unfaithful, a drinker and gambler, and violent. For Vita this marriage was 'the worst days of my life', 'nightmares', until several years later she escaped with her children to a home for battered wives. She is now contentedly remarried.

In contrast, and more common, are those who have repeated the 'strong woman' pattern of their parental couple. Thus Greta Houghton, who has stayed in Jamaica, and whose mother was the family planner, had no qualms in telling her future husband that he could not be her professional rival. 'He is not really a teacher now, because when I met him, I had let him know that I wouldn't want the both of us in the same profession.... He was obedient, he decided he switch jobs.' But this degree of dominance by the woman was less acceptable for migrants outside Jamaica in countries where domestic roles were different, more explicitly based on ideas of sharing, and some men protested in various ways. Louis May, an administrator in England, said he wanted an egalitarian marriage, rather than a man being 'a dog on a lead'. Olive Carstairs's husband, who had been a cab driver in Jamaica, since they came to Canada has imposed a regime of separate spheres, each with their own bank account, the house entirely her responsibility, and scarcely talking together. Olive is very dissatisfied, describing their marriage as 'stagnant water'.

Nevertheless, the migrant couples who have stayed together have had to find new ways of openly working out their roles and balance of power through negotiation, and more often with these younger generation migrants communication can be seen as central to the relationship. This is in line with similar changes in attitudes to marriage in Britain and North America. Thus Vivia Perrin grew up with both parents and is a strong woman like her mother, but she has rejected her parents attitude to communication. 'They didn't communicate very easily or openly with the children, so there were certain things you didn't know about ... certain things that you don't say to your parents.' So when she and her Jamaican husband decided to marry, and he wanted children soon, but Vivia wanted to qualify as a nurse in London, she negotiated with him: '"I'll strike a deal. I will have the children, as long as I can go back and do my training." And he signed the deal ... He changed his job so that he could have flexibility, so that I could go back and train. He did night work so I could go training in the daytime.' In the same spirit Stella Wadham, childcare worker in New York, after a first brief conflictual marriage with a threatening man, is now in a sharing relationship with a new partner, again Jamaican.

'We shuffle the chores in a bag. You pick, me pick!' But especially she emphasizes the importance of communication:

> One of the things I never had in my first marriage was communication. It was like … you want to be a good wife, by subjecting yourself to your husband.
>
> If you can communicate with me, and I can disagree with you first, eventually agree, that is the biggest thing that can ever happen, because you feel like you count, and then you can work over other issues.… You can understand where I'm coming from, you can understand my pain, and we can work it out together.

Lastly Donetta Macfarlane, married for over 25 years to a Jamaican electrician in Canada, describes how through communication a marriage can evolve:

> Things change gradually, every day. When I just got marry, it was just for the first two years, just the two of us. We could play as kids, chase each other all round, and make fun.
>
> And then the baby, Stafford, come. He change everything. Because now, my attention, it's split. But the one, the thing is this.… It's me complaining that I'm not getting the attention.… All his attention, a hundred per cent of the attention was just going to the baby.
>
> So, anyways, after a while it changes, and then things smooth for a while. They always say the first seven years is the worst part of it.… It was rough.… After the first seven years, things change to smoother, because at that time, we get to understand each other better, what each one expected and what we want from each other, and how to communicate better.
>
> We have an open communication line. Because we always do talk, that's one thing, even if it takes all night to get each part … we take the time to explain.… And he's okay, he's a good guy. He's my closest friend, my best friend. I have friends, I have girl friends, but the thing is this, if I have something to talk about, I don't really talk to my girlfriend.… So everything that happen is like I will just tell him. He's the closest person.

It is difficult to imagine a greater contrast in marital relationships than that between these younger migrant couples, evolving their mutual needs through communication, and the marriages typical of the older generations in their families. For most of their Jamaican parents and grandparents, living together implied taking clearly different roles, the women in charge of house and family, the man working outside, and not much talk between them. It is of course a reflection not only of migration, but also of a wider generational shift in the ideal of couple relationships, especially in North America and Britain, but also in Jamaica.

This changed ideal of couple relationships also implies more flexibility in women's and men's roles in the family, and indeed some of the younger migrants do share domestic tasks such as cooking and cleaning. But there are also signs that earlier ideas of gender roles have not been replaced. For young men this can be problematic, because there are now fewer manual jobs in which they can express their masculinity, nor is the role of an unsupportive father likely to be seen positively. Unemployed young men thus lack a clear male role in their families, which makes them more vulnerable to negative influences. This contrasts sharply with the family support given to young women in difficulty, and to the continuing strength of Jamaican women. Just as they were the thinkers and planners before migration, after migration many of these women continue to lead their families.

EIGHT

Working: Up or Down

Lola Woods had run into difficulties in trying to earn a living as a dance promoter in Kingston. 'Everybody was going away to England, look for a better life, and couldn't get jobs in Jamaica, so if you have your fare, you take a trip, because we could go easy. Just pay your fare and go. So I went.' She came in 1948 by boat, finally reaching London by train. Looking out of the train window, like the others with her she mistook the smoke from house chimneys for factories.

> And when I was coming on the train, everybody thinking we're going to get job next day, that's all in our head, because it's job we came to get. And the first £5000 and I was going back to Jamaica. I wasn't going to stay! I said, "Oh, what a lot of factories! Tomorrow we'll get jobs!" I never knew it was the houses with the fireplace.

In fact it took Lola six months to get regular work. But she remained enthusiastic, and eventually she became a ticket collector for London Underground, proud of the responsibility and the uniform which came with the job. Then in 1970 she was persuaded by a friend to make a second leap, migrating to New York. Starting without work papers, she could only find work as a caregiver, and then later as a nursing aid, so she was in lower grade work than in England, although earning a little more. But in the end, after years of manual work, Lola's double migration gamble has paid off. She has been able to save just sufficient to buy her retirement house in a Florida pinewood.

Lola has been just one of the millions who gamble their future on migration. The globalizing international economy stimulates migration through a double economic process. It destabilizes existing economies in the less-developed world, and at the same time seems to offer personal opportunities for upward mobility and material prosperity to migrants to the developed West. Jamaicans represent the more positive end of the migration spectrum. Local economic change and decline has been a significant factor, especially in migration off the land. But for over 100 years the principal driving force — as perceived either by migrants themselves or by their families — of migration out of the island has been the search for better opportunities in work and education. But how does it really work out for migrants? Did their sacrifice of nearby community and kin at home prove worthwhile? And if we think in terms of housing and work status rather than wages, might they not have fared as well by staying in Jamaica?

Working On in Jamaica

The Jamaica which migrants left has itself been transformed by economic change. The impact of change is especially striking in the countryside, where most of the families of migrants, including those now in Kingston, had originated. Forty years ago even a smallholding was sufficient for raising a family, simply but reasonably by the standards of the time. Thus Robert Austin lived with his grandparents, brother and sister in a 'small but cosy' two-room house on a two-acre plot of family land in St. Mary, sharing beds and cooking on a fire outside. His grandfather 'just farmed for us to survive from', sometimes renting an extra piece of land, while his grandmother earned as a 'hustler' [market higgler]:

> She would buy and sell stuff, like oranges. She would go to the citrus, sometimes taking us with her, to go and get the oranges.... Then the Friday, now, she would take it on the bus to the market. She never really stayed at the market for a long period of time, because she usually have her customers where she walk to their

homes and deliver the stuff…. And then, like the latter part of the evening now, she would go to the fishermen, where she had so many fishermen friends, and she would give oranges to the fishermen. In exchange she would get fishes.

But however attractive as a childhood memory, living in this style has become less and less viable. This was powerfully brought home to us when we talked to Jack Rawlings, who lives in a Hanover village in a lane close to the sea. Forty years ago the poorer families in this lane lived in thatched houses and earned from cutting sugar cane or breaking stones for the road. Mas Tim, a small farmer with land in the hills, had the best house in the lane, a three-room board house. Now the families are typically working in tourism or transport, and those with higher earnings are improving or rebuilding their houses. The thatched houses have all gone, kitchens and toilets are now inside, and many of the wooden houses have been reconstructed in concrete. Mas Tim's once smart house looks old and in need of repair, and the best house in the lane, built in white concrete with an elegant balustrade on the porch, belongs to Ms Tina. She works as a seasonal nurse in the United States. As a whole the transformed housing scene in the lane bears witness to higher general living standards, but also to a much greater inequality, an inequality generated by both the local and the global economies.

Jack's one-room wooden house is at the end of the lane. It has no electricity or other inside facilities. At night he reads — avidly — by the light of an oil lamp. He rents his land in the bush from Mas Tim and the two men are the last smallholders in the lane to set out for the hills on a donkey every day at dawn. Jack sells very little that he grows, probably just the plantains. The rest he gives away or eats himself. But beyond oil for his lamp, he has few cash needs. Most essentials come to him from family or friends, in return for the food which he gives them. 'The last time me remember buying a shirt, and the last time me buy a pair of shoes, a 1977.'

There were once many smallholders like Jack, but his bare resources explain why few young Jamaicans are following him. To make a successful living as a farmer in Jamaica today, you need more like 50 acres. But even on this scale you also need creative skill to operate in an increasingly globalized farm produce market. We talked to two larger farmers from our migrant families. Howard Beck was supervising the milking on his dairy farm — '*our* little farm, it's a joint venture with my brother'. They used to sell eggs and milk to local west coast hotels, but as a result of the new GATT international trading agreements, and the high cost of cattle feed, they are now undercut by foreign imports. 'Over the past few years, things have been bad, in that globalization has impacted negatively on us.... We allow other countries to impose conditions on us, which stifle our agriculture.... We can't continue much longer unless we have some sensible price increases.'

By contrast Carl Watts, away in the central hills, seemed more optimistic. He markets his vegetables directly to locals through his farm shop, which sells general goods as well, and he has also diversified by creating a rough and ready space where he organizes and deejays gigs. This idea came partly from playing at parties and weddings in a band, made up mainly of his own uncles when Carl was a child, 'afore me catch much height.... But the music's still in me'. But more crucially, on the advice of a daughter at college, he has found a new niche, breeding local organic goat meat. This sells at three times the price of imports: 'for real local mutton [goat meat], they give them no chemical, they just feed natural. Cause people get wise about their health now, like to eat wisely.' Carl's goat herd has built up gradually into a rewarding new enterprise. 'Me start from two, and them keep multiplying, buy a ram and then buy a she, y'know. Me start from two and me have about sixty of them now.... Me selling the ram there and buy fencing fence them off. Me wouldn't have the money to have buy the wire one time, me have plenty now'.

In short, even to be a traditional farmer you cannot afford to stand still. And this was true of most of those Jamaicans we talked to who had stayed on the island. All of them had found work of some kind, mostly reflecting the changing economy. There were two dressmakers and a retired fisherman, but much more typically the men were working as taxi or lorry drivers or as tourist guides, or in building and maintenance, and the women worked in shops or hotels or as street-sellers. At a middle class level the expansion of education provided a specially good opportunity, and there were three women teachers who had grown up in poor rural families. So it was not essential to migrate to attain social mobility: there were chances in Jamaica too.

Many also expressed pride or pleasure from working on the island. This was notably true of teachers, who are still more respected by both children and adults in Jamaica than in Britain or North America. 'I love teaching,' said Hyacinth Campbell, who has taught children of all ages. 'But I prefer dealing with the smaller ones.... The little ones, they come to me, cannot write properly, come to me, tell me they only add tens and ones, but by the time they leave me, they're multiplying by two digit numbers, they can write a letter, a composition, they can divide. I've come to think that is very rewarding to me.'

At the opposite end of the Jamaican cultural spectrum, independent taxi driving offers a flexible job, which allows Winston Lloyd to work but also participate in laid-back local ways. 'Me get up at two, three o'clock inna the early morning, and I just get up, bathe off, jump inna me ride and me come pon the street and up and down. If me make some cash me make some, if me no make none, then maybe me just drink a stout or drink a beer and smoke a joint and go back a mi bed.' But not everywhere: indeed Morris Derby eventually found taxi driving in Kingston too frightening. He described how he picked up one passenger, 'and when I look there's three man. Two in the back, one in the front. There was some shooting with the police and the criminals.... When I looked in my rear-view mirror, I can see each one of them have two guns, and I peep, the one beside me also have gun. The amount of person that die in that shoot-out, it was five'. To his surprise, they paid him. But he switched to lorry driving in the 1970s, when 'they was killing off cabmen'.

More typically, service jobs such as hotel work or nursing brought enjoyable contact with customers or patients, as well as often gifts in gratitude: 'I love to work', said Charlene Summers. 'There's good guests who come around and who maybe give you a little tips, to boost you up.' In the same spirit Joan Bower made her lively conversation one of the attractions of her roadside fruit stall on a hill above the sea: 'people enjoy me'. Trudie Brown, who grew up higglering fruit and vegetables, now sells jewellery to tourists, with the added satisfaction of helping to make it. 'We'll do carving, like I buy carving from the guys coming down from the hills. They do the rough carving and I buy it and do the finishing.... It's a craft in the bottom, a lot of craft.' But strikingly, a government office cleaner in Kingston, Alice Wadham, expressed the greatest pride of all in her promotion to supervisor: 'I'm so happy. Let me tell you this, my salary is not big, but I am proud of myself, I am proud of my job, and I am proud of the people that I am working with.'

In short, for those of our families who stayed in Jamaica there were also chances, for some of upward mobility, and for many more of satisfying work. How did this compare with the outcome of the migrant's gamble?

Working as Migrants

To consider this question we looked at 50 of our life story interviews with migrants, 23 women and 27 men, all with clear enough information about family occupational and social background over two generations. Each comes from a different family household. Out of these migrants half had ended up in manual occupations or unemployed, and half in non-manual occupations. This means that we over-represent the successful middle-class migrants, because this helps us to understand the social processes in mobility better by allowing us to contrast experience at different social levels.[1] With each migrant we compared their family work and social background in Jamaica, including whether or not they had land, with their last main occupation abroad. This resulted in four groups.

Firstly, there are 12 migrants who started from better off positions in Jamaica and ended abroad in non-manual occupations. Secondly at the other end of the spectrum there are 20 migrants who began poor and ended in manual work. We call these migrants 'stayers'. Thirdly, in between there are the more mobile migrants: 13 who rose from poorer backgrounds into non-manual work, the 'risers', and five migrants who have fallen into manual jobs. This last number of 'fallers' is low mainly for two reasons. Firstly because we have counted last main occupations, so that it misses drops in status immediately after migration, such as the teacher from Jamaica who became a school canteen assistant in London, or the travel agent whose first job was delivering pizzas in Florida. And secondly, because we have put all manual jobs together, we do not include former skilled workers who lost that status. Nevertheless, we can immediately see that the most typical migrant occupational experience was to end up at broadly the same occupational level from which they and their family had started.

So striking success was a minority experience. In general, those who moved either up or down were more likely to be younger. They were also more often women. As we shall see, this younger generation benefited from better educational opportunities, in Jamaica as well as abroad. So more recent migrants have had better chances. Reflecting this, there are slightly more 'stayers' in Britain (where the older male migrants came), and slightly more mobile, both up and down, in the USA.

One other marked overall pattern emerged. When we compared the occupations of our migrant 'movers' and 'stayers' with those of their brothers and sisters, both those who migrated and those who did not, we found that typically they had followed similar paths: twice as many shared the same pattern with their sibling group. Lone 'risers' who left their siblings behind were unusual. This suggests the significance of family relations for mobility, as well as education. We shall look for both influences as we go on to explore our migrant stories in greater depth. The ownership of land and housing, both in Jamaica and abroad, will emerge as a third crucial theme. We start with those who ended up in the middle classes.

Growing Up and Staying Middle Class

The 12 migrant 'stayers' who had grown up in middle-class families were a clearly distinctive group. They all came from families with material and cultural advantage in Jamaica. Most were rural families who had land, some extensive, farmed by family members, and they combined this advantage with administrative jobs, such as in the fire or water services, or in one family a big liquor store. Two other families were different, but each with a particularly strong model. In Roy York's family it was a very successful entrepreneurial grandfather, who 'used to deal in lobster, and supply the hotels and various tourist boats.... He's always busy because of his business.... He was a JP [Justice of the Peace], he was the mayor, [he owned] his own business. When he wasn't doing that, he had his little farm going' — ten acres close to the sea. Nearby also lived an uncle who combined fishing with running a grocery, bar and hardware store. Finally there were two families from Kingston. One had recently shifted from farming to political administration. The last family came from the city, urban professionals from the colonial era, including influential lawyer uncles, and the father a distinguished doctor.

It is true that in most of these families one can see some direct influence between a particular parental figure and the individual migrant. Thus a fire service superintendent's son becomes an English housing area manager; the granddaughter of a social worker in the USA follows in the same profession; a grandfather in car sales in Jamaica — 'which was a big thing at the time, it was the new thing' — has a grandson selling IT in Florida; one of the doctor's daughters is also a doctor, in England, where her father trained; and our lobster merchant's grandson has his own flourishing business in Canada, building and renovating houses. But since — except in one family — the migrants' brothers and sisters also go almost entirely into a variety of non-manual occupations, it appears as though what has mattered most is the cultural and material resources of the family as a whole. Similarly, for the younger generation, when we look at the work pattern of the migrants' older grown-up children, the whole family culture again seems important. For five of the seven children have married spouses also in non-manual occupations, and in two cases these marriages gave an influential upward social push. It is therefore particularly interesting that this familial cultural transmission did *not* occur through the prevalence of intact nuclear families. Indeed, only two of these migrants grew up in such a nuclear household throughout childhood. Of the others, one lived in a stepfamily with nine half-siblings, but typically they grew up with grandparents, or were shifted between parents and grandparents or an aunt, or lived with parents in an extended family household.

To these family assets were added, in all but two cases, successful schooling. Typically the parents found their children good schools in Jamaica, and although most do not mention the influence of particular teachers, the children did well. Two went on to graduate level. One became a school head pupil. In one unusual instance, Dana Howard's father was not only a farmer but also an informal maths teacher for local children as well as for his own sons and daughters. He 'steered' his daughters especially towards accounting field, and out of the nine children, only two are in manual work — one working the family farm. The remaining two sons and five daughters are all in business or professional work, including two in the USA.

Only two of these migrants have distinctly negative memories of school. One boy became more interested in making money as a marine supplier, and indeed became so prosperous that when he migrated to England and became a manual worker his earnings dropped sharply, only recovering later with his own business in Canada.

The other was a girl, Rose Lyle, who was hit by a family disaster. She had to be taken out of private school when her mother died, and was deprived of the chance of a scholarship — this was in pre-independence Jamaica — through the racist prejudice of the visiting Inspector, who coached a white girl through instead. This meant a double setback, for she was pushed back to be the family housekeeper for some years. As a result she went to England with her education incomplete, and had to start in England with manual work, but she did eventually qualify as a social worker — only to find herself ousted from her job in a second racist incident. She recovered her social position finally by creatively inventing and running one of the first London clubs for Caribbean elders.

By contrast there was one other family in which education became a protective lifeline against intergenerational falling, in this sense closer to the stories of 'risers' to which we come next. Vivia Perrin's mother, who was married to a house-improving carpenter, had been a teacher in Jamaica, but after coming to England in 1957 she was only able to get work as a canteen assistant. But Vivia's parents had not lost their ambition and persuasiveness. So when Vivia found herself in difficulties at her local primary school in West London, somehow, just as they would have done in Jamaica, they managed to get her sent to a small private girls' school instead. 'They sent me there, and I didn't pay. I don't know why they didn't pay. I went there for a while, did really well, just got on with your work.'

Vivia was the 'only black child there, but never had a problem there'. But she faced new difficulties when she went on to a selective girls' school, where by contrast the few black children were bullied and shunned: 'It was just hell.' Once again, however, she was rescued, through the influence of one teacher, who showed her understanding, and encouraged her to go on to university. 'Mrs G., wherever your children and your children's children are, you saved one soul. This is why children is my love, whether they're mine or not. Just make a difference, one day in a child's life, because you might save their life.'

Vivia eventually trained as a nurse, and she ended up as an adviser and nursing case worker developing services for black senior citizens. 'I love it.... My special skill is hand-on, dealing with a patient.' Through much the same skills in communication she has also made a remarkable contribution to her London community in two forms of voluntary work. When her two children were into adolescence, they and their friends were complaining how the police 'treat you so rough and horrible'. So Vivia became the first black person locally involved with Victim Support, and also started a local voluntary scheme for visiting young men held in cells. 'Things began to change. The youngsters began to talk to the police, we had an open door policy that we could go in and talk if we felt something wasn't going right.' And then, when her children had left home, she took up fostering. 'There was these two empty rooms, and my husband was always saying, "Oh God! There's so many children out there man, that really needs just somebody, just a bed to sleep".' Whereas in Jamaica she might have taken in children from her own extended kin informally, here in London the process was more regulated. So they trained as foster parents. 'We were short term foster parents, we fostered about thirty-two children, which we had in our home.'

So in the long run, Vivia has amply recovered her mother's original professional standing in Jamaica. She is not only a professional at work, but a respected leader in her community. Here is a migration gamble which succeeded. But in Vivia's earlier years it was a difficult struggle, in which her parents, her junior school and the sympathetic secondary school teacher all played crucial roles. And Vivia's story is in this sense a bridge to our second group, the 'risers' into non-manual work, for whom education was typically a key factor.

Rising

For these 13 'risers' into middle class, occupations present a more varied spectrum. They were also more difficult to categorize. Thus the first two families discussed here were already on the borderline with the middle class: because although the fathers were manual workers, these families did each have a shop. With them the family role was crucial, and closely tied to education. They all moved upwards as brothers and sisters together. One migrant's father was a butcher and carpenter and locally active in politics; and in the second family, the father was a lorry driver but the mother ran the local post office. They therefore had information as well as some means to finance migration. The postmistress mother was moreover the active planner of the family migration strategy. 'She set the direction,' said Arnold Houghton, 'I think their big ambition was to at least provide us with some sort of post-secondary education.' His sister Verity confirmed this: 'They always saw coming to Canada as having many opportunities for further education.'

But in the group of 'risers' as a whole, neither possession of land nor family culture seem so crucial. While half of them had grandfathers who were small farmers, the rest had little or no land. The role of family culture is also less obvious, for only half of them rise with their brothers and sisters. On the other hand, once into the middle class the family pattern for the 'risers' closely resembles the 'stayers'. Thus most of the children of the 'risers' have followed them into non-manual work, and all but one have middle-class partners — in two cases white. Family structure is also very varied: seven grew up in extended families with grandparents, two in stepfamilies, two with both parents but with one parent dying when they were teenagers, and only one with both parents throughout childhood. One child, very unusually, was living alone from the age of 12, mainly helped by local teachers who paid her for cooking and cleaning for them.

It is in fact the role of education and of particular teachers which is the strongest common theme in the whole group of risers, for in all but one family it seemed that the key influences came through school and college. This is a crucial difference between the 'risers' and the middle-class 'stayers'. With the exception of one boy who did badly at school in England, all of these migrants stayed on at school to the age of 18, one becoming head boy, and over half of them went on to further college education, two qualifying in Jamaica as accountants. Three had become teachers before migrating. Several recalled that they had 'loved school' or found school 'a wonderful experience', or spoke glowingly of 'wonderful teachers'. Such teachers included a woman vice-principal of an American high school, 'still my mentor'; another was the charismatic principal of one of the new public secondary schools established in Jamaica in the 1970s.

There were only two in this group of 'risers', both men, whose upward path was through their work rather than their education. The first was an early migrant to Britain, and his success was equally due to his shrewdness in buying and sub-letting a large London house at a time when there was little rented accommodation available for black families — a story to which we shall soon return. The other man did not do well educationally and so could only rise, as he did, through work, becoming an independent salesman. His prime model was his father.

Jacob Richards's father had migrated well ahead of him to England, and for more than 30 years was a factory worker there, until eventually he had to take early retirement. He then went in for small business, first in the ice cream trade, then a bed and breakfast hotel, and out of the profits has bought land and built his retirement house in Jamaica. Although apart from his father for his middle childhood years, Jacob returned more than once to stress his father's influence in his own success at work:

> I think my ambition side comes from my dad.... The determination, yeah. He's the one who said, "Better yourself. Always go, go." He said, "If you want anything, you've got to work for it." It's the work ethic, I think, which I've inherited from him.
>
> Because I know sometimes I've worked seven days a week. When I started the [sales] business, I worked from October right through till May, and I think I had four days off, including Christmas and Boxing Day. So I had four days in six months. And even now, if needs be, I'll work seven days a week. That's something I've inherited from him.

None of these success stories was without cost. For most there was a special pain in migration itself, with the resultant separation from Jamaican kin and friends. There were also other setbacks on the way which some experienced. These included the illness and death of a mother, which pushed one teenage woman back into the role of family caregiver, holding her back for almost ten years. Others had to overcome setbacks through racism at work. In Canada Arnold Houghton found himself in a hitherto 'lilywhite' financial services company, in which the key to promotion was membership of a private staff club — which he was not invited to join. He left for another company. Two earlier women migrants to England also remembered such difficulties at work. Dahlia Noble, another 'riser', did eventually become qualified but she was not allowed to undertake the nursing course she wanted to do in order to become a fully qualified state registered nurse — 'they didn't let me do it … I was upset over it'. We have seen how Rose Lyle, eventually a 'stayer', qualified as a social worker, but then lost her job because she was overqualified then. Such cases of discrimination suggest the extent of institutional racism in the British welfare services in the 1960s and 1970s. But it was a covert form of racism, and even Rose herself was never sure whether or not she had suffered direct discrimination.

Explicit racism, as we shall see, was probably most common with manual workers in private enterprise. Marcia Trelissick, who did later succeed in rising, certainly thought so. She had been a dressmaker in Jamaica, and when she came to London she began working in a dry cleaning shop. She found that people at her workplace could not believe that she could do high quality clothing repairs: 'Everybody was surprised to know that I was from Jamaica, and did such good work.' They were still more amazed by Marcia's knowledge of English grammar and ability to help another girl who was doing a correspondence course. 'So I was telling her, nouns, pronouns, this, that.... The lady in charge of the needlework department said, "Can you read?"' Marcia told her, 'Of course. I went to school. We don't speak any other language in Jamaica but English.' Fortunately Marcia realized her own potential and was able to move into clerical work. Before long she was administering examinations \at an international correspondence college. Like other migrants who went into professional work, she now felt herself fully respected. 'It's only in factories that they think that Jamaicans can't read, they live in trees and that sort of rubbish.' In the correspondence college, and again in her last job, 'it was fine'.

Positions won still need to be defended. It is important to remember that these 'risers' remain vulnerable to setbacks, whether through discrimination or personal misfortune. Among the older 'risers', in later life at least two have become welfare dependent. Illness and alcoholism turned one man's midlife success story into a deprived old age, while another had to retire unemployed after a serious injury at work. Jamaican migrants could come with ambition and skills, but none had significant financial capital to bring. Even their land had very little cash value in a foreign country. So they had to start in the new country effectively without assets. They most often put their savings effort into housing. So they had little with which to provide a cushion through bad times later on in life.

Falling

Let us turn now to the half of our migrants who were manual workers, or had been when they were last working. We can begin with the small but interesting group of five 'fallers', those who had grown up in or achieved middle-class status in Jamaica, but as a result of migration had become manual workers. All of them are women. One had migrated to Canada in the 1960s, became an assembly line worker, and is now unemployed. The other four had earlier risen in their own working lives to well paid and responsible managerial jobs, benefiting from Jamaica's booming tourist industry, and increasing their potential through training courses. They had migrated to New York ten to fifteen years ago with high ambitions, but became trapped in unskilled work through lack of work permits. These ambitions could yet be fulfilled, countering their current downward mobility into unregulated low paid work. For example, they are committed to education — two are adding to their qualifications. So on a closer look it seems quite possible that for some of them their fall may prove to be only temporary.

Interestingly, it is noticeable that *all* of these women have been set back at some time by familial difficulties. These were not in their earlier childhood backgrounds, for all had parents who stayed together. This is in fact a higher proportion of intact parental couples than in any other group, although probably by chance. One woman lost both parents as a teenager and had to bring up her siblings for some years, and the family problems of the others came in adulthood. Three are now single mothers, one having been devastated by the death of a partner in a motor crash; and two have suffered difficult or violent marriages. In two cases these difficulties were one major reason for taking the gamble of migrating. But possibly these less supportive family contexts also resulted in a less effective strategy for the migration move.

All these women believe in working hard. Celia says, 'I am one person who will start at any level. I will work. It is work, and I will work for my money, because I know what I want, so it didn't deter me.' They share this work ethic with many other Jamaican migrants, whether or not successful. Thus Sarah Chisholm, now an accountant in Canada, a 'stayer', contrasted work attitudes in Canada with the 'cavalier type of work atmosphere' in Jamaica, where 'if you wake up one morning and it's raining, it was, like, "Oh well, I'm not going to work". Whereas here you'd have to see a boat actually floating on the road, for you not to go to work'. Working as a migrant was clearly a challenge which she took on with enthusiasm. In Canada 'you realize that when you're given a job, you're expected to do the job to the best of your ability, and more. Being a black person, you have to be three times as good, or better, here, than a white person. You have to prove your point, and prove it damn well, to get ahead'.

Indeed, similar attitudes have been sufficiently common among Jamaican migrants at all levels to have given Jamaicans a positive stereotype of the hard-working black worker in the United States. Thus when Spurgeon White was looking for work in New Jersey after arriving as a stowaway, with no papers at all, his opening move was to announce his ethnicity, making it clear that he was not American-born. He found a lumber yard 'and see a job I like, and I went into the office and tell this man, "Well, I'm a Jamaican. I'm just here, and I'm very interested in a job at your place"…. He didn't even say much to me, I start work the same day'.

In this spirit the four New York women seem undeterred by the jobs they now have. One works as a night bakery worker and the other three as carers for children and the disabled old. But like other migrants who had also worked as carers, they were experiencing some of the special stresses of living-in work. These stresses, as with living-in domestic service in the past, revolved principally around the difficulty of demarcating work responsibilities while sharing the employer's home.[2] Perhaps the most subtle and puzzling issue was how to handle the indistinct boundaries between being in the job and being in the family, between tasks that were paid for and the human bonds which they could help to build. This relationship problem between these black nannies and carers and their white employers, was one also intrinsic to the servant relationship, but equally a form of silent racism. For while in private there could be a close human relationship with the employer, in many public situations the employee could be treated as socially invisible. Despite her private closeness with the New Jersey accountants whose twin girls she was looking after, Sandrine Porto became disenchanted with her employers as gradually she realized that they regarded not a single black person socially as a friend, a social equal. Celia Mackay similarly left a Long Island family because she felt that she was not being recognized as a full social person. 'You're just there. There's no respect, you're not counted. You're just there to work. And I couldn't take that any more.' Similarly, when she is now taking an elderly white man out in a wheelchair she is hurt by some of his friends who talk to him but ignore her.

Other points of friction were more open. One could be the use of the telephone. Audrey Callaghan, who later became a clinic assistant but started in America as a domestic worker, told her Chicago employer, 'This is where I live, and every domestic maid is entitled to two or three calls. I have no other phone.' Another problem was to distinguish between tasks as the children's caregiver and more general work duties. Both Joyce Leroy in New York and Audrey left their caring jobs after being pressurized to clean the house windows. With Audrey this dispute developed into a full-scale quarrel, ending in her leaving Chicago:

> She call me one day and tell me she was having company, and she want me to wash the garage, to clean the windows. I didn't go there for that.... Then I said, "No, Ma'am, I ain't gonna wash no garage, that's a man's job.... This Jamaican ain't gonna take it".... So she say, "You so fresh." She was pushing me, so I say, "Well, I think this fresher need salt, and you can't salt me down." Yeah, we had some good warming going on!... She keep doing it, and I was

so upset, so when my sister tell me I could come, I call everywhere possible, and run up that bill and left. I call New York, I call Washington, I call Jamaica. And I get up and go.

Another friction point was over how to handle disobedient children. These Jamaican nannies were used to a much stricter discipline of children than their American employers. As a result, some felt that the children 'didn't have respect' because their parents had failed to teach them basic manners. One nanny left a household when the children not only disobeyed, but also spat at her and hit her. But this was exceptional, and it is equally important to recognize how caring could be emotionally very satisfying, particularly for a nanny who enjoyed working with children. Sandrine Porto became very strongly attached to her employers' twin girls. 'They didn't cry for their mummy, they cry for me.... It was like they were my kids. Like, even now, I'm sure I have their picture in my purse. They were like my daughters.' And indeed, deep and lasting intergenerational bonds between black and white could sometimes be formed through nanny relationships. Joyce Leroy, a working-class 'stayer' who was earlier on a caregiver, worked for a woman doctor in suburban New York who had herself had a Jamaican nanny, 'raised with Jamaican', absorbing so much of the culture that she can still speak in patois. This was why she chose Joyce to look after her baby. Over 30 years later, that relationship continues. 'The kids are married and everything, and she send me pictures and everything. *She* keep in touch. She keep in touch.'

Nevertheless, all four New York 'fallers' found the early years tough. Stella found her first two years the worst in her life, 'one of the toughest things'. She was earning US$165 dollars a week, but over half of that went to her rent, and after she had sent money home to pay for her daughter's school she had not enough money to eat. She didn't return home at that stage because of 'this pride thing.... You don't want people to know that you weren't succeeding at it.... I couldn't pack up and go back home, that would be admitting that I'd failed at this'. It is these younger women too who most vociferously express their resentment against American racism. They were surprised by the negative stereotyping of black people, the lack of sociability between blacks and whites, and the informal enforcement of housing ghettoes. They also protest against the American immigration system, which has forced them into this unregulated job market because of their lack of work permits. But they keep their hope for the future. Thus for Stella, coming to New York has been the best and the worst thing in her life so far: 'America has been the making and the breaking point.'

Staying Workers

Finally we turn to the 20 migrants, the largest group of all, who were working-class 'stayers': brought up in poor manual working families, and ending in manual occupations themselves. This does not, however, mean that there was no movement within this manual working group. For in terms of work itself they range from a skilled craftsmen like Selvin Green in a regular job to, at the other extreme, Selassie Jordan, a travelling street trader with a stall outside a Brooklyn subway station. Some of these poorer migrants have nevertheless been successful in buying their own houses, while others are tenants. One younger man has been in repeated minor troubles with the law; and some of the older retired men and women are now partly dependent on welfare. So there is plenty of movement here, and also, as we shall see, ambition too.

Typically these working class 'stayers' are older migrant men, but four are older women. Men and women, nearly all came from the countryside, only two from urban families. Some of their families had smallholdings, but most had little land or none, and their fathers were typically small farmers, fishermen or skilled artisans, their mothers domestics or shop assistants. The poorest mother was a field worker and stone breaker. It is also interesting that their lack of upward mobility was a feature of their families as a whole: almost all their brothers and sisters also became manual workers. It looks as if their childhood family culture had a strong shaping effect. Interestingly, we did not find this pattern repeated in the second generation, whose destinies were much more scattered, including both some who were unemployed and others who have subsequently been upwardly mobile through education.

In terms of familial background, the picture is very much like the middle-class 'stayers'. Nearly all grew up in extended families, or solely with grandparents, or in stepfamilies. There were only two exceptions: one who grew up with a lone single mother, and one who was brought up in a nuclear family with both parents. Interestingly there is again a contrast with their own family lives as adults. For their stories begin with childhoods in households and villages full of people, but as they age in their new countries their lives have become increasingly solitary. There are just three men in this group in lasting marriages. Of the remainder, seven have had more than two broken marriages and four of these men and women are now living on their own, two men have remained single, and one man is out of contact with sixteen out of the seventeen children whom he has fathered.

In striking contrast particularly to the 'risers', these migrants finished school as early as they could and felt they owed little to education. The only exception was one woman who 'used to love school' — and it is no coincidence that her children have been particularly successful, both becoming graduates. More typically, another woman disliked school, where she was regarded as not bright: 'I was the one that they put down!' One man felt that his schooling had been 'messed up' when he had to change from a town to a country school, while another man confessed that 'when I left school I didn't have no ambition'. But even if a child had ambition, in many cases the sheer poverty of these rural Jamaican families meant that they needed their children to be earning as soon as possible. This was particularly true of the older children, who were finishing school when there were the largest number of children still to feed and clothe. Ted Oliver was continually taken out of school to help his grandmother on the land. 'Sometimes I would go [to school] for a week, sometimes next week change. The system was very poor, for me, in that way.'

So the vision that drove this older generation of migrant men and women was not hope of achieving through education. It was much more one of earning well abroad from steady manual work. Lola's joy at seeing the house chimneys and mistaking them for factories sums up the spirit of so many of these early migrants. And a dozen years later she brought her cousin Selvin to England too with similar hopes from manual work. Lola paid his fare. She thought he should come, 'because he's a builder, and there's so much good building going on here'.

Joyce Leroy also said that she migrated at the age of 19 in 1961 primarily for industrial work: her father 'sent me to England', telling her '"You'll go to England and get a factory work." ... That's why I went to England.' Dayton Cripps, who came a year later, could see that he had poor prospects in a Jamaican fishing village. Fishing was 'a young man occupation, once you lose the physical power, then your standard of living drops. There was no pension or nothing in it. And I thought there was a lot of cheating out there.... Fishermen will come and see the catch you had that day, and they might hurry the next day, and go and then pull your pot up and take the fish out. Yeah, yeah, yeah. So, to me, that wasn't a very steady occupation'. Similarly, Linton Black, who migrated to the USA in 1968, had found work in Jamaica as a field labourer, but he wanted something better. 'I came here legally as a farm worker, and I never go back.' His job was waiting for him and his fare paid, all organized through the Jamaican Department of Agriculture. But he moved quickly into industrial labour, ending as a construction worker.

There were many choices within manual work, so while for some their jobs were primarily means of earning money, there were several who expressed a clear satisfaction with the kind of job they had, even when at a low level. Thus Pearl Selkirk worked in a whole series of unskilled factory jobs in London, 'always on the move, looking for something else'. 'That one was hard', she remembered of an assembly line job in a skirt factory, 'everybody do a part of a skirt.... So like, one put the zip in, one put the lining in, and you never finish a skirt.... I say, "Oh no, this ain't me!"' She eventually found a job which she positively enjoyed, working as a hospital auxiliary. In Canada Ted Oliver tried serving in MacDonald's, tool dyeing in an engineering machine shop, an apprenticeship as a welder, and working as a forklift driver, before he found his present job as a truck driver for a cargo shipper. He felt he was happier working as a driver than in skilled work, which he found 'very hard', and so had dropped his apprenticeship. Similarly, Dayton Cripps, having risen from unskilled work in Jamaica to a qualified skilled trade in England, then dropped back to an unskilled job as a security guard which he feels brings variety and contact with people. And Nelson Pinnock, Toronto welder, made it clear that he was never attracted to office work. 'For like sit in one place, I fall asleep very easy. I can't see myself sitting on a desk.' He likes to load trucks and fix cars. 'Not everybody were born to be a doctor or a teacher, or a lawyer, work in an office, for who'll plant the food? Who'd build the house?'

Not surprisingly, one of the strongest expressions of satisfaction in manual work came from a skilled worker. It is interesting that Selvin Green's feeling for skilled manual work goes back to his boyhood relationship with his father, a carpenter in a sugar mill in St Thomas:

> I used to take his lunch there. Yes, I used to go in and see him.... I used to run up and down that place when I was a kid. I know that factory inside out. You know, as a kid, you could go in — and I used to love the sugar, to see where the sugar go, where the cane goes. I just follow all the line along ... until it go way up to the very top where they make the sugar.... What they do is interesting for me as a kid, because I like all these wheels turning, all these things going on, especially the mill. I always like to be there, just watching the mill.

Years later, Selvin came back briefly to work in the same mill as his father had before him, as if determined to outdo him: 'I becomes engineer, and pull that mill flat on the floor and put it right back like great big mill.' Skill in manual work was clearly very important to Selvin. He had come to England as a carpenter, but also had to undertake unskilled car factory work, and felt dissatisfied by this, so he used a government-training course to requalify as a welder. 'Just working in a factory, I didn't want to continue in that because I like my work as a trade person. So then I used to do little jobs for people at weekends — fix the kitchen, tile a little here. I wanted to continue with trade.' And Selvin, who now works as a machine setter in a London computer factory, has indeed succeeded in his goal.

Others were less fortunate. Dick Woodward's father had been a skilled craftsman in Jamaica, but he 'couldn't get a job in this country, as a tailor, which was very frustrating for him'. He was forced into labouring work. But his skills still mattered a lot to him: he would take his sons to Burtons 'to have a suit cut, and the frustration you could see. He would tell these chaps how to do it. One suit of his, took something like four years to

collect, because on every occasion he went to collect it, he found a fault!'
Similarly, when Don Bartley came to England in 1953 he had already
been a factory worker in the USA. He hoped that in England he could be
taken on as an apprentice for skilled work, and was 'very disappointed'
when he was only able to get unskilled work. He became a London gasworks
stoker, which was tough but well paid work.

Don was also shocked by the racist ignorance of some of the other
workers. Such prejudice was most often recounted by older migrants who
went into manual jobs. Thus Patrick James began working for the Post
Office as a maintenance engineer in the late 1950s in London, and recalls
how his white co-workers would behave 'like little tin gods'. 'They used to
give us the dirty work to do'. Even their earnings seemed to reflect this
prejudice.

> The whites were paid better than us … even if they were doing the
> same work…. Prospect of promotion, black people never had any
> — very little. White man used to start after you, and then he used
> to climb the ladder quick as ever…. The Union isn't like what it is
> now. Oh yes, it's changed a lot. The Union was almost useless at
> that time.

Such stories remind us of the diversity of rewards and experiences in manual
work. Skill is one issue, and so are earnings. Contact and relationships
with other people, positive and negative, could also be crucial to the job
experience. Regularity was another criterion. Thus Lola was especially proud
of her secure job as a London underground uniformed ticket collector.
When she moved to the USA, she worked in home care and then as a
nursing assistant. Although her earnings rose in America, she now feels she
had a much better job in England. 'England, to me, do better for me.' For
all these reasons, migrants could experience significant rises and falls while
remaining within the boundaries of the working class.

'Who'd Build the House?'

There was also another upward path through which migrants could rise socially, independently of their work level. This was through their housing strategy.[3] Many migrants, especially those who came earlier, started their new lives in a single rented room in a house shared with other migrants. 'He rent that one room like this, they have a kitchen, and probably they will have two cookers, to share for all the rest of the people', Pearl Selkirk remembered her first years in London in the 1960s. 'So must just make the best of a bad situation, and get on with people.' But in terms of housing the older generation of migrants also had a big advantage over their successors, especially those now in rented flats, because in Britain in the 1950s to 1970s there was plenty of cheap run-down housing to be bought, even in London. It was therefore less difficult to raise the necessary money. Some house agents would not help, but there were moneylenders willing to lend at a price to black families; and also many migrants belonged to informal saving clubs, 'partnerships' based on trust between a group of 20 to 50 who would put money in weekly, and then could choose their moment to draw their 'hand'. A shrewd buy at this time could have proved a crucial long-term financial and cultural boost for the family.

Many migrants moreover came from families who already owned houses and some land in Jamaica. Dick Woodward remembers how his father, who came to London in the 1950s, would stress the importance of owning your home. The bank might crash, but —

> if you own your own housing, or your own land, even if the economy comes to the worst, you have somewhere to sleep, and you have somewhere to grow your own food.... My father used to say, "Look, when you see a Jamaican in London, who owns a car, parked outside a home in which he lives, but that home is owned by someone else, he's not one of us. He's a Kingstonian. Urbanite. Those of us from the countryside, you may not be able to own a car, or good clothing, but you own where you live".

Indeed one of the strongest complaints of more recent migrants to the USA is that they do not have this option: they have been effectively forced to live in black ghetto districts, which may cut them off from good schools for their children, and expose them to theft and violence. Joyce Leroy was shocked by Brooklyn when she came in the late 1960s: 'Although I live in Jamaica, the first time we were really going to live in a place with only blacks, that was it…. Everybody, they were scared…. It was rough…. Garbage around…. Oh God! Where we were, a dump!'

By contrast, in Britain and Canada all our migrants, including those in council flats in Britain, live in mixed neighbourhoods. And it is striking how right from the start some migrants to Britain bought houses in neighbourhoods where there were few or no other black people, and this is a process which has continued. Selvin Green even moved 50 miles out of London to Bedford for the sake of his children. 'The children have got more room, more space. You communicate better with the teachers and the church. You get better communities…. You want this other thing for your children.' There are also signs of a similar more recent process in Canada. Sean Ismay has an unskilled job as a loader in a motor parts factory, but he now lives in the country over an hour out of Toronto, by deliberate choice.

> From I come here [14 years ago], I've never lived in any run-down area of Toronto. I lived in Toronto [city] for, like, three months, and I got out of there…. There was a certain standard of living I was used to from Jamaica, I had patched pants and barefoot, but there's always a good roof over my head, and food, and I refuse, I refuse to go to the areas where we, as black people, are supposed to live. Right?
>
> Everyone goes to me, "Man, you must be the only black guy out there." I go, "Yeah. So?" … You make enough money that you can buy a house in a better neighbourhood. You shouldn't be growing up your kids [in a poor district] … I want to break whatever mould, bad mould I have.

Sean has also broken the mould in his marriage to his school sweetheart, a white girl from a poor family who, backed by his earnings, became a graduate and professional. He sees their marriage as 'the biggest accomplishment in my life', but the house is an equally powerful symbol.

Buying a house was also an effective solution to the housing discrimination which most earlier migrants faced. Rufus Rawlings, a building worker, was driven by the difficulties he found in renting, especially because his wife Ursula was white, to buy a 15-room house in (then working class and wholly white) Islington, which he restored and filled with lodgers. Later they took in language students who paid well, but in the earlier years the house was an exceptional refuge for couples like themselves. Rufus and Ursula's daughter Sadie vividly remembers the fascination of growing up there:

> It seemed to me like a big, big castle.… It was colossal, it was an amazing house.… Loads of stairs up to the attic, lots of people living in the house.… Couples from the Caribbean and a couple of African people, people coming to England, trying to start a new life, and a few mixed couples there. There was a German woman living with a Trinidadian that lived right at the top of the house. There was an Irish girl living with a Jamaican, there was another Jamaican guy living with a blond woman … I always remember they had twins.… One of them was light and one of them was dark, it was the talk of the place that the twins were different colours.… It was a very busy house, you can imagine, and it was like a community once you got inside the front door. A big community, all very friendly.

Rufus did a lot of decorating and improving to his Islington house, and he eventually sold it at a substantial profit, enabling him to return with Ursula to Jamaica to live in some style in a big hilltop house with an adjoining bar overlooking the sea.

For those with building skills it was possible not only to buy a house but also to transform and improve it. Vivia Perrin tells how in the late 1950s her father took on an even tougher housing challenge. Vivia had been born in a Blue Mountain village, where her parents had already shown their enterprise. Her mother was a teacher, her father a carpenter. But they had also set up a small shop and bar, and had a share of a car. 'They were the only people in the village with a radio. So people would come and listen to it, and everybody would sit in the yard.' Coming to London, with both now in manual jobs, meant a sharp drop in occupational status for the family, but in no way blunted Vivia's father's determination. 'He's a workaholic. In all the time I've known my dad, I've known him probably to have maybe three days off work in his life. He's always out there, he's always looking at new ideas, looking at new ways of bringing income.' And he spotted the potential in housing.

When he went to London, the whole place was still dilapidated, the houses were still bombed.... My dad was one of the first people who started to renovate houses in London. Because we couldn't find anywhere to live, it was "No Irish, no kids, no dogs, no blacks" ... Dad went and worked for other people, those people had houses — he would fix their old chairs and beds, they didn't mind him fixing it and paying him, but they wouldn't rent him a room.

But he did that, and he saved, and he saved until he was able to buy his first house.... And it was such a horrible, nasty home. It was wet and damp, half the roof was gone. The first floor we couldn't use.... The water would come through and run down in the cold. And he fixed it. My dad had gone through and fixed one room up for us, really nice, put in new windows. Each night after work, *every* night after work, he would come in and he'd be scraping paint down off the wall, and he was replastering this room and — until he got one room finished. And then he said, "You guys are going to have to move in here, and we're going to have to work on the house like this. You're not going to get wet, you're not going to get cold." So that's what my dad did.

The rest of the house was rented out, because people were coming for work in England and they couldn't find anywhere to rent. So daddy rented the rooms out, to help people.... So when he went to work in the daytime, he was so tired, but when he got home at night, by the time he had something to eat, he had to be in the basement, and you could hear him hammering things, and sawing, and sanding, just to make the windows for the other rooms. It took him years to do this. That's how we came by our first home.

To be in manual work, in short, does not necessarily imply lack of ambition. Vivia's father's story has an epic quality, and it symbolizes a drive that was far from unique. Indeed, at least half of the stories we heard from working class migrants show in one way or another a definite element of ambition, an urge towards self-betterment.

The Migration Gamble

To sum up, what do these 50 stories tell us about work and the migration gamble?

Firstly, there is no direct relationship at all between family structure in childhood and later work achievement. The most successful migrants were typically brought up in extended families of one form or another, but this is equally so of those who have stayed in manual occupations. In the context of migration extended families could provide effective support, and grandparents were often more assured and gentler parents, transmitting work and educational values.

On the other hand, in the post-migration situation there seems to be a strong relationship between being in middle-class occupations and a marriage with a partner at the same level. By contrast, those who fell or stayed in manual work included more who were single mothers or separated lone men.

Secondly, the role of education was crucial for those who ended in non-manual work. With the 'risers' it is especially emphasized, while by contrast those in manual work typically had briefer education, sometimes interrupted, or with discouraging teachers.

In the next chapter we will therefore take a further look at how education transformed some of these migrant lives.

Thirdly, for those who lacked such educational qualifications there has been an alternative upward path, through buying and improving houses. This strategy has in the long run provided the resources for many migrants to return to a better standard of living in Jamaica.

Finally, while as a whole these Jamaicans do not constitute a strongly upwardly mobile group, in their own terms the majority of them have succeeded. Despite initial setbacks for some, more of them have risen than have fallen, and almost all of them were soon able to earn more than they had in Jamaica. Even among many of those now in manual work, one can see both continuing hope for mobility and strategies for achieving it. And particularly with the less successful, the dream of a successful return to Jamaica remains strong.

NINE

Learning and Faith

Jamaican migrants drew the strength their challenging lives demanded from a set of values, which to differing extents they held in common, and in which the secular and sacred were inextricably intertwined. On the one hand, as we have already seen, was the ambition for self-betterment, the commitment to working hard for this end, the dream of the family house and home; and on the other hand, the belief in education as a path to a better life, and the faith in church and God, which we explore here. We shall begin with the earliest schooling, and consider the challenges which were faced, first in education and then in religion, along the course of our migrants' lives.

Learning

The common roots in Jamaican culture of education and religion, family and community are nowhere more strikingly seen than in the Basic Schools which are scattered across the Jamaican countryside, voluntary community schools providing for young children in their pre-school years. These schools for three to five-year-olds are a special feature of Jamaican education. They spread through the island as a result of an educational movement in the 1930s, and they have proved very far-sighted, giving many Jamaican children the educational advantage and confidence from extra years of schooling in a particularly supportive atmosphere. Indeed their 'head start' in the basic schools must surely have played a key role in encouraging the commitment to education which is so widespread among Jamaican migrants.[1]

Edna Moore is the teacher at Watersmeet Basic School. We found Edna through her nephew in New York, where her brother and sisters have all migrated, while she has stayed on in her own village, worshipping and teaching, now close to retirement. To reach Watersmeet Basic School from the surging river below you climb steeply up the luxuriant hillside, until the lane stops below a churchyard. Hidden behind the stone Methodist church, up a flight of steps, Edna stands in her double classroom, surrounded by the children. They are close to breaking for the lunch which has been cooked for them, but first the children sing for us a mixture of religious songs and folksongs, with Edna calling out encouragement. We quickly sensed her infectious enthusiasm, her love for the children, her sense of order and the children's respect for her. In the break she talked to us, from the start linking her church with her teaching.

> This is the church I attended with my grandmother, and I didn't turn back.... God is a part of me. I shun sin, and he's keeping me and caring me and he's providing for me. Because sometimes when I may feel down, in a twinkling of an eye I just see things coming in. Yes, I tell you ... I feel good of what I am doing, I don't know for how long, but as long as God give me grace.

Edna went to basic school herself in this same Methodist church. She thinks her love for education came from 'my mother's side'. Later on, having met her soldier husband and now a mother of two children, 'when I was in my teens, I just feel to start something, and I start the Basic School at my home'. Later, at the request of the Parent–Teacher Association meeting, she moved it to the Community Hall, and then after an interval back up to the Methodist church. 'And from that I am here'. Although Edna had failed the Common Entrance Examination for high school when at school, she later made up her qualifications by taking a series of correspondence courses, so that the basic school was upgraded and awarded an extra government subsidy.

She explained the financing of the school, and its tight links with the community and families. 'The government sends a little money, we call subsidy. But the parents pay a fee, lunch fee, and a fee to pay me. All of them [can't afford to] do it, but I satisfied with what I get, because I really like this sort of work, and I like the job here'. The cooked meal is normal in basic school: 'Yes, all basic schools are supposed to cook, and the government send a little foodstuff, yes.' When children's parents have no money, 'we would give them the free lunch'. Because Edna is so rooted in the community, she can easily distinguish those who are really poor from those who are not. 'Some of them will tell us that they're not having any lunch today, and seen as I live here, I know who they all are.' Edna talks a lot to her children's parents. 'We have PTA meetings, and we meet them on the road, and sometimes they take their children to school. We have to talk to them, yes.' And for Edna, this is one of the special satisfactions of her work as a village teacher. 'I'm a people person. I love people.'

However, once children moved on to the state school they encountered a much tougher regime, which parental support could often make still harder. There are some rare memories of supportive teachers before the 1970s, such as from Morris Derby, whose primary headmaster told him encouragingly, 'You don't know nothing about losing, you must always be a winner.' But more typically, the school's tone was set by its routine of strict inspections. 'You line up, before you go inside the classroom, they come around and check your shoes, your fingernails … make sure your hair is combed, and personal hygiene, and how you present yourself,' recalled Owen Callaghan. 'Your uniform had to be ironed and not crushed. They had to be clean.' And by today's standards, the disciplining of young children could be very severe. As late as the 1970s Stella Wadham remembers being belted at primary school for going home to pee rather than using the school toilet. Owen so feared his primary school principal's belt that 'I cut class, I was in the bathroom hiding out' — for which he was then spanked at home. Furthermore at his school 'we had to weed the school yard, the boys. Every Friday we had to make sure you bring your cutlass and machete to school, to take care of that'.

Dick Woodward would usually start the day

helping to milk the cows, taking out the pigs.... So your day, as a child, is a very arduous and long one. And if you didn't do well at school, then they would know, and you would have to give an account of yourself! In those days, we didn't have exercise books, you had a piece of slate and a piece of chalk, and you'd move from one lesson to the next. And if you didn't remember, the following day, what you'd been taught, you'd be given a good caning. And if your uncle knew that you'd had a caning for not remembering, you'd have another caning!

Although most of these Jamaicans had positive memories of their school experiences, the typical severity of school discipline drove a minority, especially of boys, to hate school, and to want to get out to work as soon as possible.

A second fundamental factor in determining who could make the most of education within Jamaica was social inequality. Many children missed much school time and had to leave school early because of poverty. Others suffered from their own or their parents' ill-health, or with the girls, from early pregnancies. Some teachers were sympathetic towards children with such difficulties. Pearl Selkirk, herself from a small tobacco farm family, remembered a teacher who, 'if children come to school and didn't have a meal, he would hand them pennies to go and get a meal'. But gestures like this, however generous, did nothing to change the in-built class bias of the school system. As Pearl put it, 'We all went to the elementary school in them days. And if you'd got the big money, then you can go to big high school.' Until Michael Manley's reforming government in the 1970s, full secondary education was largely the privilege of middle-class families who could pay for their children to go to the private high schools, with only a tiny minority of children from ordinary families enabled to stay on by scholarships. So Pearl finished school at 15, not only because her higgler mother was sick and her father couldn't cope, but because that was the fate of most village children at that time. And even for those who got scholarships, the additional financial costs could be a severe challenge for parents. Howard Beck, son of a village shopkeeper, remembered how 'when I got my scholarship to high school, it was very bad then, things were very tight, economically, and he [father] said if it was necessary to sell the last shirt he had, he would want to see me through high school. Well, he didn't have to sell the last shirt, but he sold the last cow'.

The Manley reforms, creating a series of free secondary schools throughout the island, changed the educational system fundamentally, and at the same time drew in a cohort of enthusiastic and socially committed young secondary school teachers from within and beyond the island, including from Canada, some of whom made lasting influences on our migrants' lives. At both the primary and secondary levels those who were in school from the 1970s onwards have many more positive memories of their education. Thus at their primary schools, Stuart Campbell 'loved the teachers'; while Celia Mackay described her teachers as 'compassionate' people, 'you could have a problem, you could go talk with them'. Sandrine Porto similarly called her primary teachers 'very nice, very friendly, they act as if they're a big sister' — but also encouraging. 'They really push you. "You can do this".'

Still more striking was the transformed approach to secondary education. Again among the younger migrants many more remember teachers who were caring, understanding, aiming to build their pupils' self-confidence rather than to drill them. Thus Robert Austin described his teachers as 'a really positive influence ... impressional people, brilliant people, they were more like parents'. If he came late to school, he was asked by his teachers, '"Did you eat breakfast?" ... So they will make sure that we get a chance to eat.... And we will get a *free lunch* sometimes.' He described one teacher as 'like a father figure, make sure you guys are all right, and any little problem or issues you have, you can always go to him'. For Sandrine Porto too her secondary school teachers seemed like parental figures: 'more than teacher, like a mother figure, they would really talk to you, encourage you ... trying to build your self-esteem.' Joy Beck was in serious difficulties during her later years at school because of her mother's sickness, and had to leave school early, but she too found a sympathetic ear with one of the younger staff: 'She was very important in my life. I could talk to her about anything ... I would just sit down, start thinking about my mother, and I would burst into tears, and she always comfort me.' Robin Lynn named his 'special favourites' among his teachers: 'They steer me in the right direction, they see that I had the potential. They always, in my back, "I know you're going to make it".' Now in New York, he still keeps in touch with one of these teachers by phone.

One of the most remarkable of the new schools was Red River Secondary, where the Principal Russell Thorpe set the tone, combining a belief in the potential of every pupil with an old-fashioned severe discipline. While some of the boys resented his strictness, Russell Thorpe had, 'from an educational point of view, probably the most influence on many people's lives'. He insisted that the pupils all look their best: 'Your shirt has to be tucked in, shoes shine, hair well-groomed. And he didn't miss a beat.' With the girls it was 'that walk, we had to practice: head up, walk and pull your tummy in'. Pupils were required to arrive on time, avoid walking on the grass at school, and on the way home to walk on the road facing the traffic. 'He used to drive down the streets after school to make sure that everybody was doing it. If anybody was out of line, he would pick them up in his car, take them back to school and cane them. Give them a whipping sometimes.' The school premises were kept in a similar style. 'The grounds — immaculate. No paper, no leaves, nothing stray, the place was just well-groomed, manicured. It was like a breath of fresh air in Jamaica because it was so orderly.... People took pride in their work, and that was evident throughout the school ... I felt proud of being part of it.' But Russell Thorpe brought much more than order and discipline to Red River School. Most profoundly, he conveyed to the pupils that they had a potential for educational and cultural growth. He opened out new worlds to them. He would play Mozart and Handel on the school intercom. He would try to generate discussion. 'He used to stop classes and have the complete school go on the playing field, form a circle round him, and we'd talk about anything.' And most important of all, he would give personal encouragement to pupils at all levels. 'That commanding voice that is in him built up a self-confidence.... He always makes you feel as if you can achieve whatever you want to, because ... the slowest child, he'll look at you, he says, "You can do it. You can do it".'

Red River was of course a very exceptional school. Most Jamaican schools were much more ordinary, with harsh as well as sympathetic teachers. Equally important, up until the 1970s, few children from ordinary families were able to benefit from a full secondary education. Nevertheless the basic schools and the new secondary schools of the Manley era, as two of the high points of Jamaica's educational story, can be taken as symbols of a deep-rooted belief in education as a means of advancement, which influenced all social levels in the island. So what happened to these values when migrants and their children encountered new schooling systems abroad?

Because the older migrants all left Jamaica after their schooling was finished, memories of education abroad begin only in the 1960s. Two themes stand out from these recollections, whether in Britain or in North America: the undervaluing of Jamaican children's potential by their new teachers, and the vigorous attempts which some parents, and also some teachers, made to counter this. Especially in the earlier decades, Jamaican children seemed strange to many teachers, even to the point that some would examine the children's skin colour in front of the class, or touch their hair, 'because they didn't know what black people's hair felt like'. Many of the children also had pet names, and sometimes were unaware that they had been registered under another first name: Leonard Selkirk recalled, 'We registered in the school, and that's when we first realized we have two names! But we thought it made us different, made us unique, and in a sense we cherish that as part of where we come from.' In short, they came from a culture which these teachers did not understand: the teachers knew no *patois*, found it hard to grasp the children's accents and grammar, and were surprised by some of the differences in the ways they had been taught. All this could lead to an underestimation of the children. But behind this there was also an unspoken assumption, shaped by centuries of colonialism, that black students, and the educational system of a black ex-colony, must be inferior, even though in terms of formal learning, for example of grammar, Jamaican children were often ahead for their age. When Marcia Trelissick brought her children to England in the early 1960s, 'when they went to school, the teachers, they were surprised to see how advanced they were, because they always look down on West Indian children like they don't know anything.... They always think my children were from Canada'. Brigette Umber, now training as a psychologist, recalled her own encounter as an eight-year-old with the similar assumptions of a New York teacher:

> Back home, you have to learn to count with your fingers.... He says, "The reason why you cannot do math is because you're from Jamaica, and you only had it with your fingers.... If I ask you five plus five, you must know it right off the back. You don't use your fingers." And that hurt — that hurt very bad.... And I had to prove him wrong. So I competed in the math finals. And I came in first place! He was judge! ... I did it with my fingers, and I proved them wrong!

At a much later age, recently arrived from Jamaica, and already demonstrably able and ahead of most of the other girls, Deborah Gladstone, now working as a doctor in a British inner-city clinic:

> suddenly hit all the prejudice and the low expectations of black women over here, so much so that I even doubted, myself, whether I was going to apply for university.... Their surprise when I said I wanted to do medicine, shock horror!
>
> There was just a lot of ignorance, a lot of stupid things. "Gosh, you speak English well!" It wasn't anything overt ... but it was just the culture and the general expectation of, not only the school, but the society in general.... Coming from a country where it's not unusual to be black, to come to a country where everybody is caricatured, for a young person, it does have its influence. So that set me back, temporarily, and I had to overcome that. And I did.

Similarly Helena Busfield, another future professional in Britain, recalled how when she said she wanted to be a social worker, the teacher responded, 'Oh why don't you be a nurse? Black girls make lovely nurses,' Helena also noticed how the teachers would encourage black boys into sports, 'but of course, if you're going to train to do sports, you're going to miss some classes, classes which they need — because now they're motor mechanics and they are bakers, but who knows what they could have been?'

Such stories are symptomatic of a widespread failure of the schools, particularly in Britain in the 1960s and 1970s, to cope with the challenge of bringing out the talents of migrant children. But there were also stories of resilience from the children and also from their parents, signs of the continuing struggle for self-betterment which has borne fruit in the growth of a Jamaican middle class in both Britain and North America.

We asked Pearl Selkirk, then a north London factory worker, whose younger two children are both professionals, how involved she was with her children's education. 'Oh Christ! I was. I get involved with them. Whenever school wants me, I'm there. I start to work nights, I will ask for the night off … so as to go to Parent Evening for any one of them.' She organized the children's homework 'to do the work together', and made sure she checked it afterwards. In all this Pearl was a typical migrant Jamaican mother, poor but still driven by her belief in education — in this instance prophetically.

A common tactic was to try to find a better school for the children, either by settling in another neighbourhood, or by switching after their child had encountered difficulties. We have already seen how in England Vivia Perrin's parents secured her transfer to a private school, and Helena Busfield's mother, who was splitting up from her husband, 'really fought for me to go to a private college, where I did my social work, and I lived in'. Harry Davidson took similar trouble with his son. 'We moved him to three different places in New York, mostly because we were trying to get the one that fit him the best. And the one he ended up in was one where the teacher was a more rigid disciplinarian.… He thrived there.'

Another possible tactic was to approach the teacher. This sometimes worked, but more often parents were likely to be bewildered with 'the headmaster and the offending teacher … blinding them with science'. And it could go dramatically wrong. Vivia Perrin's daughter had an 'A' at A-level, but was discouraged from studying law by a school counsellor. Vivia and her husband decided to complain to the form teacher, but 'she barricaded herself in her office when we got there. And the upshot was, that my daughter became very disenchanted with school'. The whole family was branded as 'aggressive' and the daughter left school and gave up law.

Nor was this the most dramatic case of such a confrontation. Sean Ismay first went to school in Canada as a ten-year-old. He was puzzled by a child who kept calling him 'nigger', a word he had not heard in Jamaica, so 'I came home and I asked my mum, "What is a nigger?" ... So next time I went to school, the first thing I did was fight this kid'. The boy nevertheless went on harassing Sean, and despite his complaints the teachers did nothing, so finally 'I just beat him up on our way home'. The next day he and his parents were summoned to school. 'The principal wanted to kick me out. And then he started a problem, because my mum is a Kingston woman.... He was about to get his arse whopped.... My mum was defending her son.' It then emerged that the principal had been illegally striking Sean. 'The principal, he was a bigot.... He used to beat me on my hands [when I] used to throw snowballs at recess, which all boys do, and I'm the only one that he used to [punish].' The principal was by now threatening to call in the police, but his tone changed suddenly when he realized that Sean's parents understood the legal situation. His father told the principal, 'You should call the police, because we should get involved in this, because I want to know why you were hitting my child here.' Immediately, everything was straightened out: Sean was reinstated and the molestation ceased.

In contrast to such stories there were also at least some sympathetic teachers, and indeed with those Jamaican migrants or their children who succeeded professionally there was almost always, either in Jamaica or abroad, the influence of an encouraging teacher — such as the 'Miss G' who 'saved the soul' of Vivia Perrin. Another instance is Daniel Lyle, who recalls how he was struggling at his London school to play football well, 'but I was hopeless at it, couldn't play to save my life'. Daniel 'knew, deep down in my heart... what I was good at, which was performing and writing', but it took the encouragement of a teacher in his primary school for him to follow his instincts. 'She noticed in me, she just says, "You're a gifted writer, and you're a very good actor. Follow that. Because that is what you're stronger at." She always tried subtle ways to get me into that, rather than focus on the football.' And today Daniel is indeed a writer.

Two other stories are of men who have also had successful professional careers, but each might well have dropped off the educational ladder but for the encouragement of a perceptive teacher. Somewhat unusually, Leonard Selkirk arrived in London at the age of eight having had little schooling in Jamaica, and unable to read or write. He had a tough start in primary school.

> We used to have fights … asserting your position against all the other kids who were taking the mickey out of you and your accent. We got it from both black and white, it's those who were born here, rather than those who came from abroad…. We just had this rawness, and there's this rough edge, we don't take no nonsense…. You used to get knocked down, but at the end of the day, you jumped in, and that stopped the bullying.

At the same time Leonard had to rapidly learn to read and write, and at this primary school he was given supportive remedial teaching. 'I didn't get much problem in terms of primary school, I think most problems were in the secondary school.'

Leonard describes the secondary school as institutionally racist in its practice, for 'the top three classes were all white … and all the black kids were in the lower classes, we were all in the bottom three sets'. The teachers varied at lot. There were some who 'just didn't have no time for the kids', and one in particular, the head of the sixth form, 'just an obnoxious teacher', who 'put down a lot of black kids'. He did his best to persuade Leonard not to stay on for the sixth form — advice which his mother trenchantly rejected to his face. For in the meantime Leonard had found a crucial supporter in another teacher with quite different attitudes, who realized that Leonard's exam papers were as good as those in the top set. 'He could see that I would be wasted … and he actually fought the system, the structure within the school', and in an unprecedented move he got Leonard moved up four classes. This was one of the crucial turning points of Leonard's life. In the bottom sets he would have been destined for manual work; now he had the chance, which he would seize, of higher education.

Dick Woodward came with much more confidence from his schooling in Jamaica, where he and his two cousins were regularly top of the class: 'we used to compete against each other.' He also gained pleasure in reading and a sense of literature from his family's keen religious practice: he was familiar with the verses of the hymnals, and 'I knew the Bible inside out, read through it several times'. He came to London at the age of ten, unable to profit much from primary school because 'what they were doing, I'd done already, so I had a good year of doing nothing, really'. Consequently the school complained about his lack of work, and this continued when he went on to secondary school. Here he continued to lag behind with class work. and although he always did well in exams this simply annoyed the teachers more. As a result, like Leonard, he was kept drifting in the 'technical stream'. 'You do woodwork, metalwork, technical drawing and so on, and the idea was that you would leave school, and if you were lucky, you would go into things like an architect's office, or you'd go off to a factory.'

But again like Leonard, he was spotted by an idealistic teacher, in fact a man from an elite background who had come to teach in the school inspired by the 'innovatory education' of the new London comprehensives. He read a history essay which Dick had written, gave it a top mark, and asked him, 'Well, if you can do this, why are you in this class?' He got Dick moved up, taught him through the sixth form, introduced him to a much wider reading, to music and the theatre, and got him to apply to university. So Dick's life was changed in a similar way. And there is a double lesson from these two stories. Firstly the crucial influence that a true teacher can have. But secondly, because teachers of this calibre are always rare, and because they were the exceptions in an educational context permeated by racist assumptions, we also need to think of how much other talent must have been wasted among the black pupils in the bottom sets.

Faith

For Edna Moore and her young children in Watersmeet Basic School, faith and learning were intertwined in a mutually supportive atmosphere. Indeed all but two of our migrants were brought up in Jamaica as churchgoers: most of them either as Anglicans, Methodists, Pentecostals, Catholics or Seventh Day Adventists.[2] But through their lifetimes this almost universal religious practice has been challenged in many different ways. In some cases the challenge has come through education itself, but most often it has been through encountering the much wider cultural tide of secularism, strongest in Britain and least in Jamaica itself; and also through the longstanding differences in religious practice between men and women.

Hence it is interesting to contrast Dick Woodward, a man who migrated to Britain, with Hyacinth Campbell, a woman who stayed in Jamaica. Both are examples of successful professionals who originated in strongly committed religious families. For Dick, there is an explicit connection between this religious background and his educational success: 'if you take religion seriously, you have to be able to read, you have to be able to have discussions, you have to understand what others are saying.' Both were very active in their churches as teenagers, Dick as a preacher, Hyacinth as a youth leader. 'I was drawn to the church,' she said, 'I felt this spiritual in-depth thing was in me from a child.' But while to his mother's dismay, Dick gave up religion and went to university, Hyacinth's faith has deepened over the years. She has moved from the Baptists to the Pentecostals. She described to us her recent dreams, waking in tears praising God, speaking in tongues, and her conversion to 'a life full of prayer'. 'I said, "Lord, I've been holding back all along, but tonight I've given my life to you, because I know for sure that you are calling me"... I said, "Lord, you know I love luxury, jewellery. But God, if it's against everybody to wear them, strip them piece by piece, Lord".'

Hyacinth's religious experience is part of a continuing tradition in Jamaica. Charlene Summers, who works as a hotel maid, would like to go back to the religious conviction she had as a child, and has been going to the mission tent, but she is not finding it easy because so far she has not had a conversion experience. 'I'm trying right now to accept Christ as my personal Saviour ... I'm trying it out.' Charlene's uncertainty contrasts with the conviction — despite the doubts of others — with which Elisha Grant, eighty-year-old Pentecostal pastor–shoemaker, describes his own conversion.

> I get a call. I get the conviction and the Lord call me — I get saved. When I was young I never think of church. Me mother den was a Christian, but me smoke and look girls and all the rest of it. But God save me. Have put away all those things that I used to do, and I get married.

I get a conviction in me bed one night. Get save in me bed one night. I was having plenty of different vision, and one night I find myself run out of me bed wid me Bible. Say [I'm] a madman, me brother: they carry me go a doctor. But it was a conviction.

For many Jamaican families, religious conviction and activity became both a focus for family belonging and a link to the wider community. In Sandrine Porto's family, who were Anglicans, 'we have to be involved in everything'. Her mother and two sisters sang in the choir, her brother carried the processional cross, and her father was a lay preacher. Dick Woodward recalled how, even after his parents had migrated to London, they would put up some homeless people free, and were always ready to welcome an unexpected guest.

We always had a table where there was an extra plate, and it springs from this religious thing that you must always have food for the 'unknown guest' ... Sunday breakfast was a big thing in a Jamaican household in those days. But sometimes, we'd be sitting with tramps off the streets.... Our house in Jamaica, when they returned, you'd find all kinds of mad, crazy people at home.... All they had to claim that they love Jesus, or that they were in need.

There are many other similarly committed Jamaican families today, but even in Jamaica itself there have been important changes in religious practice. Firstly, there has been some degree of general secularization, and with the more conventional churches, such as the Anglicans and Presbyterians, while basic beliefs and moral values have been sustained, the intensity of practice seems to have declined. Thus Howard Beck was brought up a Wesleyan, but now only occasionally attends. 'I don't go to church very regular.' But he still feels that religion plays a 'very important' role in his family's life. He gets his children to attend when they come home for a weekend. And he believes that the church has provided them with a fundamental moral basis for life.

We all had to go to church. I think it tempers you, it teaches us values, attitudes. It is very important. We don't have members of the family who run foul of the law, in a serious way. And I think this all goes back to the initial training, the foundation. Going to church, you learn about how to respect other people, and their property, and respect for God.

Secondly, there is the diffuse influence of the small minority of Rastafarians. There were six among our interviewees. They conveyed a sense of a Rastafarianism which for most followers has become more an alternative culture, than an alternative religion to Christianity. This seemed especially so for the men, who in terms of practice need to do little more than grow their hair and from time to time smoke ganja and talk reflectively in a group. Being a Rasta helped them to relax, and to value life in the present, in contrast to worrying about sinfulness and damnation. 'The best thing out there is life, real life', Clive Henry, tourist driver, put it: 'the best thing is life, because life is out there. And my life is no really pain, no sick in my body that I say I fretting of this sick because I gonna die pretty soon. So the best thing for me is the way I have life right now.'

The most elaborate account, and the most explicitly hostile to Christianity, was given by Selassie Jordan, transnational small trader, whose parents were Rastas. He told us he was 'born a Rasta', and the best thing in his life is 'knowledge, Selassie, Rastafari'. His father taught him that the Bible 'was based upon Africans and Africa, in and around Africa. So goin to church wid a white man in deh as di Saviour, I never dig dat still, never dig dat from very early'. His family have not cut their hair for 20 years: 'Babylon teach you fe cut your hair, and you see this [hair], it's our antenna, and this makes we receive the signal from the heavens. Cause I and I not of the earth alone. I and I is of the universe…. I and I reclaim the whole universe, cosmic traveling…. Cosmic knowledge.' Selassie plans to return to Africa. He is particular about his food. 'No American food. Me eat food from Africa, because most of food inna Jamaica come from Africa…. No meat, no fish no egg, no milk no cheese, just fruits, vegetable.' He also smokes ganja regularly, and believes in 'true African love', which he sees as closely linked with reggae music. 'People like Bob Marley, Peter Tosh, their music, we used to go to the bush and listen to them with our little radio and cassette tape, smoke our little herb, and is there so the love start from. Cause all these men talk about is love. Love!'

On the other hand it was very interesting to hear a very different perspective from one of the few women Rastas, who is also one of the most regular in her practice, Joan Bower the roadside fruit seller. Joan 'grew up in church, as children', becoming a Presbyterian as an adult. Joan now combines her church attendance with being a practicing Rasta. She dances, smokes weed, has grown her hair, and goes regularly to meditations. 'It is a way of thinking. Well — it slowed me down. Slow me down, and let me think more positive about things and time, and stuff like that. Yeah man, I have a whole lot of brethren. A whole lot of sister too…. Sometimes they are at my home. We eat, we drink, we talk. Yeah man, I enjoy it.' Yet for Joan, being a Rasta and a Presbyterian feels no more problematic than being a Presbyterian and a Baptist. We sensed that the fear of Rastafarianism as recently as the 1970s has evaporated, so that the more open-minded churches can now accommodate those Rastas who are serious and moral believers. 'I don't think they have an attitude, because they accept me. I'm there. Nobody ever say anything, everybody welcome me. So I go [to the Presbyterian church].'

For most migrant families, arriving in a new country brought as profound spiritual as material challenges. Certainly there were many migrants who did sustain the religious practices which they brought from Jamaica. Thus for Stella Wadham, who was a Church of God Pentecostal in Jamaica and switched to the Nazarene Holiness Church in New York, the church 'was your social life, that was your moral upbringing — and still is'. It remains the main focus of her and her husband's social life. Robert Lynn also in New York goes to the Church of God, where both his parents are deacons, and all the grandchildren also belong, and they 'clap and so forth, and speak in tongues…. We all meet on Saturdays. Everybody meets at church on Saturday'. Afterwards, the family all go to his mother's house: 'everybody will be down there.' Similar examples in Britain include Vivia Perrins's Methodist family with their active social commitment, and Marcia Trelissick, who after migration switched from Anglican to Seventh Day, becoming a Sabbath School Superintendent and a voluntary social worker, helping to provide clothes and food for the homeless.

Nevertheless altogether half of our Jamaican migrants abandoned their faith in their new country, whether in Britain or North America, some rapidly, others more slowly. This was one of the most profound changes in their lives resulting from migration. One contributing reason in Britain in earlier decades was the lack of welcome, indeed open rejection in some instances, which the churches gave to the migrants. When Josephine Buxton, a Jamaican pastor's wife, went with a friend to a Baptist church in Paddington in the early 1960s, afterwards 'the minister shook her hand, and said to her, "Thank you for coming. Please don't come back"'. In the longer run, of course, as their white inner city congregations drained away, the clergy became only too glad to draw in the Caribbean and African faithful.

More important however, most of all in Britain, has been the rise of a secular culture focused on personal material and sexual fulfilment, into which religious practice and values fit uncomfortably. Joyce Leroy had belonged to the Church of God in Jamaica, but when she moved to Britain she dropped off 'after a while', because she found that going to church 'was one thing that people didn't do'. Interestingly, when she later moved to New York she became an active Pentecostal again. And in Canada Niama McNeep has found her children and grandchildren very resistant to taking on the Pentecostal allegiance and practices which she brought from Jamaica. One grandson has refused to join the choir because he 'thought it was going to be a pain in the butt'. The children told her they didn't want to go to 'Grandma church, because they repeat theirselves, you know when you say, "Praise the Lord, praise the Lord, praise the Lord!"' The children summed it up to us, 'The songs that the people sing is boring. I just get tired of it. Because they just sing, "Praise the Lord, Hallelujah, Praise the Lord, Hallelujah," every day on Sunday.' Reared on the constant short-span change of the media, the cultural world of the churches, which was an intrinsic part of popular culture for their parents in Jamaica, for these Canadian children is alien and incomprehensible.

Indeed, it seems that with our migrant families the impact of the secular culture has been cumulative. For among our British-born second generation interviewees, only one-fifth had any religious affiliation at all. These nonchurchgoers in both generations express a wide range of views. Some relate to their Christian heritage, calling themselves 'spiritual, not religious', 'a lapsed Christian', or 'humanitarian'; while others are directly critical of the churches: 'I find church people to be hypocritical.' Three migrant men gave up religion because it seemed incapable of challenging the social injustices of the world. One became a communist and atheist, ridiculing the Bible. Another was Arnold Houghton, who had for a while continued as an Anglican churchgoer in Canada, but today he no longer attends.

> I looked at what was going on in the world, how black people were suffering all over the place, and to a great extent, I couldn't see the relevance of the church.... I think that this whole religious thing, I think it affect our people, because we're so caught up with the hereafter, that we fail to question the here and now, some of the injustices that are going on, some of the symbolism.... Why is Jesus always depicted as white? ... The important thing is how people relate and treat one another. That is my bottom line.

It is no accident that this rationalistic view of religion comes from a migrant man, for in addition to the impact of migration and secularization there is also a crucial difference between men and women in their relationship to religion, which has been reinforced by migration, but whose roots lie in traditional popular Jamaican culture. In Jamaica women were much more consistently religious than men, partly because the churches offered them a much more socially acceptable space for public social activities than the few alternatives like the local bars, while men had a more open choice. Hence, while there were important religious roles for men as preachers and pastors in the churches and as family heads, there was also an alternative non-religious masculine role open to them, from boyhood onwards.

Nelson Pinnock recounted how as a boy he was 'the one who used to pump the organ' at the Presbyterian church, and with some pride he explained how he would evade this duty. 'If I don't want to go to church, I have to hide from the night before.' Alternatively, he would 'get up in the morning and find something that I have to go to the bush and do, and then don't come back on time. And then, of course, I'm going to pay for it', with a 'whipping' from his grandfather. Boys would have easily noticed that there were also some fathers who similarly preferred going to the bush or the bar rather than to church. This could then become an intergenerational pattern. Carl Watts and his father have both been modestly successful hill farmers. Carl recalls how as a child he went with his mother to the village Baptist chapel, but 'my father never do so much into it, because him like him juice with kinda liquor, him rum. Ye know the church and the rum, no! But me mother, she continue. Yeah, we grow up in the church'. Nevertheless, Carl now goes as rarely to church as his father. 'No, not really, no, me's not a churchman. Me go to when we have to, like wedding or funeral or a thing like that, yeah. Well really the church is, what I call it, brainwashed! Those fellows are brainwashed. But me know say there's a God, yeah, me know say there's a God, and me serve Him.'

There was no mother and daughter comparable to Carl and his father. When women stand out in these stories, it is for the strength of their convictions and the practical vigour with which they sought to help those in need. It is also striking that conversely the churches seem to have been able to give effective help to women members of their congregations who were in personal difficulty, but we heard no similar accounts from men. Typically these women's difficulties were due either to the absence or to the abusiveness of their relationship with a man.

Grace Clare has 'never seen the man they say is my father', a roadside labourer killed in an accident, and by the age of five her mother had also died. So she grew up with her strict and unsympathetic Aunt Ida, who made Grace miss school to clean the house or 'go to bush', work in the field, while paying for her own daughter Pearl to go to high school. 'Pearl went to high school … I was compelled to stay at home.' But Grace found an alternative base for support in some of the teachers whom she also saw and talked to at her Adventist church. From the age of 15, for her last three years at school, she was able to attend an Adventist school. Grace got some small financial help from 'kind-hearted people like church members, knowing what my situation was like, because I would talk to people', and similarly with the teachers, 'although they did not support me financially, morally the support was there'. For example, when exam days coincided with the sugar harvest and Grace was expected to work in the fields, 'I had to approach my teacher about Saturday', so that an alternative exam time could be arranged. 'I think most of my support, in those early days, came from the school family and the church family, not really home.' This support, and her success in school exams, gave Grace confidence and ambition. 'I said, "I am not going to stay down there in the bush where I grow up"… I realized that the Lord has blessed me with intellect; and if this is what I'm going to serve my life on, then I'm going to go for it.' Grace has fulfilled her ambition, keeping within the supportive structure of her church. She worked first as a pre-trained teacher at a rural Adventist school, saving enough to go to an Adventist training college. Grace now has her own house in a new suburban neighbourhood and works as a senior teacher in a nearby Adventist high school, bringing up her own two children in the Seventh Day Adventist faith and with the same commitment to educational ambition.

More surprisingly, there were instances in which the church community was willing to support a woman in her decision to separate from her husband. Helena Busfield grew up in the industrial north of England. Her father, a factory foundryman, was a violent drinker and gambler, who would bring home other women to the house. Her mother was a keen Adventist, but he would never go: 'no, he used to drop us off at church.' In the face of the prophesies of doom of some of her friends, Helena's mother hesitated a long time before she finally decided to separate.

> When our parents were going through their breakage, people were, "Oh, you can't leave", and we remember, really distinctly, a couple saying, "Oh, the girls are going to have lots of babies and be prostitutes, and the boys, they're going to go to prison and be drug dealers" …. Because my mum was one of the first ones, first black women in the city, to strike out and leave her husband and say she's not going back.

In fact the prophesies of doom proved altogether false, for having shed her disruptive husband Helena's mother was able to carry on with understanding support at work, eventually remarry, and raise four children who have all become professional workers. Helena sees the role of the church in supporting them through the break-up as crucial. 'We were always in the church. We joined the Seventh Day Adventist church when I was eight, but we'd always been in one denomination or another, so we had the support of the church. Really big support. And that's how we managed.'

The last story is of Sally McNeep. It shows how sometimes the strongest religious commitment could overrun not only educational ambition, as we saw with Dick's mother, but even a normal concern for the well-being of the family itself. Sally is a Pentecostalist. As her daughter Niama put it, 'She devote herself in her Christianity.... God came first, then her children.' She was still less prepared to sacrifice her faith for her husband David. He was a Baptist preacher in Jamaica, but 'he used to drink a lot, and have a lot of womans around'. Hence he was a serious blemish on Sally's Christian reputation. So eventually, when David was already over 40, she decided to rid herself of him by sending him to England.

> She say, he was like a stumbling block in her way, and she got to remove him. So prayer she said she go down and pray and fast then, and the Lord did remove him out of her way, for her to continue with her Christianity. There was this opportunity come up, when England were opening in the fifties, to take in immigrants, so that's the time my mum hear about people going to England. So they sell the house, and she take that money and pay his passage. She send him away. So that's about it with him. He went away.

David was under the illusion that his wife and children were going to follow him to England, but that was never Sally's intention, and indeed when several of their children did migrate it was to Canada. David's plan was for Sally to join him first in England, and then for the children to follow in stages, as was the practice of many migrant families. But Sally used the children as a reason for refusing to rejoin her husband.

> Then I think what happened, he sent for her. But she refused. She said, "If he was good, God wouldn't take her out of his way." So she refused from going. He want her to leave us when we were still a kid growing up, to come to England. So she write him and tell him, no, she's not going to give away her kids, because, like, "Just puss pickney you give away."[5]

For Jamaican women, in short, whether or not they were migrants, the churches were much more likely to offer a forum for public respect and personal fulfilment than they were for men. On the other hand, the link between religion and educational ambition which was so common in Jamaica was severely weakened, and indeed for half of these families effectively broken, through their experiences of migration. This was partly because of the racism and discouragement which even the cleverest migrant children encountered in most schools; for the earlier migrants partly also because of the racism of many of the churches; and especially in Britain, but also to a lesser extent in North America, by the secularism of the society in which migrant families, both men and women, now found themselves.

TEN

The Dream of Return

Ted Oliver, truck driver from Jamaica, lives comfortably in Canada with his white wife Candy and their two children in the three-bedroom house they have bought in a Toronto suburb. They chose this suburb because it has a good school. Ted has been in Canada since he was 20, and Candy comes from a Canadian farm family. A crucial bond between them has been that they were both brought up by their grandparents: despite such different ethnic origins, he feels that 'we have the same background'. Ted now sees his own identity as mixed — 'I'm part of Jamaica, I'm part of Canada' — and they have brought up the children to enjoy both cultures, taking them on holidays to Jamaica and introducing them to relatives there. They play both Jamaican and American music, and they cook a mixture of Italian and Jamaican food, with Jamaican most Sundays: 'yam, fried plantain, ackee and saltfish, callaloo.' But Ted's ultimate dream is not of more success and more mixing in Canada. It is of return. 'I still have my grandfather land.' He would like to build his new family a house on his family land back in Jamaica, in the Trelawny hills where he grew up, and with Candy this has become a shared vision for their future lives together:

> My wife now, she's this type of person who likes to move. She have this type of feeling, "Oh yes, let's go to Jamaica and live in the woods." Up to this morning we were travelling on the highway, she said, "Why you wanna live in this mess?"

Because the first place I take her in Jamaica, in the mountain, and take her in Cockpit mountain, and she loved it. First when I take her, I went to — they have a spring in the mountain, so we take our shoes off, they have these kind of plants in Jamaica, but they are big vines, and we take it and wrap it round her feet, tie it up…. We walk across the canefield, we go to the spring and drink water, catch the water coming up from the ground, drink it. Go in the mountain, see the difference. She love that.

She said to me this morning, "Let us sell the house and go and live freely." I see that. I can match myself to that.

There is a poetic note in Ted's vision which is not unique. Spurgeon White, stowaway and lumberman, has not been back to Jamaica because he lacks official papers, but he dreams of building a log cabin on his family land. He imagines being back in his childhood home: 'The first sunset, the first one ever come in my heart was from Jamaica…. I was in the hills. It wasn't polluted, everything was perfect to me. The sunset, the moon, the banana trees, the sugar cane, the beauty of the island.' And in discussing land and community earlier we encountered other lyrical testimonies, such as Selvin Green's,[1] portraying the beauty of the island, its climate, its rivers, birds and fruit. For many Jamaican migrants locked in the dispiriting climates and unappealing environments of North American and British cities, the image of Jamaica as a lost paradise where they could relax in the sunshine seems to be one key element in their dreams of return. But it was intertwined with the longing 'to go back home', to build a house, to be together again with family and childhood friends, to revisit roots, even eventually to be buried in the family land.

To these we should add some less typical reasons for returning. One young adult had migrated to London as a child, but never settled: 'I was always dying to come back to Jamaica.' In the Manley era in the mid-1970s Audley Rawlings, British-born, migrated in the opposite direction to the general current, going out to join his returnee parents in western Jamaica, full of optimism: 'I felt I was going nowhere in England … but at that time, Jamaica was a lot different from what it is now…. I said, "Jamaica is the land of opportunity"… Jamaica was underdeveloped, and there was less crime, and it was like paradise.' There was also one migrant in the same era of hope who saw return as a chance to share some of what she had gained abroad. Stephanie Gladstone came back from Canada full of idealism to Jamaica to teach in one of the new secondary schools set up by Michael Manley: 'This is where I want to be. This is home. And I want to give back some of what was given to me.'

Most likely for the great majority of migrants their original dream was to do well enough to make a successful return in later life to Jamaica.[2] Dick Woodward thought his family, who came to London in the 1950s, were typical in originally hoping to return within three years, and for long after living in a state of readiness to travel back, with 'grips under their beds'. And indeed still among our interviewees, despite the passage of time over half still cherish this dream, and these would-be returnees come from right across the occupational spectrum. However, among the older migrants, especially those with modest resources, many have come eventually to accept that they will live out their lives in the countries where they are now settled. David McNeep, retired London railwayman, cited the proverb, 'Where the tree falls, it lies there.' Conversely, among the younger migrants there were many who felt that it was too early for them to return, although 'if I could afford it tomorrow, I would'. Robert Lynn, New York highway maintenance man, does plan to return, 'but not now. We have to make a foundation here first. Basically, like my own home, and then go down there and … build a nice house'. It was important for a migrant to be able to return with pride, so that paradoxically, the worse their situation the harder it became for them to return. Stella Wadham had some very rough years in New York after her husband left her, earning so little as a caregiver that after paying for the rent and sending money to Jamaica for her daughter she had not enough to eat. She would stand and cry in the shower: 'I cried, cried until I had no voice.' She only survived because her Jamaican landlady insisted on giving her free meals. Why didn't Stella return to Jamaica? 'It's this pride thing … I couldn't pack up and go back home, that would be admitting that I'd failed.'

There was also a minority who had decisively rejected any thought of return, principally for two reasons. The first was that they were too put off by the lower standard of living in Jamaica than they had become used to in their host country, the power cuts, the lack of hot water: 'the island would have to change — 360 degrees.' The second was their fear of violence. 'Jamaica was a very very good country that you could go any part of the country, and nobody interfere with you, nobody trouble you,' remembered David McNeep. 'When we was growing in Jamaica, you could leave your house open and gone a bush, gone do anything.' Many older migrants regret the passing of 'the old-fashioned Jamaica' they knew as children. Now, fanned by the press, rumours are constantly circulated of returnees who have been robbed or murdered, even on the way from the airport. 'People come over from the States to live, and then they are being killed'. For some would-be returnees, the answer is to be pragmatic, to avoid provocative displays of wealth. 'I don't dress up with a chain, and this flashing of dollars and so forth,' says Robert Lynn, New York highways maintenance worker. 'No. I'm going to the market, I'm in the same pants, same, I just blend with it.' For others, fear has put return out of the question: as Arnold Houghton, Canadian accountant, remarked, 'I don't want to be living in Jamaica behind some barbed wire fence, six guard dogs.'

However, rumours and fear have been so stimulated that even some well-educated migrants have developed fantasy views of current life in Jamaica. Thus a health professional in England asserted that in Jamaica today 'everybody lives in a prison, locked gates, burglar alarms, bad dogs in the garden'. This is not remotely true even of Kingston, let alone the smaller towns and countryside. Hence other migrants are arguing for a more balanced view. 'I want people to understand that Jamaica's not all about guns and violence and drugs,' says Belle Dickens, a writer who has recently returned from New York. 'There's a side of Jamaica that's warm, that's friendly, where people can sleep with their door open, where people can walk late at night.' Similarly Joy Beck, New York health worker, points out that Jamaican society still is caring, and robbery and violence are not a Jamaican monopoly. In New York 'people are not as caring, like back home. You know, you can always go to your neighbour and say, "Can you watch my child for me? I'm going to the store." Here you can't do that.' The previous week a thief among the staff had got into her office and stolen $80 from her, but nobody would say who it was. When she was mugged in the Bronx some years earlier, her daughter had been screaming, '"Help my mummy! He's going to kill my mother!" And people were just walking by…. People, they just hold their heads straight, they see nothing, they hear nothing. I'm not used to living like that.' For all the changes in Jamaica, that is where she hopes to return to live.

Of our Jamaican migrants, 12 have returned to Jamaica for substantial periods, and six of them are still living on the island. All of them, whether they stayed or not, were positive about their decision to come back. 'I love it. I wouldn't trade it!' Nevertheless, for half of them the return proved only temporary. Not surprisingly, most of the reasons for not staying on are similar to those for migrating in the first place. Although all those who were of working age found suitable jobs with little difficulty, one reason for not staying on was economic: 'it's very hard to make an honest living in Jamaica.' Of the others who have left, one man came back to Britain to give his children better educational opportunities; and another as a way of splitting up with his wife. 'My wife and I just couldn't see eye to eye', and he could see that the children were taking sides, 'So I said, "Well if that's the case, I'll go"… If you don't want to live that way, you get out of it. That's what I did.' The main difference with younger initial migrants is that some older returnees are forced back because they need the free health care to which they are entitled in Britain.

These few returnees are part of a much wider migratory current which is changing the face of Jamaica. It is having a crucial impact on the Jamaican economy too, for the pensions and other incomes of returnees are now second only to tourism in their contribution to the island's foreign currency earnings.[3] The pioneers of return migration have principally been English, who constitute ten of our twelve returnees. This is partly because the English Jamaicans migrated earlier and so are closer to retirement age, but also because those who bought their own houses can now cash in on a very substantial capital appreciation. And while some Jamaicans have returned from England to Florida, for them this is a much less easy compromise alternative than it is for Jamaicans in New York. So it is above all the English Jamaicans who are changing the face of Jamaica with their new houses.

You can find clusters of these new houses right around the Jamaican coastline, and they also climb up to the cooler heights of the central spine around Mandeville and Spaldings: walking the side roads there, their grey concrete frames thrust up through the bright green foliage like a regatta of dinghy sails in the Caribbean sea. When you look more closely, quite often they are unfinished, great three-storey frames with yawning unfilled gaps, sometimes half-abandoned with trees taking over the structures, somebody's abandoned gothic dream. More often with time they are finished, painted sparkling white, doors and windows filled with elaborately twisted metal grilles, and rooms inside big enough for a complete family reunion.

These houses are the fruit of years of struggle, first of all in Britain or America, but then in Jamaica too. It is very difficult to get a house built satisfactorily at a distance, so that it often takes months of visits stretched over several years before it is completed. When we met Esau Blackett, a tailor from northern England who also runs a wedding car business, he had a load of drainpipes for his house, sticking out of the car windows. He comes out for a month twice a year to push the building on, meanwhile letting both floors which he has finished, keeping only one room for himself. Winnie Busfield, a nursing assistant also from the north, used to come to Jamaica once in every two years to visit her mother, and in the early 1990s, with the help of a niece, she found a plot of land for a house close to the sea, part of a cluster of returnees' houses. Three years later the house was partly built: 'we finish the downstairs, the lower part of the house, and my husband came out to help look after my mother.' Her mother died before Winnie could follow. For another six years she kept working in the hospital, but raised substantially more cash by selling her house there and renting a flat, 'because the children now grown and they taking their own paths and working in London'. Once her house was sold, she sent out her furniture: 'well, things came out from England — shipment of all our house, household goods, furnitures and things.' But the upper part of the house was still little more than a shell, and it was a good ten years before it was completed. Finally Winnie and her husband could relax in their very spacious house, with guest rooms for their children and a glimpse of the sea down the valley.

Completing the house was one step in the dream of return. But in many ways a still tougher challenge, which took some returnees by surprise, was to reintegrate in Jamaican society. Winnie had one strong advantage, that she had been a Seventh Day Adventist from childhood, and continued to be active in England, where she 'used to be a missionary, I used to go with literature, proclaiming the word of God.... I brought up my children to love the Lord'. Now Winnie feels that 'the major part of getting back into the system is over', but nevertheless, even for her reintegrating was hard.

> It was difficult at first. Very very difficult. Certainly was very hard. As if the whole custom had changed. People attitude was rougher, not like most of the people I knew when I was small — they're all gone to foreign. So it was a whole generation with the new ideas, more disrespectful to adults, and so forth, so it was hard.
>
> But I am a very determined person, I overcome all those ... I am now well into the system. I fight my way into the system! Even the churches! Oh yes! Barriers in the churches.

Today Winnie's local friends are 'mainly through the church'. She has got over her initial surprise, after living for years as an exception in a world of white faces, that here in Jamaica, 'everywhere I go, there were all these black faces, and for a while, it took me a good while really to grasp it, that this was a black country'. She has learnt to speak *patois* again, and she has become a travelling missionary in Jamaica. But this very process of resettling has brought a profound change in her sense of identity. She has come to feel that she is perhaps as much English as Jamaican.

> Now, if you look at my community here, you will see that it's mainly returning residents, so that makes it much easier, because you have so much in common.... If it was all the everyday Jamaicans, I could not cope with it ... I could not relate to somebody that I hadn't shared the same culture with for 40 years. You understand? ... We go from England, so you have a lot of things in common.... You know more about them [returnees] than you know about your own Jamaicans [neighbours and family],

because most of your years you've spent with them.… You can talk about a place in England, and they can chat about the place. Now, when I got back to Jamaica here, there is hardly any place I know … I know more of England than Jamaica.

Now, if you have gone back straight into the heart of the community, you will have more problems. Because sometimes they call us "foreigners", oh yes. In England we were foreigners, you come back to Jamaica, your country, you're foreigners. So you get it from both sides.

Belle Dickens, who has recently returned from America, expressed rather similar feelings. She has moved into a cousin's newly built house, and is happy to be back in Jamaica. 'I love it, because it's more laid back, and it's really me. It has changed a lot. But I am more relaxed here, as opposed to being in New York, where one is uptight, and you're constantly going. I love it. I wouldn't trade it!' Nevertheless she feels much more comfortable living with a group of returnees.

I feel more at home with the returned residents, for the fact that they have a wider scope. In rural Jamaica, everybody knows everything you do.… Living in this [returnee] community now, it's kind of cool, because everybody — they have been exposed, everybody's into their own thing, nobody pays much mind. They seem to be doing their own thing. So it's cool.

Let us end with Vivia Perrin's story of return. Vivia is a professional nurse, and in London she has been a church goer and community activist. She has come back in that spirit — 'for me, coming back, I needed that purpose' — but she has no illusions that succeeding as a returnee is easy. She reflected on how she has watched too many others fail.

If they were from Jamaica, 20 years is enough to get them into the culture of the United States, or the culture of Britain. Then they come back, but most of them come back and they have not moved Jamaica on. Somewhere they left it. So a lot of them are disappointed, a lot of them are disheartened. And a lot of the people here, I've seen a big number going back to England. I don't know what it is going to do for them, because they have sold their homes, they have severed their ties with the church, with their communities, and the money they bring here, to build a house that they've got here, they cannot resell at a price to go back and buy again.

Vivia says that returnees need 'a network of support', and many are disappointed not to get that from their families: 'the biggest complaint you have from returning residents is from families.' She advises would-be returnees to come out for four or five years on 'fact-finding tours', checking out finances, security and so on: taking it gradually as she and her husband Albert did.

Vivia and Albert had been exploring the idea of a retirement house for some years. They tried a house briefly in Florida, and then Portugal. But Albert had retired much before Vivia, and after spending six months in Jamaica, 'he looked so good. He was so fit, he was like the young man I knew'. His mother had given him a piece of land, close to Albert's brother. Vivia was still unsure, but when Albert asked her, 'What do you think of building?' she said, 'OK, up to you.' Albert then got her involved in the project. 'I'd like you to help me design this house, because it's for you, even if you don't want to come there.'

It was some six years between their first thinking of the retirement house and moving into it. For the main push, Albert had to come back to Jamaica for six months. 'He says, "Love, I think I'm going to start building." And I said, "OK. But I don't earn enough money to build that sort of house you're going to build." He said, "Oh, we'll just build one room and then add onto it." I said, "OK." But by the time my husband come back, the house was nearly done.' The next time they came out to Jamaica, they moved into the completed house, beginning by cooking outside under a mango tree.

Vivia and Albert have thrown themselves into the social life of their southern Jamaican village, Guanjo Pen. This had always been central to their dream of return. Twenty years before, sitting at their family table in west London, Albert had said: '"So many of us have left Jamaica, and have come away. We are so blessed by the knowledge that we've gained. Wouldn't it be nice for us to go back and do something on the island?" … We jest and we joke, but we discussed it, and that seed was planted.' Vivia's original idea was to open a nursing home, and she does indeed work full time as a nurse in the nearest town. But once they had returned they were soon into other activities. They have been helping to provide new board houses for the poorest families. They sit as governors on three local school boards. The village has new signposts they designed. They have set up a Neighbourhood Watch involving over 100 households. And they have created a wider network in the whole area, the Returning Residents Group.

> We look at the community needs, we're working on a basic school at the moment, trying to help them rebuild a basic school. But it's mainly for us, for camaraderie. Because when you come back, people don't accept you readily. They rip you off. So what we do, we've got a list of dentists and doctors we all use, and plumbers, and these people know where their bread is buttered, you know? So we have a togetherness.

The project which most of all engages Vivia, however, is for a health centre which would bring some of the services which are currently only available in Kingston. Vivia has thrown herself into this project, raising money through the churches in Jamaica, England and America. Poorer people gave vegetables and fish, and the church gave a cell phone. Land was given by the church, and the structure has now been built with the help of volunteer labour from abroad. We stood in its shell, trying to imagine it in use. It stands waiting for windows, doors and tiling. Vivia pays for many of the smaller items from her salary, 'whatever is left over there, I put towards buying whatever is needed — paint and stuff for it. So this is the purpose, this is what's keeping me here, and I'm not leaving until it's done. It's nearly finished, it's nearly finished.'

Although all this campaigning activity has not pleased all of the existing local leadership, there is no doubt that combined with her work as a nurse, Vivia has won a local standing. 'I had to work to make myself, and to make people accept you, because they don't accept you readily, once you've traveled.' Being a nurse brings her many confidences, and also gifts. She has learnt *patois*, which she never spoke at home in England. But in spite of all this, returning to Jamaica has brought home to Vivia her Englishness. Both emotionally and culturally, she feels 'the pull of England'.

One of Vivia's main hesitations about returning was that she did not wish to inflict the same migration pain which she had suffered herself as a child on her children. 'I hated the fact that my parents left me, and I had to cope, and I was mindful that I didn't want my children to feel that way.' Hence she keeps returning to London, partly fund-raising, partly to enjoy the shops, but above all to see her children and grandchildren, 'because I need to have close contact with my family'. When in Jamaica she texts them all weekly. 'I think the pull of England will always be there, because that's where my nuclear family is.'

Vivia calls herself 'the lady with a purpose. That's just how I see myself now. If you ask me, I say "I'm British" first. I don't care who don't like it, I am English first. But I will do what I need to do, where I am.... Well I say "home", England! I can't say that in front of my husband, because he says [of Jamaica], "This is your home now."'

ELEVEN

Living with Family Complexities

We have now followed our migrants and their families from their Jamaican childhoods, though migration to their later lives and dreams. As migrants they are all actors in one of the most important movements in modern times, part of a global search by men and women from less prosperous countries for work in the most advanced economies: migratory movements which are transforming both the countries which send and those which receive. For this reason alone we are sure that it is worthwhile in itself to hear their own accounts of their own experiences, of their struggles for a better life, their setbacks and successes.

Nevertheless we believe that Jamaican transnational families have a special interest beyond that. In the last 30 years there has been a rapid transformation of British and North American family systems, primarily due to the rise of divorce and repartnering and hence, where there are children by the first marriage, of stepfamilies. The same kind of pattern, although not termed as a 'stepfamily', has been very common in Jamaica since the slave era. This experience of ways of coping with complex families over many generations means, firstly, that British and American commentators could well look to see how Jamaicans handle such potentially difficult family transitions. But Caribbean family experience is not a static legacy from the past: on the contrary, it is adaptive and dynamic. So we also need to consider how it has developed in the migrant situation, and how far this might be seen as an effective response to the new context of global living.

Growing Up in Complex Families

The complexities of transnational Jamaican family relationships come partly from pre-migration family patterns in Jamaica, and especially for three reasons. The first was that in the grandparental generation many mothers had five or even ten children, so that their numerous descendants often created a dense network of multiple cousins living in the same district. A second reason was that while most often our migrants grew up in childhood with a couple, whether parents or grandparents, this was nevertheless very often as part of a family which in Anglo-American terms would be called a 'stepfamily' or a 'double stepfamily', because even in earlier generations repartnering was common. Hence very often one or both parents had outside children from another relationship, and half brothers or half sisters who sometimes grew up in the same household, and sometimes not. There were indeed some whose own childhood households in themselves encapsulated the complications of their wider family, with adults raising children from a variety of different parents. The third element generating complexity was migration itself, which scattered grandparents, parents and children, and brothers and sisters, on different sides of the oceans, so often disrupting old patterns and creating new ones. How did these Jamaican migrants experience and cope with these complexities?

Their childhood experiences of complex large households were all in Jamaica before migration. The memories we heard of them — here mostly from the 1970s to the 1980s — were strikingly positive. Rickie Constable enjoyed his summers with his farming grandmother, 'well respected in the community', who also 'brought up my cousins. She would cook easily for 15 to 20 kids, they'd all come up into the front yard.... We'd all sit there, and have our plateful, and we'd be eating. Yeah, very giving woman, caring'. Owen Callaghan describes growing up in a household with his grandmother, a country dressmaker, his aunt and uncle and eight cousins, as 'a lot of fun', with 'all kinds of games' as well as fights and mischief. Sean Ismay, whose mother had gone to Canada, grew up with his grandparents and eight children from three different sets of parents, all the children helping on the farm. But that was not all the children his grandmother raised.

Later on, his grandmother, Sean recalls, 'now that we left, she took in more kids. She's always had kids there.... Some of them were grandkids, and others was like from friends and family that she knew could not provide for their kids.' Ted Oliver, whose mother was in Kingston, was similarly raised by his farming grandmother, 'the one who's really there for me', along with his sister and a group of cousins, 'so we have four families in the house'. In addition, his grandfather Simon was also in the house much of the time. For Simon maintained a visiting relationship as a couple with Ted's grandmother, while living in his own house, 'very close, like three doors down': she would cook and wash for him, 'do everything for him'.

Stella Wadham deliberately chose to live in one such complex grandparental household rather than with her own parents. She could have lived with her mother in Kingston, but chose to live with her father's mother in the country. 'My mother went to a wedding in the country, and she [grandma] "borrowed" me for a week.... So it went from a week to two weeks, to a month, to "when she's ready for school".' Stella went back to her mother at three, but 'I'd barely eat, and I would just sit and suck my fingers', and 'started getting skinny', until eventually, 'I broke down, and I started crying, and I said, "I wanna go to my grandma! Grandma let me feed"'. They sent Stella back to her grandmother until she was a teenager. And for Stella, 'my grandmother was everything to me'. But they were also living with an aunt and uncle, and up to a dozen other children. 'We always had, like, extended family — cousins who lived further up in the country that needed to go to school nearer, so they would stay over. So we always had … just one big extended family.'

Stella's upbringing also helped her to understand that having children with more than one partner did not have to lead to friction. She is one of seven children herself, and although only three came from both parents she is fully in touch with them all. A still stronger influence came through the aunt she lived with, who Stella sees as a model in dealing with family transitions. 'There's been situations with her husband, and she's just dealt with it so well. He has had outside children, during the marriage, and when push comes to shove, she ends up with the kids.' She not only took in these outside children, but was an 'inspiration' to them, providing an example which for some of them was to be relevant to stepfamily relationships in the post-migration situation:

> She was just telling me that, Mother's Day, she got this big card, and this is one of his daughters that she grew, and she's now in Canada. Not hers. And she sent a letter back in the card, and said to her, "Thank you for everything you did for me. Because now, what you did, has taught me now to deal with my husband's kids" — which is now her step kids. Because each time anything happens, she just remember that she had taken her in. And she never treated her less than her kids.

Because the wider network of cousins were left behind, and also sometimes the migrants' own elder children, one immediate effect of migration was to make such large and complex households very rare in the new country. With these families, the most complex household arrangement after migration is unique. Ben Bell, Sid and Crichton's father, domineering, 'articulate' and 'stubborn', from the 1960s right through to the 1990s maintained two households in London with different women, supporting them both, and coming regularly for short visits. 'He might stay for a couple of days, or might visit today, put down some money, or "Do you need this? Do you need that?" Boom boom. Might go shopping.' But Ben kept the different parts of his life separate, so that the boys did not know about the rival household until they were 10, and they were strongly discouraged from visiting him in his other home. At the same time they also discovered that there was a third woman, who was mother of Nell, their half sister by Ben, as well as of other children. Ben's secrecy is untypical, and in later years his children decided to ignore his wish to keep the parts of the family separated. The two brothers, their half brother on their mother's side and this half sister are all in touch today, taking part in large family parties and celebrations with many other cousins and kin: an extended cousinage in the new country, although all living divided up into small family households.

The same progression can be seen with Rodney Scott's family. His childhood was again unique, for he grew up as a transnational child, alternating between his grandmother in Florida and his great-grandmother in London. However, his great-grandmother took in children with a truly Jamaican enthusiasm, including hungry children off the street, and at any one time usually had a household of nine children. Eventually she became an award-winning pioneer of fostering, 'the first black foster parent' in her London borough. Interestingly, Vivia Perrin also became a foster parent in London, another example of a similar switch from informal extended family parenting in Jamaica to formally recognized fostering abroad. But Rodney Scott's family also again illustrates the parallel development over time of large kin networks abroad, for by the time his great-grandmother died in the 1990s, she had 60 known relatives within a mile in west London, and 25 family cars came to her funeral.

There were continuities in Leonard Selkirk's experience too. Until rejoining his parents in Britain in the 1960s he had been brought up with his grandparents, but often also staying with cousins. 'We were meeting up, we were all, like, with other cousins … but weren't necessarily in the same household every day and every night. We would have been backwards and forwards.' Leonard now encourages similar informal contact with his children's cousins, who stay over, and share joint holidays. On the other hand, for other families who now lacked nearby kin there might now be an alternative focus: a church, or a group of old school friends — we attended one such gathering in the Bronx — or a village or district reunion, which could give the feeling 'like we're all family'. Similarly Leonard describes how earlier he had been able to share his understanding of Jamaican family life with other migrant children. 'In school, we'd always talk about our experiences. Virtually all my friends lived with their grandparents or uncles whilst their parents came over.' Through this mutual sharing of experience they unconsciously came to accept that there was nothing wrong with their kind of family arrangement. 'So we presumed, without thinking, we probably lived off each other knowing that it was okay.' So that another effect of migration was to force reflection about Jamaican family patterns, which had previously been taken for granted.

Thinking about Families

So how did migrants make sense of their often extensive and complicated family networks? The key was the informality and pragmatic adaptability of Jamaican family relationships. We have suggested earlier how the Jamaican family system was symbolized by family land, with rights given equally to all descendants from the original owners, but priority in practice allowed to those in most need. There are similar practical simplifications which our migrants used, both conceptually in thinking about relationships, and also practically in handling transitions.

Part of this shows up through basing the use of kin terms on personal experience rather than on descent. Hence half brothers and sisters who grew up together are treated as full siblings.[1] As Nelson Pinnock, who has two full and six half-siblings, put it, 'as children, we didn't grow up as no half nor nothing. We just grew up as brothers and sisters.' Two other men also refer to cousins who grew up with them as sisters, using the same phrase again, 'so we all grew up like sisters and brothers'.

The complexity of attitudes resulting from this pragmatism can be understood in a similar way. Sarah Chisholm, now a Canadian administrator, was brought up in Jamaica belonging to a family of 12 full and half-siblings on both her father's and her mother's sides. Her father had a good job with the Parish Council. She declares forcefully:

> We are very close, and I don't refer to them, I don't consider them as half-brothers or half-sisters. They are my sisters, they are my brothers, irrespective of whether we share the same mother: they are my sisters. I think it's ridiculous people talking about, "That's not my full brother. He's my half-brother." I think that's — very low.

But she does in fact make some clear distinctions. She recalled of her eldest sister, 'at one time I thought she was my mother, because she was very very caring'. And particularly strikingly, when her father adopted the sister of a half-sister abroad who was not a blood relative, she was able to treat her as a full sibling: 'the bond is so close, so tight ... that eventually you say, "Oh this is my sister".... We had that closeness.' In both of these instances one can see how the term from one formal relationship can be substituted by another term for positive reasons.

On the other hand, she also says later that she is not close to two older sisters who were abroad when she was a child. It seems clear that half-siblings who were not known in childhood could eventually be disregarded as kin, particularly when their common parent had not maintained regular contact. Isabelle Woods, who grew up in London, took a similar attitude. Her father, who had been in little contact and provided scarcely any support for her as a child, reappeared when she was 20 and told her, 'You'll have to meet your stepbrothers and sisters.' But she felt no interest in meeting them: 'Not at all. Like I told him, "I'd rather get to know him first, before I start to learn about the rest of the family."' She could not get on with him and has been out of touch for ten years, nor has she taken up contact with her half-siblings.

The same kind of transfer of naming terms took place when a child was parented by another relative. In one exceptional case the grandmother pretended to be the real mother, but such deceptions were not necessary. Dayton Cripps speaks for most who grew up with grandparents in declaring: 'I'd have to say that my real mother was my grandmother.' Equally typical, Sean Ismay called his grandmother 'mum', and his mother by her first name. Stella Wadham, who called her grandmother 'momma', remarks, 'my mother never got "mother" title from me.' Robert Austin grew up with his grandmother and her partner, whom he called 'my grandfather'. He explained, 'Actually he's not our grandfather, but there. I accept him as my grandfather because we never knew my grandfather.... He was pretty nice to us, especially me.' There were also sometimes non-blood relatives who became, through their active roles, called members of the family. Sid Bell remembers a Jamaican family friend, 'a very cheeky woman, brown skin, chubby, very loving', from his London childhood:

> There was a lady called "grandma", who used to look after me. She wasn't my grandma, but I always thought of her as my grandma because she used to look after me, and her family became my family, it's like an extended thing. I call them cousins. They're not really

my cousins, but because of the friendship between my mum and her family, it's this … Jamaican or West Indian thing, it's a cultural thing, which accepts you as part of the family because they've known you from knee-high.

Similarly, descriptions of family patterns were above all shaped by personal selectivity. Trudie Brown, who lives in Jamaica with her mother and her two children, has six brothers and sisters and an immense cousinage, including most of one village on their family land. But while acknowledging these other relatives, she focuses sharply on 'the close family, the immediate.… My family is three members. That's myself, my son, and my daughter.… That's my family — three. They're the close family'. It is surprising that she does not include her mother, but very typical that she omits the unsupportive fathers of her children: 'I was there, I was alone.' There are parallel examples of close families among migrant families abroad, typically small families of strong women, such as Yolande, Isabelle and Lola Woods, or Celine Parris, who in the 1980s lived as a London teenager with her adored grandmother, sharing her bed and her bottle of rum, confiding together.

Connie Dixon also simplified and incorporated her own experience. She grew up close to the sea with at least 30 relatives on her mother's side living within a mile. Today, when she returns from Canada it takes two or three days for her to walk round the village lanes, exchanging news as she calls from house to house, 'Whappen gal?' She has other sets of relatives in the parish through the fathers of her three half-sisters. Overseas she has one sister and her uncle — her mother's brother — in America, to whom she is close; and another cluster of cousins descended from her great-grandmother in London, with whom she has little shared experience, although is in contact. But within this very complicated web she has always strongly focused on a small core group of kin. Connie never knew her father, and after her mother's early death she grew up with her grandmother. She recalls how, when at school, 'we were supposed to draw our family, and where we come from and all that; and I remember I always drew my grandmother and myself. I was always helping my grandmother.… If I were ever asked where I came from, I always said, "My mother drew me on a piece of paper and cut me out. That's how I came into the world"'.

Looking back, she sees this as her 'childish way ... to cope with it'. She describes how the number of relatives who surrounded her was 'just overwhelming. I think that's why, over the years, I've just blocked it out, thinking, "Okay, these are important, these aren't important". It's just too much, especially when they don't play an active role'. She has knitted together a close family of her own, consisting of her three half-sisters, her two sons, her husband, and her uncle, who was especially supportive to her as a child. Most of this closeness developed through living experience, but Connie has also shown a striking ability to reshape or to forge new links. Thus as a migrant she later became a successful stepmother and step-grandmother, making an active link with the mother of her stepchildren. And even the relationship between the four sisters, who after very early childhood grew up apart, was a creation of adulthood. As one of her sisters put it, Connie was 'the person for keeping the bond among us'. Their present closeness has been largely due to her urgings, from Canada, with one sister in the United States and the other two in Jamaica. As Connie wrote to Grace, 'we are sisters, although we didn't grow up together, it's important that we're always in touch,' and offer support to each other.

Handling Transitions

This ability to adapt and to forge new bonds after family breaks, which we may call creative pragmatism, was especially important in the very common context of repartnering and outside relationships. It seems likely that it built on a traditional willingness of many Jamaican women to bring up their men's children by another mother, which in the past may have happened with very little explicit negotiation. For example, Celia Mackay's father had six outside children by two women, and Celia's mother was willing for several years, apparently without protest, to bring up three of these children, until her father's first wife, who had migrated, was eventually able to send for all three — not all hers either — to come to England. Some migrants continued to favour these quieter old Jamaican ways. Ted Oliver grew up with a grandmother, whose ex-husband was a regular visitor to her house: 'I saw my grandmother husband come around.' Ted himself has an elder child whose mother he supports. Now in Canada and happily married, he is shocked by the amount of conflict in a typical Canadian divorce. 'That's what I found very different here. These parents here are totally different. They lock you off so you can't get to see your kids, you can't get to — so it work on your brain, you do things crazy.'

Nevertheless more recently it has become increasingly common among migrant families to discuss these and other more everyday problems much more openly. Verity Houghton, for example, now in Canada, describes how in her family strategic thinking became more shared when she had become an adult: 'I think the way we've grown up, you tend to bounce ideas off of them [other close family members].... So they're in the know as to what's happening in everyone's life, and be able to say, "Well, that doesn't sound right".... It means helping out with the kids ... or if they need a short term loan or whatever, then you always try to be there to provide that as well.' In a similar spirit of discussion and negotiation, before Sarah Chisholm and her second husband Duane started living together in Toronto, she talked to her sons and her nieces who were living with her. 'Before he and I decided to live together, I discussed it to ask their opinion ... I told them what my plans were in the future, and that I do not expect anyone to be disrespectful to him.' Duane has proved a friendly, affectionate and helpful partner, and with time the children 'grow to accept him and to love him, and now they call him "Daddy"'.

There are also signs of more expressed concern among separating mothers to keep their children in touch with their ex-husband's kin.[2] So Stella Wadham speaks regularly on the phone from New York to her ex-husband and his mother, because Stella believes that she should not 'take away her father's side of people from her, because she's half mine and half his'. Sandrine Porto tries to get her two older daughters to phone their father themselves from New York, saying, 'You really have to talk to your dad. He needs to let you know his family.'

It is particularly interesting that we encountered instances of a similar inclusiveness in two second generation Jamaican families in London. In the first family the mother is Sadie Rawlings, whose parents were Jamaican and Irish and who is a professional counsellor. Sadie keeps her own four children in touch with her ex-husband's son by another mother, and especially notably, invites both this child and his mother to family social occasions — although by white English conventions neither mother nor child would be regarded as kin. Equally striking is the story of Crichton Bell's children. When we first met Crichton he was an unemployed building worker with one daughter from his long-term girlfriend Katrina, who is herself the child of a mixed relationship between a West Indian and a Scotswoman. Crichton describes Katrina as 'dysfunctional' and this first daughter has been brought up with her Scottish granny in Liverpool. Katrina's other children were growing up with her sister and her brother. More recently Katrina had another daughter, conceived as she was breaking up with Crichton. Crichton first of all insisted on testing to prove that the child was his own, and then took responsibility for it — but within the context of his extended family. He turned to his half sister Nell, and discussed the question with her and her family. The outcome was that one of Nell's daughters took in and is now raising the infant girl.

Not surprisingly, the accounts by these migrants of living with remarried parents are very varied, but they are much more often positive than negative. Stepfathers range from some such as Winnie Busfield's, who was an abusive 'beater' — 'I didn't see my stepfather as a father' — to others like Josephine Buxton's, who was 'the only father that I know. Gentle and good. I was well cared for. And I don't miss any daddy, because I was very much near, close to him'. Jacob Richards talks at length about his English 'stepmum' as 'a very steadying influence', who helped to teach him 'prudence, patience'. Two women also mentioned the role of mothers who acted as a 'good stepmother' in ensuring that their husbands' children by other women were given their share of support from their fathers. Joy Beck recounted how her own mother played this part in their Jamaican village. Her husband had many outside relationships, but she nevertheless 'made sure that he [Joy's father] supported all the kids that they [the mothers] said was his. She would make sure that, in the summer time, they would come to the house, they would spend a week or two. She would make sure that when they leave they will have a new set of uniform, books, shoes, everything to go back to school. So it's like a summer camp here'.

The pains which some children experienced through the transition into a family of repartnering run in close parallel with the emotional difficulties others felt when, after growing up with grandparents or other kin, they became migrants and rejoined parents who for several years had not been their caregivers. Sean Ismay migrated to Canada in the 1970s at the age of 10 to rejoin his mother, after living through his early childhood with his grandmother. He was particularly interested in comparing his rejoining his mother with entry into a stepfamily. For Sean felt his own mother was as much a stranger as her husband, whom he did not know at all. Sean felt himself as his grandmother's rather than his mother's son. So from a pragmatic point of view, rejoining a separated parent and joining a stepparent, one a blood relative and the other not, were in practice very similar transitions: 'not being my biological parents, that wasn't the problem'. Sean felt that his mother should have given him time to adjust.

> That was definitely a problem, because, here is a strange lady that I don't know, laying down all these rules and regulation.... She jumped in with both legs, trying to be my mother straight away, setting down the rules.... Scolding me, and wanting to beat me, and it's like, "You can't beat me. You're not my mother" ... I said this to her, "Listen, you don't have to make up for nothing". She's trying to be over motherly. "Second best is not always a bad thing. And in this case, it's the only thing that you're gonna get, as the best is already taken." Like, she wants the number one spot, and it's impossible, right? ... "Don't try to be that mother from one year old, up. You missed that. That part was already filled. Continue now you know me. Start off slow and build."

Sean contrasted the difficulty he had in bonding with his mother with the more subtle and successful approach of his stepfather, with whom he now has an 'excellent relationship', calling him 'dad' and hugging him. His stepfather started quite differently, avoiding any attempt to impose himself as a father figure. 'No, no, no, no, he didn't. He introduce himself to me, right away, at the airport.... My stepdad gave me a choice, he goes, "My name is Leslie. You can call me Leslie, you can call me "dad".' So Sean calls his stepfather 'dad' of choice, while his mother, who 'insisted on me calling her "mummy"', he calls her by her first name.

On one hand it is important to recognize that Jamaican extended families had clear limits to their flexibility in such transitions. There were bad as well as good stories, and always there were pragmatic limits to the boundaries of kinship recognition and obligation. Thus most of the transitions following parental breaks and repartnering also involved half brothers and sisters. Broadly speaking, those who grew up in the same households saw themselves as full brothers and sisters and remained in touch as adults.

On the other hand, contact was often lost with those who grew up in other districts. However, often this was not because of parental separation in itself. Sometimes there had been contact, but the siblings simply did not like each other. For example, Russell Peel, who is in Britain, on his father's side has three half brothers living in America. He met them while they were all still in Jamaica, but he disliked them because he found them 'boasie'.[3] This was 'before my sisters and me start travelling, their mum was living in America … so they felt themselves better. So I don't deal with them'. But lack of contact was most often because as children they had lacked any shared experience, and were therefore often in effect disregarded as siblings.

Thus Winnie Busfield, now back from Britain in Jamaica, never knew her two oldest sisters: 'they are from another father, which I do not know much about.' Similarly, while Greta Houghton, who has remained in Jamaica throughout, regarded the five half siblings she grew up with, two by her father and three by her mother, as 'all one, we were a family', she described a sixth half sister whom she never met as quite separate, someone 'we didn't really know much of'. Marcia Trelissick, who lived with her grandmother three hours away from her mother in later childhood, is now only in touch with one of her six younger half sisters on her mother's side, and she explains this separation in the same way:

> Those six children, I know them, but we don't have anything in common, because I didn't grow up with them, I just visit my mother and that's it.… I don't know much about them really. You see, I was not living there. You know much about your sisters and your brothers when you live together. If you don't, you don't know much.

The Strengths of Transnational Kinship Networks

Just as the handling of transitions in Jamaican transnational families takes on particular configurations reflecting attitudes to kin relationships, so do the sources of resilience and strength which they reveal. Inevitably again the message of these life stories is mixed. Thus, there are many accounts of effective kin mobilization to help relatives, but it is principally children and mature adults who receive this help. This kin mobilization is least effective with young men in difficulties — as we saw earlier in this book.[4]

Equally striking, however, is the resilience of the kin system. The most extreme instances are those in which it seems that migrants have succeeded in recreating a Jamaican family network or neighbourliness within their new context: a reinventing of tradition in new forms, which is sometimes quite deliberate. Thus Arnold Houghton describes his situation in Toronto:

> Two sisters close by. Parents not far away. It used to be like every Saturday, we just hang out at mother's.... We still get together quite a lot, unrehearsed. You just pick up and end up at G's, and then you might end up at Verity's. My parents I see at least twice, sometimes three times a week, sometimes every day, because I might pop by at lunchtime.

When Tracey Scott moved to Florida five years ago, there were already kin in three other houses in the same road, the homes of an aunt, and uncle and a grandmother.

Such regrouping does not just involve immediate family. One particularly remarkable migrant woman seems not only to have recreated a community for herself through friends as well as kin, but to have done this successively in three different locations. As Yolande Woods puts it:

> When [my mother] left Jamaica, and she went to England, there were friends that came around the same time, lived in the same area. When she left England, she moved to the Bronx, I remember the whole street was like full of people that we knew back in England.... And then when she decided to move down to Florida, she was one of the first ones to move down there. Now, every time

you go there she goes, "Oh yeah, do you know Blablabla moved down here?" It's like she's created this little community for herself.

More commonly, many migrants were helped by other West Indians especially in finding lodgings immediately after arrival, and later on they often also provided mutual support in savings clubs.

However, given that we are concerned with geographically mobile migrant families, some of whose members will always be contemplating another move, such regroupings or friendships are most often peripheral to the mainstay of kin support. The four most typical forms of kin help are firstly, practical assistance in migrating; secondly through sending financial remittances, usually to kin in Jamaica; thirdly, caring for older kin; and fourthly, help with child-rearing, very often to enable a young mother to work or to migrate. All these exchanges of help operate on a transnational basis.

Practical help in migrating — including paying for tickets, providing an initial home, and help in finding work — is the normal practice in most of these families; and similarly, remittances in the form of money and gifts are sent back to kin in Jamaica by most migrant families — and by both men and women.

Caring for the old who are left behind in another country is a form of help which is mentioned much less often, by only a quarter of these families. This was partly because for a sick grandparent or parent in Jamaica, it was a bad moment to think of migrating abroad to rejoin a child. But often migrants were at pains to ensure that a parent was receiving proper care; and in other families a younger member did return to Jamaica to live with them. What help was given to the old depended — as with Jamaican kin relations more generally — very much on whether any feeling of reciprocal obligation had developed. Thus David McNeep, now sick and in his eighties in England, had ten children in Jamaica and Canada, but he had been out of contact with all but one and none was now willing to come to take care of him. By contrast Louis May had been brought up by his grandmother, and when the family called from Jamaica to England to tell him that she had suffered a stroke, 'I had to grab everything, everything, and spend the next night coming, on the plane to Jamaica. And I tell you after this stage, because the thing is that I had to lift her up like a baby.... And what came back to me is what she used to do to me when I was a baby.'

Help with children, by contrast, is a much more common form of mutual aid. Child fostering among kin, either temporary or permanent, is a very widespread practice in Jamaican families, probably dating back at least to the slave era, maybe even to Africa.[5] Sometimes it is a response to a disaster, such as a parental death; but more often it is a positive strategy chosen so as to help the young adult parent to get into work, or to go ahead as a migrant. Some children are sent back to kin in Jamaica in the hope of a better education. The initiator can be either the parent, or the grandparent, or occasionally the child. Thus, Stella Wadham in Jamaica effectively insisted on staying with her grandmother, by refusing to eat whenever she was returned to her mother; and Stella in turn chose to leave her young daughter behind, with care shared by both of the child's grandmothers, when she migrated to New York. And Greta Houghton's Jamaican mother must have specially liked the role of fostering:

> My mother actually raised, took care of other people's children, who might not have been relatives of hers, immediate relatives... who would have come in and ask her, somebody might be migrating to England, a mother might be migrating to England and ask her to let the children stay for a little while, so she did that too.

We have found this 'child-shifting' operating in almost all of our families, and in over half of them there are transnational instances.

Childcare is typically provided by a grandmother or aunt living nearby to enable the mother to leave to work, but it may be the caregiver who moves. When Isabelle Woods' mother Lola decided to move from London to New York, Lola summoned the children's grandmother from Jamaica to fill the gap: who as a result committed herself to spending twelve years of her life in England. 'It was a big decision my nan had to make, but she did.'

While the key axis of exchanges of help is between parents, children and grandchildren, it is notable how the possibilities extend well beyond this. Aunts are common caregivers. Cousins are taken in to assist migration.

Remittances are sent not only to parents, but often also to siblings or to in-laws. Temporary help with migration may extend to very distant kin, including even ex-in-laws.

Underlying this is a sense not only of the potential importance of extended family kin, but also of how strong obligation with more distant kin can be built through individual life experiences. When Patsy Clark decided to migrate to the United States, she received crucial support not only from her mother's brother, who was already there and had been sending remittances to his nieces, but also from this uncle's ex-girlfriend, who had her to stay in her house, and found her a job.

In another family, as a child Sarah Chisholm had been particularly close to her eldest sister, who she describes as being like a mother to her, 'a protector.' When this sister died, Sarah decided to help by bringing two of her daughters to Canada, and indeed as one of these nieces says, has in turn played the role of a mother figure: 'She's my mother, she took care of us after my mum died, and she has just been making sure that everything goes okay for us.' Sarah herself is in no doubt why she has taken on this role, and explains precisely how she felt a clear reciprocal obligation to help her sister's children: 'I brought them here, because of the kindness of my sister, of what she did for me. I thought it was necessary to return the kindness to her children.'

These examples also reinforce another point: the key role of women as activators of these kin networks. In contradiction to those who have argued that women are salient in Caribbean families only by 'default' in 'incomplete' families whose men are missing,[6] we have found women taking such roles whether or not husbands or fathers are present in their households. In general, while both men and women are likely to send financial remittances, the responsibility for caring, and also as we saw earlier, for the organizing of kin migration, seem most often to rest with women.

Keeping Contact

It is not surprising that if geographical separations within Jamaica could cut the bonds between siblings, the impact of long distance migration was inevitably more drastic, endangering the closeness between husbands and wives, grandparents, parents and children, as well as less immediate kin links. In a Jamaican country village maintaining the multiple cousin network required little more than acknowledgement when passing in the road or outside their houses. But migrations pushed these networks into the background, bringing the focus much more onto the inner circle of kin with whom it was practical to maintain contact. And even the inner family might gradually take on a new shape, recentring on a geographical basis. Sean Ismay, who migrated to Canada, has a large group of relatives in England as well as the multiple extended family back in Jamaica. 'There's like two circles. The ones that never got sent to foreign were really close, because they were back in Jamaica. And the ones that are, was a different circle, because they were all in England, so they all up there.'

Yet distance did not deter Jamaican migrants from trying to hold their families together. Indeed, a commitment to maintaining transnational kin links was already evident 40 years ago, when Sheila Patterson wrote of how among British West Indians, the key to the family was not seen as the household: for there was such a frequent exchange of letters, remittances and visitors, that 'the links with close kin at home are often as strong or stronger than any bonds between the members of a Brixton domestic unit'.[7] We found that both men and women migrants maintained contact with relatives in other countries, but it seems likely that in many families women were more active in sustaining kin links. Thus Owen Callaghan in the United States remarks how 'my mother is the one who keep in touch much more than I do, because she always curse me, "Owen, you don't call anybody, you don't visit"'. In Rodney Scott's family the hub of contact had been his London great-grandmother, and after her death he felt that the family was 'drifting apart'. '[My wife] might be more in touch with her family, than I,' reflected Bill Fox, Jamaican agricultural adviser. 'The woman seem to be able to maintain links, family links, better than men.... The men feel that's the woman's affair. That's a woman's duty. She should keep the connection.' This partly explains why contact seems more often lost on the paternal side. Bill continued: 'Do you know what a gentleman told me yesterday? What he finds is that the womenfolk, the wives, always look after their side of the family better than they look after the husband's side of the family!'

It is certainly true, as we have already seen, that women play the predominant role in the exchange of help in childrearing in these transnational Jamaican families, the help of a grandmother recurrently enabling a mother to move in search of work. We have also discovered how in many families women have played the strategic role in thinking and planning for migration. But even if to a lesser extent, men are also active in maintaining these transnational Jamaican families.

There are in fact plenty of examples of men among our migrants who actively sustain contact with their kin in other countries. From London Jack Constable regularly phones his six brothers and sisters in Canada, the United States, Britain and Jamaica. From Canada Sean Ismay writes frequent letters to his grandmother, and also sends her parcels regularly, although somewhat frustrated by how little of it she enjoys for herself: 'half of it she's dividing among everybody around where we lived, yeah, not just her family.' In particular, the men send money as their form of contact. Russell Peel is in Britain, his brothers and sisters in America and Jamaica. 'I'm here, I'm sending her money when she's home [from her travels abroad]', he says of his mother. 'The good thing about her, a good thing she had so many of us, because we are now her pension.' Russell, who is single, sends almost half his earnings from England back to his mother.

It has required particular ingenuity, usually by the women of the family, to maintain effective contact with young children who were temporarily left behind by migrants, and we have already encountered instances of children who felt their parents were strangers when they were eventually able to follow and rejoin them. But there were also successes. Ted Oliver lived with his grandmother from the age of three until he rejoined his mother in Canada at 20, but it was very important for him that his mother always kept in close touch. 'She would be sending anything we need, she would be always sending things for us.' She also phoned exceptionally frequently. 'I would say we grown up far away, but relationships, as a mother, I still cannot throw it away. The relationship is still there. You know, she will call me and tell me this, do this — every day. Every day.'

Sean Ismay's mother and grandmother relied on letters and parcels. 'Money and stuff she [mother] will send.... The parcels we'd see, and then

I used to read the letter to my grandma, because my grandma can't read.... We took turns, because okay, not just letters from my mum, but my grandma used to receive letters from her other kids in England.' His grandmother also dictated their letters to their mother:

> She taught me. I remember sitting out with my grandma writing, writing my first letter to my mum here. Me and my cousin, and my mum's other sister was here too, so we wrote the letter at the same time. We actually put the same word in each letter, because my grandma was telling us what to put, so we were writing it word for word.... She knew how to write letters while we didn't, but yet she can't read or write.

Letters were, however, at best a clumsy way of maintaining contact. This is brought home through the memories of one family who tried to keep in touch systematically through letters alone. Pearl Selkirk wrote from London to her children in Jamaica every week, 'I write to my mum every weekend'. She also sent photos, so that the children would 'always have a feeling what we look like'. Her son Leonard recalls how when the letters arrived at the grandmother's village home, she would solemnly summon the children, 'call us in the room. "Your mother write". And it would be read to us, and she'd tell us what she said'. But it was very difficult for the children to make sense of her news. For example, in one letter she wrote, 'she's actually saying, "It's snowing in England, and it's cold out here". But no one knew, we just couldn't imagine what cold could be ... we didn't have no concept of cold or snow'. Even the photos misfired, because the children could not remember who the people were in them, so much so that Leonard became convinced that one of his uncles was his father, and when he arrived at London airport hugged the wrong man. With the phone, the sound of the voice and the dialogue which it enables, an altogether deeper level of intimate contact becomes possible.

Nowadays there are many more ways of keeping in touch. Cheaper flights have encouraged much more frequent visits to distant kin. Some older women have become regular fliers, visiting children and grandchildren. Russell Peel is in London and his mother, a retired school janitor in Jamaica, who Russell visits there annually, now spends almost half her year in America with her daughters, who 'always fight [over] which one to send a ticket for her to come over'. These are mostly individual visits, but another interesting and apparently growing phenomenon is the transnational family reunion. Jacob Richards, for example, had recently flown out from England to Jamaica for a seaside wedding in which two-thirds of the 80 guests, including the bride and groom themselves, lived overseas. Another family have been developing transatlantic plans for a family history with oral history recording as well as genealogical research — which has already linked their descent to a 1747 slave ship on one side and to Arawak Indians on another — as well as a reunion in Jamaica and a family website on the internet.

Some of the professional families have been experimenting with faster alternatives to the post. 'The younger people are trying email', Verity Houghton commented from Canada. 'Now we're getting to email,' and her brother Arnold remarks optimistically, 'Distances have shrunk big time. You never know!' Audley Rawlings in Jamaica told us that communication with his daughter at school in England 'is left to modern technology. Email and telephone. I'll email her a couple of times a week. [Her mother] speaks to her every day'. Audley is even able to help her with her homework despite the distance between them. 'Well now, she's doing an IT project, where she's setting up a computer system, a computerized system for a movie store, movie rentals, video rentals.... She puts together her draft, she'll type it up and send it to me, and I will edit it. I don't basically change what she's doing, but I might make some grammatical changes, change it to make it make more sense.'

Nevertheless phoning, because it has become so much cheaper, at least for those in Britain and North America, is now the dominant form of communication between family members. Mostly this is technically straightforward, but at least one family has used the conference facility to create a regular weekly transnational chatroom. In Brigette Umber's family the pivotal figure is her father, Hopeton, a New York builder, 'the icon of the family.... He tries to keep the family very close'. They organize a family reunion every five years in Jamaica, hiring one of the biggest hotels in

Montego Bay. More modestly, most Sunday mornings Hopeton gets on the phone.

> He call one family member in Jamaica, and then he'll put that one family member onto the family member in Canada. Then she'll hook that one to the family member in England. Then England will hook that one back up to the family in Brooklyn, and then all of them is on the phone. Sunday morning it's chaotic in my house. It's always been like that, every Sunday, because that's the only time they get to talk.

This is when family business is sorted out. 'The wedding is coming up, it's even more chaotic, because they're trying to figure out how they're going to get from here…. They're all over the place.' But often it is just chatting to share their ordinary life experience.

> Every Sunday morning, the routine is still the same — ackee and saltfish and fried dumpling, and callaloo. Every family member does it. And then they'll call over, "What did you cook?" "Ackee." "Okay, I'll come and I'll have the callaloo." Then they go, "You bringing over the callaloo?" "Yes." "Okay." Then they call the next one, "What did you cook?" "Dumpling." And then it all start all over again! They are chaotic! … My family's insane! They call one another, you're in Brooklyn and they're in Connecticut, all of them get on the phone, and they call…. "Uncle Hopeton, what are your eating?" "Oh, ackee." "What are you doing?" "Nothing." "All right. You going to church?" "Yes, ten o'clock." "Okay, what time is it?" "Oh, around eight."

And so this regular weekly round continues, bringing more and more news of ackee and saltfish and fried dumplings, punctuated — even after just a week's interval — with the refrain, 'Sure thing, a long time I don't hear from you'. In such a family ritual the new and the old, the world of globalized migration and information technology and the country practices of church and cooking in Jamaica, fuse into new forms.

Towards a New Form of Modern Family

To conclude, while migrant transnational families have been around for many centuries, these Jamaican families are essentially a modern form developed in the context of a globalizing economy, sucking in labour and sending out goods and money from one continent to another, and increasingly tightly linked by cheap transport and by modern communication technology. This makes it for the first time possible for ordinary migrant families to maintain active practical and emotional links over immense distances and to sustain exchanges of help. Connected by such transnational families, communities in different continents become mutually dependent on each other.[8]

There are clearly dangers to all families in these developments. The separations brought by migration itself are especially painful when they result in the rupture of parent-child bonds, which subsequently may only be rebuilt with difficulty. There can be dangers especially for young men, whom these families seem less able to support protectively than young women, and also for older men, who may end their lives in a loneliness inconceivable in their earlier years so full of people.

On the other hand, hearing these life stories brings out how transnational Jamaican families have special features, particularly their flexibility in formal terms and pragmatism, which help them to mobilize aid through the kin network in ways which we suggest would be much less likely with white Anglo-American families. These strengths provide some mitigation of the pains of migration. In any case much of their fragmentation through migration is itself an active response to the poor economic situations from which they set out. Raymond Smith concludes that earlier onslaughts on the fragmented mother-centred black family have been 'grossly misplaced.... There is no evidence that poverty is caused by family structure, and a good deal of evidence that kinship ties continue to represent the major ameliorating factor making life bearable among the urban poor.'[9]

How reasonable, however, is it to see these families as providing, not only vital mitigation of economic and social disadvantage, but also a progressive and pioneering 'modern' family form which anticipates aspects of family life which will become much more generally common in the near future? There are in our view five features of Jamaican transnational families which would support such a claim.

The first is their development of a transnational networking which uses the global economy and modern technology both in their search for income and in maintaining practical and emotional contact. Certainly migrations have scattered families around the world for centuries, and letters have sustained some irregular degree of contact since the coming of the nineteenth-century postal service, but it was really only from the late twentieth century that regular intimate contact could be maintained across the oceans, above all through the advent of cheap air flights, the telephone and email. Although in this respect far from unique, Jamaicans have certainly seized this chance and built and sustained their families around it.

A second and much more unusual progressive feature is the scope and influence they have given for generations, and continue to give, to women. We have seen how in many families, even where men are present and significant, particular women became dynamic activating figures around whom the kin system revolves. In several families there is one woman above all responsible for the family's migration strategy, who is described as 'the mother of the family' or even as 'the father of the whole family'. For generations — perhaps back to the slave era, when women were already marketers for family produce — it is women in Jamaican families who have been expected to take the strategic role, to '*tink and plan.*' For the present generation, thinking and planning needs to be international as well as local: it needs 'a very global vision.'

Beyond that there were certainly also other families, where fathers had moved on, in which the men could seem still more marginal to the kin network's direction: as one woman put it, 'phantom figures,' lacking any real masculine role. One can see from these instances why Jamaicans might have coined the proverb, 'Mother blood is stronger than father blood'. And from an anthropologist's perspective, such dynamic kin systems, while definitely neither 'matriarchal' nor 'matrilocal,' can indeed be plausibly seen as based on broader social processes in which 'there was a salience of women,' a form of family which Raymond Smith has termed 'matrifocal'.[10] Be that as it may, Jamaican families provide a rare example in the modern world of families which really do operate on the principle that women have at least as much family power as men.

The third feature is the pragmatic complexity of Jamaican family forms and their ongoing creativity. We have seen how this has facilitated the migration process itself. But it is particularly interesting that some of the second generation are also finding solutions to family problems through seeing these in the perspective of complex extended families rather than moving towards a household-centred view. In other words, thinking in this way is not simply traditional: on the contrary, it is likely to outlast the original migrants. This is partly because there is an urgent need to find better ways of handling family issues in Britain and North America, where stepfamilies are now a highly significant and rapidly growing element in the population as a whole. Complex families with repartnering have been common in Jamaica for centuries. It does look as if the familiarity of parental separation and repartnering has led to a healthily pragmatic approach to it in Jamaican families from which important lessons could be learnt. These interviews suggest that there is much less long-term acrimony between ex-partners and rarely struggles over the possession of children, as well as much more readiness of kin, immediate or more distant, to step in to help 'single mothers' or 'single fathers' with child-rearing. There are, of course, a few bitter experiences of suffering under unfair and harsh substitute parents among the life stories which we have recorded. But these are the exception, and we certainly more often heard more stories of those who were caring and inspiring.

A fourth forward-looking quality of Jamaican families is their inter-racialism. Mixed race partnerships between black Caribbeans and whites are of increasing importance both in Britain and in Canada. While mixed marriages of many kinds have been growing increasingly frequent in western countries,[11] they draw on longer traditions in Jamaica, where although racist attitudes have also been common for centuries, so have mixed race unions. Now these contemporary Jamaican families can often be both transnational and interracial; and they do seem to have an openness of attitude which helps them to accept kin from other ethnic groups. For example, Nelson Pinnock was quite happy that one of his daughters has a white Canadian boyfriend, and explains with some pride, 'I have four uncles married to four different nation women. One married to a Chinese, one married to a white — he died in England, one married to a black, and the other married to a Jamaican Indian.' In some instances this is taken still further, to become a positive family ethic encouraging interracial social relationships. Thus Isabelle Woods recalls how in her London childhood, 'my grandmother, she always used to say, "You mix. You always have to work a bit harder, but mix"'. These families are especially well-functioning models for the multicultural cities of the new globalized economy.

A final forward-looking aspect of these families is in their modifying of national consciousness. Frequently one can sense the evolution of a sense of identity which cuts across national boundaries, and could be seen as pointing in a direction which our current conflict-ridden world might gain by following. And with a few of our migrants, these new identities transcend locally based double identities to form 'global visions', humanist and cosmopolitan, harbingers perhaps of world citizenship. Most of our Jamaicans share a dream of return to Jamaica, and many of them realize it. A few have a more elusive dream, of a wider world in which they and others can move freely, always at home, as if world citizens.

Whether dreamers or workers or both, for us these Jamaicans exemplify, as we heard Jesse Jackson put it recently to a London audience, 'the power of a creative minority sharing history and sharing experiences'. In making their own histories in North America, in Britain, in Jamaica itself, these families, linking hands across the Atlantic, have also helped to strengthen and enrich each of the societies in which they live today.

Notes

Jamaican Transnational Families

1. Harry Goulbourne, 'Questions of Theory, Definition, Purpose', in *Caribbean Transnational Experience* (London: Pluto Press, 2002), chapter 1.
2. Jean Besson, *Martha Brae's Two Histories: European Expansion and Caribbean Culture-Building in Jamaica* (Chapel Hill: University of North Carolina Press, Chapel Hill, 2002).
3. Jean Besson and Janet Momsen, *Land and Development in the Caribbean* (London: Macmillan, 1987), 15.
4. Gill Gorell Barnes, Paul Thompson, Gwyn Daniel and Natasha Burchardt, *Growing Up in Stepfamilies* (Oxford: Oxford University Press, 1997).
5. Christine Barrow, *Family in the Caribbean: Themes and Perspectives* (Kingston and Oxford: Ian Randle Publishers and James Currey, 1996), 9–17, 61.
6. Erna Brodber, *Abandonment of Children in Jamaica* (Kingston: Institute of Social and Economic Research, University of West Indies, 1974), 49. Surprisingly, in one of the best recent books on Caribbean families from a social work perspective, these comments by Brodber are still cited approvingly: Jaipaul L. Roopnarine and Janet Brown, *Caribbean Families: Diversity Among Ethnic Groups* (Greenwich, Connecticut: Ablex, 1997), 7.
7. Stephen Davis, *Bob Marley: Conquering Lion of Reggae* (London: Plexus, 1984).

Contexts: Past to Present

1. The estimate of one million Jamaicans living abroad is based on 550,000 Jamaican-born in the United States (to whom could be added their US-born descendants), 200,000 Jamaicans and their families in Canada, over 300,000 Jamaicans and their families in Britain, plus an unknown number of earlier migrants and their families in Panama and other Caribbean countries (see note

16 and 19). The Canadian and British figures are based on ethnic self-identification in the census.

2. Barry W. Higman, *Slave Population and Economy in Jamaica, 1807–1834* (Cambridge: Cambridge University Press, 1976), 140.

3. Roger Abrahams and John F. Szwed, *After Africa: Extracts from British Travel Accounts* (New Haven: Yale University Press, 1983), 163, 289, 340.

4. Douglas Hall, ed., *In Miserable Slavery: Thomas Thistlewood in Jamaica, 1750-86* (Kingston: The University of West Indies Press, 1999), 158–9.

5. James Boswell, *The Life of Samuel Johnson* (London 1791; abridged edition, London: Penguin Books, 1979).

6. Paul Gilroy, *The Black Atlantic: Modernity and Double Consciousness* (London: Verso, 1993).

7. Michael G. Smith, *West Indian Family Structure* (Seattle: University of Washington Press, 1962); Mervyn Alleyne, *Roots of Jamaican Culture* (London: Pluto, 1988); Orlando Patterson, 'Persistence, Continuity and Change in the Jamaican Working Class Family', *Journal of Family History* 7 (1982): 135–61; Raymond Smith, *Kinship and Class in the West Indies: A Genealogical Study of Jamaica and Guyana* (Cambridge: Cambridge University Press, 1988).

8. James Walvin, *Black and White: the Negro and English Society 1555–1945* (London: Allen Lane, 1973); Kenneth Little, *Negroes in Britain: A Study of Race Relations in English Society* (London: Kegan Paul, 1948) on Cardiff; Michael Banton, *The Coloured Quarter* (London: Jonathan Cape, 1955) on Stepney, London.

9. Irma Watkins-Owens, *Blood Relations: Caribbean Immigrants and the Harlem Community, 1900-30* (Bloomington: Indiana University Press, 1996).

10. Fernando Henriques, *Family and Colour in Jamaica* (London: Eyre and Spottiswoode, 1953).

11. Rex Nettleford, ed., *Jamaica in Independence* (London: James Currey, 1989); Michael Manley, *Jamaica: Struggle in the Periphery* (London: Writers and Readers Co-operative, 1982); Leonard E. Barrett, Senr. *The Rastafarians: Sounds of Cultural Dissonance* (revised edition, Boston: Beacon Press, 1988).

12. Heather Horst and Daniel Miller, 'From Kinship to Link-up: Cell Phones and Social Networking in Jamaica', *Current Anthropology* (December 2005).

13. According to the 1991 Census, 57 per cent of West Indians in Britain had arrived between 1955 and 1964. On the perceptions of migrants to Britain and North America as part of migration dynamics, see Elizabeth Thomas-Hope, *Explanation in Caribbean Migration: Perception and the Image: Jamaica, Barbados, St Vincent* (London: Macmillan Caribbean, 1992).

14. Sam Selvon, *The Lonely Londoners* (London: Allan Wingate, 1956); for the atmosphere from the mid-1950s, also see Andrea Levy's recent novel *Small Island* (London: Review, 2004).

15. Mike Phillips and Trevor Phillips, *Windrush: The Irresistible Rise of Multi-Racial Britain* (London: HarperCollins, 1998); Dilip Hiro, *Black British, White British*

(London: Eyre and Spottiswoode, 1971); Ceri Peach, *West Indian Migration to Britain: A Social Geography* (London: Oxford University Press, 1968); Ceri Peach, 'Black-Caribbeans: Class, Gender and Geography', in *Ethnicity in the 1991 Census*, ed. Ceri Peach (London: HMSO, 1996), vol. 2, 25–43.

16. This figure is based on the 565,000 who identified as Black Caribbean in the 2001 Census, plus a small allowance for descendants of West Indians who identified themselves as Black Other (including Black British) or Mixed (National Statistics Online).

17. Richard Berthoud, *Family Formation in Multi-Cultural Britain: Three Patterns of Diversity* (Colchester: Institute of Social and Economic Research, University of Essex, 2000).

18. In comparison with other migrant groups in economic terms, Caribbean families in Britain have a middle profile, behind whites, Indians and Chinese, but well ahead of Pakistanis and Bangladeshis. Richard Berthoud, *The Incomes of Ethnic Minorities* (Colchester: Institute for Social and Economic Research, Report 98–1, 1998); and Richard Berthoud, 'Ethnic diversity and inequality', *ISER Newsletter* (June 2002): 3. A very recent social mobility study by Lucinda Platt has found that 45 per cent Caribbeans from working-class backgrounds have professional or managerial jobs, slightly more than the 43 per cent of those from white non-immigrant working class families (Joseph Rowntree Foundation website). According to the 2001 Census, unemployment rates were recorded as follows: white men, 5 per cent, women 4 per cent; Black Caribbean men 14 per cent, women 8 per cent; Bangladeshi men, 20 per cent, women 24 per cent. Black Caribbean women have an economic activity rate almost level with white women, which is a major reason for the relative prosperity of their households (National Statistics Online).

19. For the United States, the 2000 Census reported altogether 553,000 Jamaican-born in the whole country. For a full total, their children would need to be added, and a further addition made for illegal immigrants not reported in the Census: with these counted, one recent estimate of the New York Caribbean community was a total of one million (Philip Kasinitz, *Caribbean New York: Black Immigrants and the Politics of Race* (Ithaca: Cornell University Press, 1992), 4. For the Toronto Metropolitan Area, the 2001 Canadian Census reported 150,000 Jamaicans and their children, of whom a third were born in Canada.

20. For the United States, the 2000 Census reported unemployment rates as: whites 3.0 per cent, Jamaicans 5.1 per cent (almost identical for men and women), Hispanic or Latino 5.5 per cent, African American 6.9 per cent. The median annual income of Jamaican households was $40,000, a little below the white median of $44,000, but well ahead of Hispanic households with $33,000 and Black Americans with $30,000. As in Britain, Jamaicans had a high economic activity rate, Jamaican women 69 per cent in the workforce compared with 66 per cent white women (US Census Bureau, *Census 2000 Special Tabulations*). According to the Canadian 1996 Census, Jamaican economic activity was

similarly high in Toronto, but rates of unemployment were generally higher: 9 per cent for Canadian-born whites, 20 per cent for Jamaicans, only exceeded by some African ethnic groups. Median household incomes for Canadian families are Cdn$57,000, for Jamaicans $28,000, one of the poorest groups, partly because 62 per cent of households with children are headed by single mothers (Michael Ormstein, *Ethno-Racial Inequality in the City of Toronto: An Analysis of the 1996 Census* (Toronto: City of Toronto, Department of Community and Neighbourhood Services, 2000), 54–55, 104–6.

21. Edith Clarke, *My Mother Who Fathered Me: A Study of the Family in Three Selected Communities in Jamaica* (London: Allen and Unwin, 1957; third edition, Kingston: University of West Indies Press, 1999); Raymond T. Smith, *Kinship and Class in the West Indies: A Genealogical Study of Jamaica and Guyana* (Cambridge: Cambridge University Press, 1988); Jean Besson, *Martha Brae's Two Histories: European Expansion and Caribbean Culture-Building in Jamaica* (Chapel Hill: University of North Carolina Press, 2002); Christine Barrow, *Family in the Caribbean: Themes and Perspectives* (Kingston and Oxford: Ian Randle Publishers and James Currey, 1996); Verene Shepherd, *Women in Caribbean History* (Kingston: Ian Randle Publishers, 1999); Christine Barrow, ed., *Caribbean Portraits: Essays on Gender Ideologies and Identities* (Kingston: Ian Randle, 1998); and Barry Chevannes, *Leaning to Be a Man: Culture, Socialization and Gender Identity in Five Caribbean Communities* (Kingston: The University of West Indies Press, 2001). Two other interesting earlier studies are Judith Blake, *Family Structure in Jamaica, the Social Context of Reproduction* (New York: Free Press, 1961); Madeline Kerr, *Personality and Conflict in Jamaica* (Liverpool: Liverpool University Press, 1952).

22. Sheila Patterson, *Dark Strangers: A Sociological Study of the Absorption of a Recent West Indian Migrant Group in Brixton, South London* (London: Tavistock, 1963); Nancy Foner, *Jamaica Farewell: Jamaican Migrants in London* (London: Routledge and Kegan Paul, 1979); Sandra Wallman, *Eight London Households* (London: Tavistock, 1984); Ken Pryce, *Endless Pressure: A Study of West Indian Life-Styles in Bristol* (Harmondsworth: Penguin, 1979); Harry Goulbourne and Mary Chamberlain, eds., *Caribbean Families in Britain and the Trans-Atlantic World* (London: Macmillan Caribbean, 2001). Clifford Hill, *How Colour Prejudiced is Britain?* (London: Victor Gollancz, 1965) is an unusual early study with a section on mixed marriages. More generally with other migrants, Colin Holmes, *John Bull's Island: Immigration and British Society, 1871–1971* (London: Macmillan, 1988); and on housing, race and class, John Rex and Robert Moore, *Race, Community and Conflict: A Study of Sparkbrook* (London: Oxford University Press, 1967).

23. E. Franklin Frazier, *The Negro Family in the United States* (Chicago: University of Chicago Press, 1939); Herbert G. Gutman, *The Black Family in Slavery and Freedom, 1750-1925* (Oxford: Blackwell, 1976); Daniel Moynihan, *The Negro Family: The Case for National Action* (Washington: Department of Labor, 1965).

24. Frances Henry, *The Caribbean Diaspora in Toronto: Learning to Live with Racism* (Toronto: University of Toronto Press, 1994); Nancy Foner, *From Ellis Island to JFK: New York's Two Great Waves of Immigration* (New Haven: Yale University Press, 2000); Constance R. Sutton and Elsa M. Chaney, eds., *Caribbean Life in New York City: Sociocultural Dimensions* (New York: Center for Migration Studies of New York, 1987); Mary C. Waters, *Black Identities: West Indian Immigrant Dreams and American Realities* (Cambridge, MA: Harvard University Press, 1999). Also important are Philip Kasinitz, *Caribbean New York: Black Immigrants and the Politics of Race* (Ithaca: Cornell University Press, 1992); Milton Vickerman, *Crosscurrents: West Indian Immigrants and Race* (New York: Oxford University Press, 1999); and Paule Marshall's novel, *Brown Girl, Brownstones* (New York: Feminist Press, 1959). Among parallel studies, Christine Ho, *Saltwater Trinnies: African-Trinidadian Immigrant Networks and Non-Assimilation in Los Angeles* (New York: AMS Press, 1991); and Peggy Levitt, *The Transnational Villagers* (Berkeley: University of California Press, 2001).

25. Tamara Hareven, *Family Time and Industrial Time: The Relationship Between the Family and Work in a New England Industrial Community* (Cambridge: Cambridge University Press, 1982), 116–9; Sherri Grasmuck and Patricia R. Pessar, *Between Two Islands: Dominican International Migration* (Berkeley: University of California Press, 1991); Pierrette Hondagneu and Ernestine Avila, "'I'm here but there": The Meanings of Transnational Motherhood', *Gender and Society* 11 (1997): 548–71; Barbara Ehrenreich and Arlie Hochschild, *Global Women: Nannies, Maids, and Sex Workers in the New Economy* (New York: Metropolitan Books, 2003); Ronald Keldon, ed., *Reluctant Exiles? Migration from Hong Kong and the New Overseas Chinese* (Hong Kong: Hong Kong University Press, 1994); Pheng Chea and Bruce Robbins, eds., *Cosmopolitans: Thinking and Feeling Beyond the Nation* (Minneapolis: University of Minnesota Press, 1998); Pierrette Hondagneu-Sotelo, *Gendered Transitions: Mexican Experiences of Immigration* (Berkeley: University of California Press, 1994); Nina Glick Schiller, 'From Immigrant to Transmigrant: Theorizing Transnational Migrants', *Anthropological Quarterly* 61, no. 1 (1995): 48–63; Linda Basch, Nina Glick Schiller and Cristina Blanc Szanton, eds., *Towards a Transnational Perspective on Migration: Race, Class, Ethnicity and Nationalism Reconsidered* (Basel: Gordon and Breach, 1994), especially 164–72; Edward Said, *Out of Place: A Memoir* (London: Granta, 1999). Some well-established migration researchers have now also adopted the new transnational perspectives: for example, Alejandro Portes, 'Globalization from Below: The Rise of Transnational Communities', in *The Ends of Globalization: Bringing Society Back In*, eds. Don Kalb et al. (Lanham, Maryland: Rowman and Littlefield, 2000), 253–70.

26. Karen Fog Olwig, *Global Culture, Island Identity: Continuity and Change in the Afro-Caribbean Community of Nevis* (Chur: Harwood Academic, 1993); Deborah Bryceson and Ulla Vuorela, *The Transnational Family: New European Frontiers and Global Networks* (Oxford: Berg, 2002); and for another change of perspective

by well-established researchers, Sallie Westwood and Annie Phizacklea, *Transnationalism and the Politics of Belonging* (London: Routledge, 2000). Gilroy, *The Black Atlantic*; Robin Cohen, *Global Diasporas* (London: UCL Press, 1997). Also on hybrid cultures, Les Back, *New Ethnicities and Urban Culture: Racisms and Multiculture in Young Lives* (London: UCL Press, 1996); Stuart Hall, 'New Ethnicities', in *'Race', Culture and Difference*, eds. James Donald and Ali Rattansi (London: Sage, 1992), 252–59.

27. Harry Goulbourne, 'The Transnational Character of Caribbean Kinship in Britain', in *Changing Britain: Families and Households in the 1990s*, ed. Susan McRae (Oxford: Oxford University Press, 1999), 176–97; also in Harry Goulbourne, *Caribbean Transnational Experience* (London: Pluto Press, 2002), 160–183; Harry Goulbourne and Mary Chamberlain, eds., *Caribbean Families in Britain and the Trans-Atlantic World* (London: Macmillan Caribbean, 2001). The project's oral history/life story interviews have been archived through the Data Archive as a resource for future researchers at the British Library Sound Archive. We were greatly helped by reading some of these transcribed interviews at the start of our own research.

28. Sidney Mintz, *Worker in the Cane: A Puerto Rican Life History* (New Haven: Yale University Press, 1960); Oscar Lewis, *La Vida: A Puerto Rican Family in the Culture of Poverty in San Juan and New York* (London: Secker and Warburg, 1967) — which is an unrealized transnational family study; Erna Brodber, *Myal* (London: New Beacon, 1988). In the early 1970s Brodber carried out a major oral history project, interviewing Jamaican men and women born around 1900, which would have made a fascinating comparison with our own later generations, but 30 years later when we were interpreting our own project the results had not yet been published. Fortunately Brodber has very recently published two valuable books from her original project: *The Second Generation of Freemen in Jamaica, 1907–1944* (Gainesville: University Press of Florida, 2004); *Standing Tall: Affirmations of the Jamaican Male* (Kingston: Sir Arthur Lewis Institute for Social and Economic Studies, 2003).

29. Mary Chamberlain, 'Family and Identity: Barbadian Migrants to Britain', in *Migration and Identity*, eds. Rina Benmayor and Andor Skotnes (Oxford: Oxford University Press, 1994), 119–36; Mary Chamberlain, *Narratives of Exile and Return* (London: Macmillan Caribbean, 1997); Mary Chamberlain, 'The Family as Model and Metaphor in Caribbean Migration to Britain', *Journal of Ethnic and Migration Studies* 25, no. 2 (1999): 251–66.

30. Paul Thompson, *The Voice of the Past* (Oxford: Oxford University Press, 1978; third edition 2000); Daniel Bertaux and Paul Thompson. eds., *Between Generations: Family Models, Myths and Memories* (Oxford: Oxford University Press, 1993); Daniel Bertaux and Paul Thompson, *Pathways to Social Class* (Oxford: Clarendon Press, 1997); Gill Gorell Barnes, Paul Thompson, Gwyn Daniel and Natasha Burchardt, *Growing Up in Stepfamilies* (Oxford: Oxford University Press, 1998).

31. 'Oral History and Black History', 1975–78, funded by the Nuffield Foundation: the interviews are now in the British Library Sound Archive (C707).
32. Thompson, *Voice of the Past*; Raphael Samuel and Paul Thompson, eds., *The Myths We Live By* (London: Routledge, 1990); Alessandro Portelli, *The Death of Luigi Trastulli and Other Stories* (Albany: State University of New York Press, 1991); Elizabeth Tonkin, *Narrating Our Pasts: the Social Construction of Oral History* (Cambridge: Cambridge University Press, 1992); Alastair Thomson, *Anzac Memories: Living with the Legend* (Oxford: Oxford University Press, 1994).

Jamaica: Recapturing Family Memories

1. Anancy stories are about a spider who gets his way through talk, craftiness and deviousness (for example, Louise Bennett, *Anancy and Miss Lou* (Kingston: Sangsters, 1979)). There are parallel folktales in Brazil. They originate from West African stories about Anansi Krokoko, the great spider, the symbol of wisdom in Ashanti.
2. Jean Besson, *Martha Brae's Two Histories: European Expansion and Caribbean Culture-Building in Jamaica* (Chapel Hill: University of North Carolina Press, 2002).
3. Fernando Henriques, *Family and Colour in Jamaica* (London: Eyre and Spottiswoode, 1953), 47; David Lowenthal, *West Indian Societies* (Oxford: Oxford University Press, 1972), 93–100.
4. Jack Alexander, 'Love, Race, Slavery, and Sexuality in Jamaican Images of the Family', in *Kinship Ideology and Practice in North America*, ed. Raymond Smith (Chapel Hill, NC: University of North Carolina Press, 1984), 147–80.
5. Louise Bennett, *Jamaica Labrish* (Kingston: Sangster's, 1966), 214–15.
6. SISTREN with Honor Ford Smith, ed., *Lionheart Gal: Life Stories of Jamaican Women* (London: Women's Press, 1986), 68, cf. a denial of slave ancestry, 179; Werner Zips, *Black Rebels: African Caribbean Freedom Fighters in Jamaica* (Princeton, NJ and Kingston: Marcus Wiener and Ian Randle Publishers, 1999).
7. Catherine Hall, *White, Male and Middle Class: Explorations in Feminism and History* (London: Polity Press, 1992), 233, 'Missionary stories'.
8. Christine Barrow, *Family in the Caribbean: Themes and Perspectives* (Kingston: Ian Randle, 1996), 397–429 on child socialization.
9. Barrow, *Family in the Caribbean*, 171–75, 'male marginality revisited'.

Staying or Leaving

1. Mary Chamberlain, *Narratives of Exile and Return* (London: Warwick Caribbean Studies, 1997), 91–112. Similar gender differences in migration narratives had been earlier suggested by Isabelle Bertaux-Wiame in her work on Breton migrants

to Paris: 'The life history approach to the study of internal migration', *Oral History* 7, no. 1 (1979): 26–32. For a fuller discussion of this theme, Elaine Bauer and Paul Thompson, '"She's always the person with a very global vision", the gender dynamics of migration, narrative interpretation and the case of Jamaican transnational families', *Gender and History* 16, no. 2 (2004): 334–75. An outstanding recent study of the role of gender in migration is Pierrette Hondagneu-Sotelo, *Gendered Transitions: Mexican Experiences of Immigration* (Berkeley: University of California Press, 1994).

2.   Cf. Hilary Beckles, *Natural Rebels: A Social History of Enslaved Black Women in Barbados* (London: Zed Books, 1989); Barbara Bush, *Slave Women in Caribbean Society* (London: James Currey, 1990); Sidney Mintz, *Caribbean Transformations* (Chicago: Aldine, 1974), chapters 7–8 on Jamaican markets past and present.

3.   Douglas Hall, ed., *In Miserable Slavery: Thomas Thistlewood in Jamaica, 1750–86* (London: Macmillan, 1989), 79.

4.   For an overview, Verene Shepherd, *Women in Caribbean History* (Kingston: Ian Randle Publishers, 1999).

5.   Nancy Foner, 'Male and Female: Jamaican Migrants in London', *Anthropological Quarterly* 49, no. 1 (1976): 28–35.

6.   SISTREN with Honor Ford Smith, ed., *Lionheart Girl: Life Stories of Jamaican Women* (London: Women's Press, 1986), 151.

7.   Henrietta De Veer, 'Sex Roles and Social Stratification in a Rapidly Growing Area: May Pen, Jamaica' (PhD dissertation, Chicago University 1979), 186–7.

Jamaicans in their New World

1.   Mary C. Waters, *Black Identities: West Indian Immigrant Dreams and American Realities.* (Cambridge, MA: Harvard University Press, 1999), 65, 84–7; Milton Vickerman, *Crosscurrents: West Indian Immigrants and Race* (New York: Oxford University Press, 1999), 170–1.

2.   Stephen Small, *Racialised Barriers: The Black Experience in the United States and England in the 1980s* (London: Routledge, 1994); Frances Henry, *The Caribbean Diaspora in Toronto: Learning to Live with Racism* (Toronto: University of Toronto Press, 1994).

3.   Vickerman, *Crosscurrents*, 92.

4.   This has also been shown with undocumented Mexican women migrants to Los Angeles (Rita James Simon and Margo Corona DeLey, 'Undocumented Mexican Women: Their Work and Personal Experiences', in *International Migration: The Female Experience*, eds. Rita James Simon and Caroline B. Brettell (Totowa, NJ: Rowman and Allanheld, 1986), 118–9, 124–5.

5.   Cf. Sheila Patterson, *Dark Strangers: A Sociological Study of the Absorption of a Recent West Indian Migrant Group in Brixton, South London* (London: Tavistock, 1963), 226–33.

6. Henry, *Caribbean Diaspora in Toronto*, 28.

7. Waters, *Black Identities*, 246; Constance R. Sutton and Elsa M. Chaney, eds., *Caribbean Life in New York City: Sociocultural Dimensions* (New York: Center for Migration Studies of New York, 1987), 79–81.

8. Cf. Patterson, *Dark Strangers*, 282–5.

9. Sam Selvon, *The Lonely Londoners* (London: Alan Wingate, 1956).

10. Richard Berthoud, *The Incomes of Ethnic Minorities* (Colchester: Institute for Social and Economic Research, University of Essex, Report 98-1, 1998), table 22.

11. Stuart Hall, 'New Ethnicities', in *'Race', Culture and Differences*, eds. James Donald and Ali Rattansi (London: Sage, 1992), 252–9; Paul Gilroy, *The Black Atlantic: Modernity and Double Consciousness* (London: Verso, 1993).

12. Alejandro Portes and Ruben G. Rumbaut, *Legacies: The Story of the Immigrant Second Generation* (Berkeley: University of California Press and Russell Sage Foundation, 2001), 6, 39, 50–1, 208.

Women and Men

1. On gender in the Caribbean, especially Christine Barrow, *Caribbean Portraits: Essays on Gender Ideologies and Identities* (Kingston: Ian Randle Publishers, 1998); Christine Barrow, *Family in the Caribbean: Themes and Perspectives* (Kingston and Oxford: Ian Randle Publishers and James Currey, 1996), 69–79, 170–75; and Olive Senior, *Working Miracles: Women's Lives in the English-Speaking Caribbean* (London: James Currey, 1991). On masculinity, Barry Chevannes, *Learning to Be a Man: Culture, Socialization and Gender Identity in Five Caribbean Communities* (Kingston: The University of West Indies Press, 2001). The classic earlier discussion is Edith Clarke, *My Mother Who Fathered Me* (London: Allen and Unwin, 1957; 3rd edition, Kingston: The University of West Indies Press, 1999). On gender roles after migration, Nancy Foner, *Jamaica Farewell: Jamaican Migrants in London* (London: Routledge and Kegan Paul, 1979), 55–85, 'Women and men'.

2. See Chevannes, *Learning to be a Man*, 43, 136–40, 183–5, 225. However, in contrast to his findings, as we saw earlier in chapter three, among the families we recorded the mother was most often the disciplinarian.

3. This attitude is also reported by Chevannes, *Learning to be a Man*, 39, 49–50, 158–9; and by Erna Brodber, *A Study of Yards in the City of Kingston* (Kingston: Institute of Social and Economic Research, University of the West Indies, 1975), 38.

4. The United States Census figures for Jamaicans do not show such striking gender differences. However, among American blacks, twice as many girls as boys go on to higher education (Gerald Graff, *Clueless in Academe: How Schooling Obscures the Life of the Mind* (New Haven: Yale University Press, 2003)). On work and unemployment among ethnic groups in Britain, Anne Green, 'Patterns of Ethnic

Minority Employment in the Context of Industrial and Occupational Growth and Decline', in *Ethnicity in the 1991 Census*, ed. Valerie Karn, vol. 4, (London: Office for National Statistics, 1997), 67–90: Table 4.5 shows 45 per cent of white men in non-manual occupations compared with 35 per cent of black men, but by contrast black women (with 61 per cent) just ahead of white women (with 59 per cent). Black men were almost twice as likely as black women to be unemployed: see chapter two, note 18. On education, Robert M. Blackburn, Angela Dale and Jennifer Jarman, 'Ethnic Differences in Attainment in Education, Occupation and Life-Style', *Ethnicity in the 1991 Census*, ed. Karn, vol 4, 242–64. Table 12.2 shows that of black Caribbeans born abroad, 9 per cent of men and 19 per cent of women had higher education qualifications, and of black Caribbeans born in Britain 8 per cent of men and 11 per cent of women. This compares with 19 per cent of white men and 16 per cent of white women. In other words, the gender gap was greater before migration from the Caribbean, and women migrants came with higher qualifications than white women in Britain, but their daughters have not maintained this lead. At the GCSE level the 2001 Census found Indian and white girls well in the lead, black girls in the middle level just ahead of white boys, with black boys trailing, although still well ahead of Pakistani and Bangladeshi boys (National Statistics Online).

5. A small recent study of 124 young Jamaican males found that the presence or absence of the father had no significant impact on whether or not they were delinquent: Claudette Crawford-Brown cited in Jaipaul L. Roopnarine and Janet Brown, *Caribbean Families: Diversity Among Ethnic Groups* (Greenwich, Connecticut: Ablex, 1997), 215.

6. Edith Clarke describes this traditional masculinity in *My Mother Who Fathered Me* (London: Allen and Unwin, 1957), for example, 96. For more recent interpretations, Christine Barrow, 'Masculinity and Family', in *Family in the Caribbean*, ed. Barrow, 354–7; Peter J. Wilson, 'Reputation and Respectability: A Suggestion for Caribbean Ethnology', *Man* 4 (1969): 70–84; and the response of Jean Besson, 'Reputation and Respectability Reconsidered: A New Perspective on Afro-Caribbean Peasant Women', in *Women and Change in the Caribbean*, ed. Janet Momsen (Kingston: Ian Randle Publishers, 1993).

7. Janet Brown, Arthur Newland, Patricia Anderson, and Barry Chevannes, 'Caribbean Fatherhood: Under-researched, Misunderstood', in *Caribbean Families*, eds. Roopnarine and Brown, 85–114.

Working: Up or Down

1. In Britain in 1991, 35 per cent of black men and 61 per cent of black women were in non-manual jobs, compared with 45 per cent of white men and 59 per cent of white women: Anne Green, 'Patterns of ethnic minority employment in the context of industrial and occupational growth and decline', in *Ethnicity in*

the 1991 Census, ed. Valerie Karn, vol. 4 (London: Office for National Statistics, 1997), 67–90, Table 4.5. In the United States 53 per cent of Jamaicans were recorded working in professional, managerial, sales and office occupations, compared with 62 per cent of whites and 41 per cent of Latinos (US Census Bureau, *Census 2000 Special Tabulations*, online).

2. Leonore Davidoff, *Worlds Between: Historical Perspectives on Gender and Class* (Cambridge: Polity Press, 1995), 18–40, 'Mastered for life'; Barbara Ehrenreich and Arlie Hochschild, *Global Women: Nannies, Maids, and Sex Workers in the New Economy* (New York: Metropolitan Books, 2003).

3. For the long-standing importance of housing to West Indian migrants, Sheila Patterson, *Dark Strangers: A Sociological Study of the Absorption of a Recent West Indian Migrant Group in Brixton, South London* (London: Tavistock, 1963), 161–62, 174; Nancy Foner, *Jamaica Farewell: Jamaican Migrants in London* (London: Routledge and Kegan Paul, 1979), 138–39; Peter Ratcliffe, '"Race", Ethnicity and Housing Differentials in Britain', in *Ethnicity in the 1991 Census*, ed. Karn, 130–46. In 1991 36 per cent of black Caribbean households in Britain were tenants in local authority housing, 48 per cent were owner-occupiers (compared with 21 per cent and 67 per cent white households respectively). This put them midway in the range of immigrant groups. But strikingly, those black Caribbean households most financially able to buy, that is couples without dependent children, were as likely to be homeowners as white couples in the same position. The importance of housing is also the theme of two novels, the first set in London, Samuel Selvon, *The Housing Lark* (London: MacGibbon and Kee, 1955), the second in Trinidad, V.S. Naipaul, *A House for Mr Biswas* (London: André Deutsch, 1961).

Learning and Faith

1. On popular educational ambition and change in Jamaica after 1946, see Nancy Foner, *Status and Power in Rural Jamaica* (New York: Teachers College Press, 1973). In the 1990s over 90 per cent of Jamaican children were attending basic schools or other pre-school education, a high proportion by world standards, but the quality of Jamaican education at this and at higher levels was criticized as too much based on lecturing, with not enough discussion and problem-solving by the children: Hyancinth Evans and Rose Davies, 'Overview Issues in Childhood Socialisation in the Caribbean', in *Caribbean Families: Diversity Among Ethnic Groups*, eds. Jaipaul L. Roopnarine and Janet Brown, (Greenwich, Connecticut: Ablex, 1997), 1–24. The continuing commitment to education among migrants is most evident in the United States, where 45 per cent of Jamaicans have some college education (compared with 54 per cent of whites and 30 per cent of Hispanics) (US Census Bureau, *Census 2000 Special Tabulations*).

2. On the educational experiences of migrants in Britain, Raymond Giles, *The West Indian Experience in British Schools* (London: Heineman, 1977); V.K. Edwards, *The West Indian Language Issue in British Schools* (London: Routledge and Kegan Paul, 1979); Mairtin Mac an Ghaill, *Young, Gifted and Black: Student–Teacher Relations in the Schooling of Black Youth* (Milton Keynes: Open University Press, 1988). In North America, Frances Henry, *The Caribbean Diaspora in Toronto* (Toronto: University of Toronto Press, 1994), chapter 6; Mary C. Waters, *Black Identities: West Indian Immigrant Dreams and America Realities* (Cambridge, MA: Harvard University Press, 1999), chapter 7.

3. One of the most vivid accounts of recent religious practice in Jamaica is Diane J. Austin-Broos, *Jamaica Genesis: Religion and the Politics of Moral Orders* (Chicago: University of Chicago Press, 1997); also Jean Besson, 'The Baptist Church, Revival Ideology, and Rastafarian Movement', in *Martha Brae's Two Histories: European Expansion and Caribbean Culture-Building in Jamaica* (Chapel Hill: University of North Carolina Press, 2002), 239–76.

4. Leonard E. Barrett, *The Rastafarians: Sounds of Cultural Dissonance* (Boston: Beacon Press, 1988); Barry Chevannes ed., *Rastafari and Other African-Caribbean World Views* (London: Macmillan, 1995).

5. 'You only give away kittens.'

The Dream of Return

1. Selvin Green, see chapter four, 'Jamaica: Communities in the Land'.

2. Nancy Foner in the 1970s found just over half of London Jamaicans hoped eventually to return home: *Jamaica Farewell* (London: Routledge and Kegan Paul, 1979), 210–13, 234–36.

3. Harry Goulbourne, 'Returning "Home" from the "Mother Country" in the 1990s', in *Caribbean Transnational Experience* (London: Pluto Press, 2002), 184–205; Elizabeth Thomas-Hope, 'Transients and Settlers: Varieties of Caribbean Migrants and the Socio-economic Implications of Their Return', *Interrnational Migration* 24 (1986): 559–70.

Living with Family Complexities

1. As also documented by Raymond T. Smith, *Kinship and Class in the West Indies: A Genealogical Study of Jamaica and Guyana* (Cambridge: Cambridge University Press, 1988), 58–60. The complexities brought by sibling relationships have been given little attention by social researchers: one other rare exception is Mary Chamberlain, 'Brothers and Sisters, Uncles and Aunts: A Lateral Perspective on Caribbean Families', in *The New Family*, eds. Elizabeth Silva and Carol Smart (London: Sage, 1999), 129–42.

2. C.f. Smith, *Kinship and Class*, 45.
3. Boastful.
4. See chapter seven.
5. Esther Goody, *Parenthood and Social Reproduction: Fostering and Occupational Roles in West Africa* (Cambridge: Cambridge University Press, 1982).
6. Christine Barrow, *Family in the Caribbean: Themes and Perspectives* (Kingston and Oxford: Ian Randle Publishers and James Currey, 1996), 61.
7. Sheila Patterson, *Dark Strangers* (London: Tavistock, 1963), 298.
8. For a vivid account of this mutual exchange between a village in the Dominican Republic and a neighbourhood in Boston, Peggy Levitt, *The Transnational Villagers* (Berkeley: University of California Press, 2001).
9. Smith, *Kinship and Class*, 183.
10. Smith, *Kinship and Class*, 7–8.
11. Rosemary Bregar and Rosanna Hill, *Cross-Cultural Marriage: Identity and Choice* (New York: Berg, 1998); Yasmin Alibhai-Brown and Anne Montague, *The Colour of Love: Mixed Race Relationships* (London: Virago, 1992).

Interviewees for *Jamaican Hands*: Birth and Migration Decades

Decade of birth:

1910s   David McNeep (b. J; to UK 50s)

1920s   Don Bartley (b. J; to US 40s, UK 50s)
Josephine Buxton (b. J; to UK 60s)
Len Chuckens 1927(b. J; to US 40s, UK 50s)
Bill Fox (b. J)
Anna Gladstone (b. J; to UK 40s, 50s, 70s, returning to J)
Elisha Grant (b. J)
Edley Keat (b. J)
Marisa Keat (b. J)
Rose Lyle (b. J; to UK 50s)
Lloyd Porto (b. J)
Tamara Porto (b. J)
Rufus Rawlings (b. J; to UK 40s, J 70s, UK 90s)
Jack Rawlings (b. J)
Marcia Trelissick (b. J; to UK 60s)

1930s   Chris Bartley (b. J; to US 40s, UK 50s)
Jack Constable (b. J; to UK 50s)
Sid Constable (b. J)
Selvin Green (b J; to UK 60s, J 70s, US 80s, UK 80s)

Patrick James (b. J; to UK 50s)
Edna Moore (b. J)
Spencer Vaughan (b. J; to UK 50s, to J 70s)
Randolph Morgan (b. J)
Ursula Rawlings (b. Ireland; to J 70s, UK 90s)
Pearl Selkirk (b. J; to UK 60s)
Spurgeon White (b. J; to US 60s)
Lola Woods (b. J; to UK 40s, US 70s)
Clark Woodward (b. J)

1940s

Linton Black (b J; to US 60s)
Winnie Busfield (b. J; to UK 60s, J 90s)
Audrey Callaghan (b. J; to US 60s)
Dayton Cripps (b. J; to UK 60s)
Morris Derby (b. J; to UK 90s)
Greta Houghton (b. J)
Neil Knight (b. J)
Joyce Leroy (b. J; to UK 60s, US 60s)
Daisy McNeep (b. J)
Dahlia Noble (b J; to UK 60s)
Vivia Perrin (b. J; to UK 50s, J00s)
Alice Wadham (b. J)
Dick Woodward (b. J; to UK 50s)
Roy York (b. J; to UK 60s, C 60s)

1950s

Howard Beck (b. J)
Nell Bell (b. UK)
Joan Bower (b. J)
Hyacinth Campbell (b. J)
Stuart Campbell (b. J; to US 80s)
Olive Carstairs (b. J; to C 60s)
Sarah Chisholm (b. J; to C 70s)
Patsy Clark (b. J; to US 80s)
Connie Dixon (b. J; to C 70s)
Stephanie Gladstone (b. UK; to J and UK 50s, J 60s, C 70s)

Deborah Gladstone (b. J; to UK 50s, J 60s and UK 70s)

Verene Gladstone (b. J; to UK 50s and 70s, returning to J)

Verity Houghton (b. J; to C 70s)

Donetta Macfarlane (b. J; to C 70s)

Celia Mackay (b. J; to US 90s)

Eva McNeep (b. J; to C 80s)

Louis May (b. J; to UK 80s)

Ted Oliver (b. J; to C 70s)

Nelson Pinnock (b. J; to C 70s)

Juliet Pinnock (b. UK)

Morris Pinnock (b. J)

Audley Rawlings (b. UK; to J 70s)

Sadie Rawlings (b. UK)

Jacob Richards (b. J; to UK 60s)

Leonard Selkirk (b. J; to UK 60s)

Charlene Summers (b. J)

Carl Watts (b. J)

1960s Robert Austin (b. J; to US 80s)

Joy Beck (b. J; to US 80s)

Crichton Bell (b. UK)

Esau Blackett (b. J; to UK 60s)

Judith Bowes (b. J)

Clover Brown (b. J; to US 90s)

Trudie Brown (b. J)

Helena Busfield (b. UK)

Owen Callaghan (b. J; to US 70s)

Grace Clare (b. J)

Harry Davidson (b. J; to US 80s)

Belle Dickens (b. J; to US 70s, to J 00s)

Blossom Grant (b. J)

Dana Harrod (b. J; to US 80s)

Clive Henry (b. J)

Arnold Houghton (b. J; to C 70s)

Sean Ismay (b. J; to C 70s)

Winston Leroy (b. UK)
Winston Lloyd (b. J; to C and return 80s)
Daniel Lyle (b. UK)
Roshana Lyle (b. J; to US 80s)
Robin Lynn (b. J; to US 90s)
Frankie Mackay (b. J)
Russell Peel (b. J ; to UK 90s)
Sandrine Porto (b. J; to US 90s)
Gene Trelissick (b. J; to US 80s)
Stella Wadham (b. J; to US 90s)
Isabelle Woods (b. UK; to US 80s, UK, 80s)
Yolande Woods (b. UK; to US 80s, UK 90s)

1970s   Sid Bell (b. UK)
Rickie Constable (b. J; to US 70s, UK 00s)
Selassie Jordan (b. J; to US 90s)
Celine Parris (b. UK)
Rodney Scott (b. UK; to US and return, 70s, 80s, 90s)
Tracey Scott (b. UK; to J 70s, UK 90s, US and return 90s)
Andrea Sole (b. J; to C 80s)
Brigette Umber (b. J; to US 80s)

b. J – born in Jamaica; UK – United Kingdom; US – United States; C – Canada